Tucker's
Deadlinc

In memory of Irv

Tucker's Deadline

A True Story

Robin Binckes

30° South Publishers

Also by Robin Binckes:
Canvas under the Sky (2011)
The Great Trek—Escape from British Rule: The Boer Exodus from the Cape Colony, 1836 (2013)

Published in 2014 by:
30° South Publishers (Pty) Ltd.
16 Ivy Road
Pinetown
Durban 3610
South Africa
www.30degreessouth.co.za

Designed & typeset by SA Publishing Services, South Africa
(kerrincocks@gmail.com)
Cover design by SA Publishing Services, South Africa
Cover image by Jeremy Hall
Printed in South Africa by Pinetown Printers, Durban, KwaZulu-Natal

ISBN 978-1-920143-97-8
ebook 978-1-928211-21-1

CONTENTS

PROLOGUE

"What a great day I've had," said Irving, as we walked into the house.

"Nightcap?" I asked.

"Not for me," Margie laughed, "I know when I've had enough! I'm off to bed. Goodnight!" She kissed me then kissed Irving and climbed the stairs to the bedroom.

Irving and I walked into the lounge. He flopped onto the settee with a big sigh.

"Whew! That was fun."

I poured him a glass of Bin 257 from Checkers, a very pleasant merlot, and opened a can of Windhoek beer for myself, the can making a *shook* sound as I pulled on the ring-top and sank into my favourite armchair. I took a deep, long drink of the ice-cold beer; the bubbles burst gently on my tongue.

"Lovely ... that's a real refresher. Cheers Irv. Here's to you," I held up the can in salute.

"Cheers Robbie."

We were silent for a few moments. Irving leaned over and tickled the tummy of Campbell, one of our two Scottie dogs, lying on the floor. I watched him.

"He's a fat little bugger, isn't he?"

"*Ja*, we spoil him."

"You shouldn't you know, Robbie. I don't spoil my dog. He's a working dog, though."

"What is he?"

"What do you think?" he asked, flippantly, "a sheep dog of course."

Irving Tucker was visiting us in Johannesburg, having come all the way from his farm, Bryn Uchaf, outside the small village of Oswestry in England, on the border with Wales. His stopover with us was part of the annual pilgrimage to South Africa that he and his wife, Yvonne, had kept up for the past twenty years. But this was his first visit alone—Yvonne had died of cancer four months earlier, in August of 2009.

Irving had told us some months before that he would be coming to town and that he wanted to stay with us for a few nights, as he and Yvonne had done, for many years. During one of our many telephone conversations I had suggested that I take him on an historical tour while he was staying with us, which, despite his ongoing sniping at everything South African, he had agreed to do; we had now returned home after the tour and dinner in Rosebank.

"Hey! This wine's not bad." He held the glass up to the light and peered at the ruby red liquid. "Good colour, from Checkers you say?"

I nodded.

"Not bad, not bad at all." He filled his mouth with the wine, swirled it around, set the glass down on the coffee table and leaned back in the couch, clasping his hands behind his head and looking at me.

"*Ja* Robbie," he said, in a resigned tone, "and you and Margie? Are you over all that crap with those bastards who screwed you? How are you coping financially? Yvonne was always worried about you, you know. She was concerned that you and Margie had no money."

"No, we're okay, Irv. We cope. Being a tour guide has been very good to me. I've been very fortunate and have built up a good little business with my guiding. Fortunately I earn quite good money from it."

"Are you able to put aside for when you retire?"

He was opening a cupboard I preferred not only to keep closed, but tightly locked. I felt a stab of uneasiness at the question. It was a concern that was always present but deeply hidden, never really discussed.

"Not really, Irv, but then we live quite well on a day-to-day basis."

"Having seen how you worked today, doing that tour for us, I can see how hard you have to work. How many days a month do you work like that?"

"Probably about twenty-five days in an average month."

He looked horrified. "Hell, that's really hard work, and you're not getting any younger. But is it really necessary? Surely you didn't lose all your money, did you?"

"Afraid I did, Irv. At the end of the day what I didn't have to pay back to the bank for sureties signed was taken by our two 'friends'," I indicated air quotes with my index fingers, "our new partners, who snookered us."

"Still. You shouldn't have to work so hard. Put your feet up, smell the roses."

I laughed. "Quite honestly, there are no alternatives. I have to work like this now that we've lost our money. My fault. Still, no good crying over spilt milk, is there?"

I tipped my head back and swigged my beer.

"Anyway, enough about us, let's talk about you. You're looking quite thin, which I'm not surprised to see, now that you've had to learn to look after yourself; but apart from that, Irv, you seem to be doing good?"

He looked at me, wiggled his fingers behind his head and slid further down into the soft plump cushions of the sofa.

"I won't deny that it's been tough. Very tough ... since Yvonne ... died ..." he faltered. "You see, what most people never realized is that Yvonne was everything, and I mean every little thing, to me. She was the wise one, the one who did the farm finances, in fact the one who really farmed. She was the leader, the person who supported and guided me, who made the decisions. I mean, she even looked up telephone numbers for me."

I frowned in puzzlement and Irving saw my look.

"Ja, she did everything for me, and apart from that I loved her like you cannot believe. You know I was never one to be chasing after women? Well, when I met Yvonne I fell, I fell hard. I never recovered from that fall."

He stared into the distance as if he had forgotten that he was talking to me; then shook his head as if to clear away the thoughts. "I miss her Robbie; God knows how much."

I nodded, "Well, you do seem to be holding up well in the circumstances."

He blinked away the tears that had sprung to his eyes and forced a smile, the corners of his lips curled slightly upward.

"Ja, Robbie, I've had quite a stroke of good luck happen."

I was surprised to hear this from a man who had only recently lost his life companion.

He looked at me as if deciding whether or not to talk, the smile still flickering at the edges of his mouth, then he appeared to make up his mind, leaned forward and said: "Remember when Yvonne and I left South Africa in 1976, I had some paintings from our neighbour in Broederstroom, Gordon Voster?"

"Ye-es … I seem to remember you had a painting of his."

"A painting? We had twelve of the buggers. When we were leaving Gordon wanted to buy my Land Rover, so he gave me twelve of his paintings for the Landy. When we arrived in England I sold one of the paintings for more than the landy was worth. Ja, two thousand quid. A lot of money then."

"You're kidding? That's fantastic." I had a pull at my beer. "Have you still got the other eleven?"

He nodded.

"Shit, they must be worth a few bob by now?" I said, doing a quick mental calculation. Eleven times at least two thousand pounds, twenty-two thousand pounds or two hundred and twenty thousand rand. Wow.

"Ja, well, together with our other paintings, they're all quite valuable."

"What other paintings have you got?"

"When Yvonne's dad died a few years ago we got some of his paintings; Yvonne's brother Michael also got some. In addition, over the years Yvonne and I collected art."

"Really?" I said, as I walked to the kitchen and fetched another beer from the fridge.

"I didn't know you had that much culture in you, Irv."

"Oh, I've always been keen on art. Even when I was at school I used to spend a lot of time at the Johannesburg art gallery. I used to go there with your friend, you know? Old Ray Johnson, the guy who likes you so much because you tried to get into his wife." He grinned at his own joke.

I felt my face flush. "I never did, Irv, and you know it."

"Well, anyway, you knew that Yvonne's dad was a Hess, didn't you? They were refugees from Germany during the Second World War and he managed to escape with some of his art. That apart, Yvonne and I used to visit art galleries all over the world and we started to collect paintings."

I had the feeling that this was the introduction to a story, so remained silent.

"Before Yvonne died we decided to realize the children's inheritance by selling a painting or two."

I laughed at his joke. He and Yvonne had no children and no dependants.

He continued: "So I called the managing director of Sotheby's in London and he came down to the farm."

"Ha ha!" I chortled, "sure thing. The managing director of Sotheby's? He came to you? You have to be joking."

"Serious Robbie, he came to the farm and agreed to take the picture we had chosen to sell back to London."

I looked at him to see if he was teasing me, but he was deadly serious.

"Wow, it must have been quite a painting. What was it?"

"It was a Frank Auerbach."

I quaffed my beer. "Never heard of him. Pity he didn't take a Gordon Voster, Irv. Clearly they're really worth something."

Irving ignored my comment. "Well, a few months after he had taken the painting, Yvonne became ill and I forgot all about the painting and Sotheby's. Then Sotheby's phoned to tell me they had scheduled the painting for auction on 11 November 2009—together with Richard Attenborough's art collection."

"What? Serious? Jeez, that's something, isn't it?"

He nodded.

"Soon after that the brochure arrived for the auction; wait, I've got a copy, I'll fetch it from my case. I brought it to show you and Margie."

He bounded up the stairs and returned moments later, carrying the brochure for the Sotheby's Attenborough auction.

He tossed it across the room so that it landed in my lap.

"Turn to the last page."

I did as he instructed and there it was: "Auction of Frank Auerbach's painting 'Head of Leon Kossoff', Expected Sale price £200,000." It took a second or two to register.

"My God, Irv. Two hundred thousand pounds? For that? That's a bloody fortune. Shit a brick, man! Is that what you got? Fantastic!"

Irving shook his head.

"No, it's not. Let me finish. I decided to go up to London for the auction—"

"Don't tell me," I interrupted, "after Attenborough's paintings, it didn't sell?"

"—No, no, nothing like that. So, I decided to take a trip up to the smoke to attend the auction; there was a big crowd on the day and Attenborough's paintings sold for pretty much what the estimates had been. The highest price any of them achieved was two hundred and twenty thousand quid. When they had finished most of the people left the auction and headed for home. Of course my heart sank. In fact it was as if the whole thing was over. I doubted whether anyone would even bid on the Auerbach." He sipped his wine. "They give the sellers a special room upstairs you know, where you can watch the bidding."

I nodded.

He continued: "After Attenborough's paintings were sold, so few people remained that I left the private room, came downstairs and sat in the front row among the few people who had waited. Getting a seat wasn't difficult. Well, the bidding opened at two hundred thousand. Straight away there was a higher bid; up it went. There were two telephone bidders bidding against each other, nobody in the room was bidding. But up the bidding went—up and up, up and up."

I sat entranced by Irving's story, hanging onto his every word.

"There were only two people bidding. The bidding went higher and higher. Each of the two bidders was determined to have the painting."

"Shit!" I cried, "put me out of my misery. What did it go for?"

He smiled, almost sadly.

"It went for one million, seven hundred thousand, seven hundred and seventy-seven British pounds."

I whooped with delight and leaped to my feet, laughing and shouting as I cavorted around the room.

"Well done, Irv! Let's drink to that! Well done! Shit! That's over twenty million rand—twenty million rand. Holy shit! You can do anything you want with that. Cruise the world, travel, anything. Fuck, the world's your oyster, Irv! What are you going to do?"

The smile had disappeared. He looked at me as if seeing me for the first time. He stared at me, then blinked, slowly. And that was when he told me he was going to kill himself.

Chapter One

HOMECOMING

It was December 2009 and Irving had arrived from England the day before. His rented Toyota was loaded with suitcases when he pulled into our driveway. He climbed out, squinting against the glare. He looked thinner when last I had seen him a year earlier.

We hugged each other and I saw him wipe his eyes with the back of his hand as tears threatened. I blinked, clearing my own eyes which had filled with tears as I witnessed his sadness. This was the first time we had seen each other since the death of his wife, Yvonne, four months ago.

"Hello bugger," he said, his voice unsteady, "good to see you again."

He turned and reached into the car. When he emerged again he had an enormous bouquet of sixty red roses in his hands. He smiled as he passed them to me.

"Put them in some water, Robbie, they're for Margie."

That was Irv, always remembering his manners.

After putting the roses into four separate vases, I returned to the car to help Irving with his luggage.

"Hell Irv, what have you got in here? Lead?" I asked, as I helped carry the heavy cases up the stairs to the spare room.

He laughed. "Oh, it's stuff for the Malans, plus stuff for the school at Haga Haga [a village on the southeast coast near the town of East London] and, you know, all sorts of stuff." He sounded embarrassed as he continued, "There's some of Yvonne's stuff as well, I don't know if it will fit Margie?"

That night we chatted in the kitchen about our tour the next day, while Margie, my wife, prepared a fresh green salad. She looked up from what she was doing and said, "I've never been to Soweto, Rob. I think I'll join you guys tomorrow, if that's okay?"

"Of course," I said looking at Irving for confirmation.

"Absolutely, Margs, we would love you to come along."

A few years after my first wife, Jean, and I were divorced, Margie and I had met at the birthday party of a mutual friend. Six months later she moved in with me, with her two sons—Greg, aged eight, and his younger brother Christopher, aged six—plus three dogs. A year later we were married in a simple ceremony on the lawn of the house I had built overlooking the deep blue sea at Haga Haga.

Every marriage is a balancing act and Margie was the perfect balance for me. A librarian for one of the larger law firms in Johannesburg, she was everything I was not. Quiet by nature, balanced, sensible, her feet firmly on the ground, she proved the perfect personality to counteract my own shoot-from-the-hip temperament. Despite being unobtrusive, Margie was a great deal of fun with a sense of humour to match the best.

Michael, my forty-year-old son, who was in Johannesburg at the time, kicking his heels as he waited to finalize his documentation and all the red tape to start a new life in the Cayman Islands, had decided to join us for the tour; so there would be the three of them and me.

While Margie prepared dinner I selected a bottle of Meerlust Cabernet from my small stock of wine, which I kept in the garage next to my car.

Irving was talking to Margie about his farm in England. I took a corkscrew, plunged the tip through the foil wrapping around the cork and into the cork and was about to pull the cork from the bottle, through the wrapping, when Irving saw what I was doing.

"Christ! Robbie! Don't do that—" he said, snatching the bottle out of my hands. "Don't you know how to open a bottle of wine properly?" he snapped. He pulled open the cutlery drawer, took a sharp paring knife and cut around the top of the foil, as carefully as if circumcising a newborn baby, exposing the bare neck of the bottle.

"There. Haven't you got a foil cutter? I'll have to get you one. I can't have you opening a good wine like an idiot. Shit. This is as hot as hell. Where have you been keeping this wine? I hope it's still drinkable."

Our townhouse did not have a great deal of space so I stored our wine in cooler bricks stacked inside the garage, against the garage wall. I knew it wasn't the right place but had little option. I answered like a chastized schoolboy: "In my garage, Irv."

"No wonder it's so bloody warm. You can't keep wine like that, Robbie. Anyway, if that's all you have, let's drink it."

I didn't answer.

He handed the bottle back to me and I poured two glasses. Margie preferred white. I took a bottle of Sauvignon Blanc from the fridge, which I had opened the night before, and quickly cleaned and neatened the foil at the neck of the bottle, hoping that Irv wouldn't notice. He didn't.

The next morning, lying in bed, drinking coffee, I said to Margie, "You know, I'm quite nervous about doing this tour with you guys and Irving today."

"Why on earth? I know that you always get tensed up before a tour but Irving is your friend. I'm sure there's no need to be nervous."

"You know what he's like. He's always putting us and the country down. I just hope he shuts up and listens, and doesn't spend the day telling us what a bunch of arseholes we all are."

Michael arrived while we were having our breakfast of paw paw and watermelon, standing in the kitchen.

"Hello Mike," said Irving, giving him a bear hug. Michael, at six three, stood a full three inches above Irving. The two of them pumped hands.

"So Mister Tour Guide," said Irving to me, while I was drinking my second cup of coffee for the day, "what's the programme?"

I looked at him before answering. Despite the weight he had lost since Yvonne's death, he was still a handsome man. Golden curly hair which had greyed peacefully, blending into a beard that looked as though his sideburns had meandered down his face, around his chin, and over his upper lip, but had missed a strip under his lower lip; the naked skin under his mouth gave the impression of a second lower lip. He looked like a young Santa Claus. His brown eyes crinkled when he smiled and his grin was broad and sharing. Although he had shed some weight he was still heavier than me, at about eighty-two kilograms. Quite fit for a man of sixty-three.

Irving was waiting for an answer and looked at me quizzically, head cocked slightly to one side.

"Well, I thought we could go to Soweto first. Margs hasn't been there before."

"Nor have I," chipped in Michael.

"We can do a tour of Soweto and then have lunch there, at Sakhumzi's restaurant and then—"

"Are you sure the food is okay to eat in Soweto?" Irving interrupted.

"—Of course it is! It's as good as here."

"Hey! That's not very complimentary about your wife's cooking—only kidding Margie," as he saw the rattled look on Margie's face. He chuckled at his own joke.

"Then, after lunch, I suggest we go to the Constitutional Court, popularly called the 'ConCourt'."

"That sounds boring," said Irving, "isn't there anywhere else in Johannesburg that you can take me? Your overseas visitors must think you are scratching the barrel Robbie. Constitutional Court? Come on! Surely there are more interesting places in Joburg?"

"Well, I rate the ConCourt as one of the priorities for any thinking visitor here who wants to see where we are as a country today, and where we aspire to be in the future. Please note, Irving, I said *thinking* visitor; but maybe I can't put you into that category?"

He gave a little laugh in response.

"Also, I've just realized something; you're interested in art, aren't you?"

He nodded, watching me over the lip of his coffee cup as he drained it.

"As it happens, there is a magnificent art collection at the Court, in fact, the whole symbolism of the Court is linked to art."

He looked sceptical. "South African art?"

"Yes, some of the best."

"Okay, let's have a look then. Is that it?"

"No, if we have time I'll take you into Alexandra township as well."

Irving looked as though I had invited him to dine with the devil.

"Are you mad? Isn't that a dangerous place? I know it used to be. When we were in the army you couldn't even go there."

"It's fine now," I said, "my charity, or rather, the non-governmental organization called Friends of Alexandra is there, where I work with orphans and under-privileged kids. If you're interested I'll show it to you."

"Yes, please, I'd love to see your work. Yvonne would have liked to have seen it too. Not so sure about going into the township though; still, if you say it's okay ..."

Michael put his cup in the sink, rubbed his hands together, looked at me and said, "Right. Let's hit the road, Dad. Let's rock 'n' roll."

"Why don't you put your cup in the dishwasher?" asked Irving.

Margie's glance collided with mine in mid-air. Dishwasher? What dishwasher?

It was a Sunday so there wasn't much traffic. We drove along the highway passing Wits University on both sides. I nodded to my right. "You see this area down here, in what today is Newtown? This is where blacks and Indians lived after the Boer War, together with some whites, also *boers* [a term for Afrikaners which today has taken on negative connotations]. Then bubonic plague broke out and they were all forcibly removed to the south-west, to what much later became Soweto, but that was the start of forced evictions. Way back in 1904."

Irving was silent, looking around as if seeing Johannesburg for the first time.

"That mosque over there," I said, nodding my head in its direction while steering, "that's where Mahatma Ghandi burned his identity documents in 1907 as a protest against government oppression of Indian people."

"Not the British," said Irving, "you mean the *boers*?"

"No, the *Zuid Afrikanse Republiek* as it was then, was still under British control, so his protest was against the British."

"That's crap," said Irving, with a chuckle. "Is this what you do, Binckes, make up stories and bullshit your American clients?"

I felt my face flush and my knuckles whiten as I gripped the steering wheel more firmly.

"It's not crap, Irving. Ghandi lived here for twenty-one years and it was here that he developed his whole philosophy of *satyagraha*, soul force, which he applied so successfully in India."

"Serious?" asked Irving.

"You had better listen to him, Irv. I can assure you the last thing Rob would do is bullshit a client. He knows what he's talking about," said Margie, quietly, from the back seat.

"So you've learned a bit, have you, Robbie? I'll have to treat you with newfound respect."

Cars whipped past us on both sides. I was in the centre lane so that Irving could have a view of the city, and it seemed I was the only person heeding the speed limit.

"You remember that building, don't you Irv?" I said, indicating a tall blue-clad office block next to the highway. "John Vorster Square. Police headquarters. Where people mysteriously fell out of windows to their death."

"Oh yes," said Irving, looking at the building.

"Of course they never fell—they were pushed."

"Bastards," said Irving, with all the venom of a cobra, "and we all did bugger all."

I didn't answer.

"There's Soccer City, the stadium for the World Cup," I said looking to the right, "a ninety-four-thousand seater."

"What a waste of money, hey Robbie? I mean there are thousands of people here living below the poverty line and without houses—so your government goes ahead and builds stadiums for soccer. Talk about fiddling while Rome burns. I suppose one of your big fat politicians had a share of the action with that stadium. How many did they build?" he asked.

"Eleven."

"Eleven? Eleven! What on earth are they going to do with them after the World Cup. Typical African state. Total waste of money. Good thing Yvonne isn't here—she would tell you what bullshit it is."

"But we South Africans all think the World Cup will be a fantastic opportunity for this country to showcase itself, and I'm sure the major stadiums will be used after the event," I countered. "Maybe there'll be some problems in the smaller centres, we'll have to wait and see."

"What are they going to showcase? Out-of-work people?"

"Come on, Irv. Stop being so cynical. It'll be great for us."

"Not according to our newspapers. They say you'll never be ready in time and I think they're right. Look at your roads: all being repaired, roadworks everywhere; stadiums still under construction. They also say that nobody will come because of the crime. You don't understand, Robbie, your crime here is terrible. Look here," as he locked his door, "here we are going into Soweto, and I had forgotten to lock my door." He laughed at his foolishness.

I smiled, shook my head and kept quiet.

"So this is Soweto," said Irving, as we entered the massive, sprawling township on Chris Hani Road, passing the suburb of Diepkloof on our right. "Doesn't look too bad, does it?" he observed.

"Well, that's one of the more affluent suburbs. You should remember that Soweto is where black people had to live, by law. But they were not allowed to own property; they had to pay rent to the local government. Everybody lived in matchbox houses, small one-roomed homes with few services, no electricity. As such nobody improved their homes ... why should they? They didn't own them. Today of course, with ownership, many of the matchbox houses have been renovated; in some cases they've been knocked down altogether and replaced with better homes. But there are still a large number of matchbox houses, as you can see."

Half a kilometre farther I slowed down.

"This is the Chris Hani Baragwanath Hospital, largest hospital in the world; well, it was listed in the Guinness Book of records as such in 1995. Over three thousand beds and six hundred doctors. They deliver on average sixty babies a day here, and handle over a million patients a year."

Irving peered out the window.

"The hospital was built by the British in 1943 as a medical facility during World War Two, for their troops 'up north' who, they figured, might require medical treatment. When General Smuts, the prime minister at the time, opened this hospital, he stated that at the end of the war it would become a hospital for the people of this area. Of course Soweto had no such name until 1963; prior to that it was just a collection of black townships. As you know, Soweto is an acronym for South Western Townships." I stressed the final 's' of townships. "It's townships plural, not township."

"So it was built by us?" Irving said with a wry smile.

"What do you mean? Who's us?"

"Us—the Brits, the poms—we built this hospital."

"Come on, Irv. You're not British. You were born and bred here. You're as South African as a *naartjie*. Stop bullshitting about being British."

"Oh yes, I am. That's where I live and that's what I am. British, and proud of it."

I ignored the bait he'd tossed at me.

Chapter Two

A TASTE OF JOBURG

We parked next to Walter Sisulu Square in Kliptown, Soweto while I related the story of the signing of the Freedom Charter in 1955 and the subsequent arrest of 156 leaders in 1956, including Mandela, which resulted in the Treason Trial.

"So that was when he was sent to prison for all that time?" asked Irving.

"No, actually, it wasn't. After the trial, which went on for five years, they were all found not guilty and—"

"Not guilty?" Irving interjected. "How could that be? Those Dutchmen [a derogatory term for Afrikaners] judges were all part of the *apartheid* system. How could they have been found not guilty?"

"—Well they were. The police figured the document, the Charter, was part of the *rooi gevaar*; you remember that, don't you, Irv?"

He nodded. "Sure. The red danger, the fear of communism."

"As a result, despite the court finding them not guilty, that document was not allowed to be shown in this country until 1990, because of its perceived communist links."

"Ridiculous; that the Nats blamed it all on communism."

"Not so ridiculous, you know, Irv." I looked in the rear-view mirror and saw Margie and Mike listening attentively. "When our Nats were so paranoid about communism, they were not alone. I mean, in the fifties, in the USA, you had the McCarthy congressional hearings; in the early sixties, the Bay of Pigs and the Cuban missile crisis. When Russia rattled its sabre the whole world trembled."

Irving nodded his head slightly, as if agreement had been squeezed out of him.

"In 1989 the Berlin Wall came down and communism was no longer a threat. The Cold War was over. In 1990 we released Nelson Mandela."

"I don't see the connection. Mandela wasn't a communist," Irving stated emphatically.

"Well, the jury is still out on that one and is likely never to return," I said with a laugh. "What I do know is that when the police finally arrested his group of the High Command of *Umkhonto we Sizwe*, on 11 July 1963, they found a great deal of evidence that linked Mandela to the communists."

"Come on you two," said Margie, "let's move on. We'll never finish if you don't stop arguing."

We drove on through Kliptown, past the small settlement of tin and cardboard shacks where hundreds of 'un-housed' people lived.

"Look at this! I can't believe your government allows people to live in conditions like this while those fat cat politicians feed at the trough," Irving snorted, disgustedly.

Next to the river three pigs rummaged their way through the piles of rubbish surrounding the shacks.

"Speak of the devil—there they are! They must have heard you Irv!" I said, trying to lighten the mood. I was rewarded with a slight smile, acknowledging my attempt at humour.

We stopped outside the gates of the Morris Isaacson High School and talked of the events of 16 June 1976—the march of the high-school children which ended in the shooting of thirteen-year-old Hector Pieterson, and many more. Continuing our tour, we followed the route of the march and stopped opposite the wall commemorating the site where Hector Pieterson fell to the ground, dying.

"And that's when we left," said Irving.

I shot a glance at him.

He was looking straight ahead at the wall. He shook his head and grimaced. "We didn't want to live in a country that allowed that kind of thing to happen. Those Dutchmen were out of control. Yet they managed to hang on to power for another twenty-four years."

"I didn't realize that that was when you left the country," I said.

"Sure. What do you think? That we were mad or something? Yvonne and I were not like the rest of you silly sods."

I ignored him and busied myself parking the car. We were instantly surrounded by a bunch of a half-dozen grinning, laughing, scruffy 'parking attendant' teenagers, angling for the obligatory car wash at a price well over the market price. They greeted us with shouts of "*Umkhonto! Umkhonto!*"

"What are they calling you?"

"*Umkhonto*," I replied, "it's my township name."

"What does it mean?"

"Spear," I answered.

Irving guffawed, slapping his thigh. "I can guess why they call you that."

"And you would be wrong. It's because my company is called Spear of the Nation."

"How can you have a name like that? Isn't that *Umkhonto we Sizwe*? That's the name of the military wing of the African National Congress, the ANC, isn't it?" He looked as though I had stolen his own name. "How can you have the English translation as the name of your company?"

"Because I registered it. Prior to that it had never been registered in English."

Outside the car the shouting and jostling continued.

"Clean your car, *Umkhonto?*"

"My turn today!"

"I'll watch your car for you."

"Please *Umkhonto*, you promised me last time."

"What's going on?" Irving asked, frowning.

"Oh, they all want to clean my car. They know I'll pay whoever cleans the car."

Irving's mouth curled. "They must really love you," he said sarcastically.

I climbed out the car and nodded my assent to Emmanuel. The other faces looked as though they had lost the lotto.

"*Ja*, they do. It's cupboard love though. They love me as long as there's money, or food, in the cupboard. Come on, let's have some lunch."

I led the way and found a table and chairs under the trees at Sakhumzi's restaurant in Vilikazi Street. The three of us exchanged amused looks as we watched Irving tuck into a plate which he had piled high with mutton, *mieliepap* (a porridge made from maize meal), an onion and tomato gravy and *umngqusho* (samp and beans).

"Lovely food," he said between mouthfuls, "love mutton cooked properly. Mind you, not as good as the lamb on our farm, that Yvonne and I raise."

When we returned to the car I paid Emmanuel and went through the usual ritual we performed every time I visited.

"Right," I said, looking around me, "who watched my car?"

Two of the street kids raised their arms.

"And did you do anything to earn this money?" I asked.

"Yes *Umkhonto*. We watched it."

"I know you watched it, but did anyone try to take it? Did you work for your money?"

The penny dropped.

"*Auw! Umkhonto*, there were five of them."

"Five of them? What did they try to do?"

"*Umkhonto*, they attacked us, but we fought them off with our bare hands."

"And they had guns, *Umkhonto!*" the other added, with a broad grin.

Irving, Margie and Michael roared with laughter at this exchange.

"*Ja, ja*. I'm sure. Here's your money." I gave them each ten rand. "See you next week."

We left Soweto and moved on to our next stop in Braamfontein, Johannesburg.

As we strolled towards the entrance to the Constitutional Court, Irving's attention was attracted to the bronze sculpture by the late Dumile Feni. He stopped.

"That's titled 'History'," I said. "It shows the oppression of the people of South Africa at the hands of the colonial powers. In this case the British."

"How do you know it's the British?"

I pointed to the bowler-hatted figure sitting on the back of a black man, "If that isn't enough," and then to the sagging, shrivelled breasts of the women in the sculpture, "you can see by the breasts of the women—obviously British."

Irving snorted, while the three of us chuckled.

After we had walked through the ConCourt and I had explained the symbolism of the building and its design features, I could see that even Irving was impressed. I hid a sigh of relief that we had finished viewing the interior of the court without an argument.

"Of course," I said, now on a roll, "we legalized same-sex marriages some five years ago in 2005—"

Irving interrupted. "You have same-sex marriages here in South Africa?"

"Yes," I said proudly, "not bad for a backward African state, hey, Irv? Particularly when countries like the USA are still battling with the issue."

"You allow *moffies* [South African slang for homosexual men] to marry? You call that progress?" He looked at me as though I had just broken out in leprosy. "You mean *poeftes*? [Afrikaans for 'poofter', another slang term for homosexual men]. They allow *poeftes* to marry?" he repeated, as if I must have misheard him.

I nodded. "Yes, except those terms are totally unacceptable here nowadays. Homosexuals are known as gays."

He looked as if he was going to explode and then, like a balloon with a leak, he deflated. "Oh well, it takes all sorts. Where's that art collection you were bragging about?"

I stopped at the first piece of art hanging above the Great African Steps outside the Concourt.

"This is by Marlene Dumas, she lives in the Netherlands and today is the highest paid female artist in the world."

"You mean highest paid South African artist in the world," he corrected me.

"No, I don't," I said, "I mean artist *in the world*."

"Irma Stern sells for much more. I've heard of Marlene Dumas but she's not in the same class as Irma Stern."

"I mean *living* artist, Irv; an artist alive *now*."

The day was slipping away so I shortened the visit, shepherded my three 'tourists' into the car and headed for Alexandra, noting the 'click' when Irving locked his door as we drove up London Road into the township.

"Look, we don't have a lot of time so let's just go to the hostel and you can see my projects."

Irving was silent, gazing out of the window.

I swung left at the clinic and as we passed the first of the tin shacks.

"Jeez!" Irving said, as though stung by a bee. "Are people living here?"

"Sure. Those are their toilets, there's a communal tap, this is where they live."

The streets were bustling with people. Noise, smells and colour bombarded the senses.

"We are in an area of one square mile—with four hundred thousand people living in it."

Irving had lowered his window to take pictures when we arrived, and as I turned down Roosevelt Road, from the corner of my eye I saw him push the button to close his window, glancing around nervously.

We cruised down Roosevelt Road with taxis whizzing past us, hooting at our slow pace, and Irving spotted the Madala Hostel.

"Shit! I can't believe it!"

"What?"

"There are people living there! Look at the goats, and the filth—Christ, Robbie, what's your government doing about this? How can people be living like this thirteen, fourteen, years after democracy? Is this what Mandela wanted? It's a bloody disgrace."

"Well, these hostels were inherited from the Nats. They were intended for migrant workers, Zulus, at the time. This one was designed to house two thousand five hundred men; instead, it housed five thousand. For those five thousand there was one wash basin per seventy men; one toilet for the same number. This one had electronically operated steel doors to seal off one hundred and fifty men at a time, in separate sections of the hostel. The Nats said that it was for their own protection but actually it was to keep them under control."

I stopped the car and we all gazed at the hostel on our right. While I was talking I faced Irving, who had his back to the car window. I could see a youngster of about thirteen approaching us, and recognized him as one of our orphans, Alfred. He came up behind Irving and punched his window with his fist. BANG!

"Fuck!" yelled Irving, spinning around to be confronted by a black face with a row of flashing white teeth, pressed against the glass.

"Get going Robbie! Go! Go!" he shouted.

The three of us roared with laughter.

"Don't worry, Irv, it's Alfred," I spluttered.

"Who the hell is Alfred?"

I was doubled over with laughter, tears spilling from my eyes, so Margie spoke.

"He's one of the orphans that Rob takes care of in Alexandra, at the centre for orphans and vulnerable children. Rob and some other people started it about four years ago and today it takes care of three hundred orphans and vulnerable children, every day."

While Margie spoke, I leaned over and lowered Irving's window, to speak to the smiling Alfred.

"Hello, Alfred."

"Hello *Umkhonto*. *Umkhonto* I need shoes." He held up a foot in a shoe without laces, with a sole that flapped like one hand clapping.

"How much, Alfred?"

"Two hundred, *Umkhonto*."

I saw Irving's hand go into his pocket.

"Here, let me."

"No, Irv, this will be from the Friends of Alexandra, not my own money. I'll claim it back."

I took two hundred rand from my wallet and passed the money to Alfred.

"I want to see the shoes, Alfred, and get them from the Indian shop, okay?"

"Yes *Umkhonto*. Thank you *Umkhonto*, thank you."

We left Alfred and turned right towards the Nobuhle Hostel.

"He is one of twenty-nine orphans who are luckier than the rest," I said.

Irving, having recovered his composure, said, "Lucky? You must be joking. How can he be called lucky?"

"We have twenty-nine of those orphans, including Alfred, who are sponsored by individuals, mainly from the USA, and they get special treatment like clothes at Christmas time, food parcels and so on—all arranged through the Friends of Alexandra, Here we are."

I turned into the deeply rutted road leading to the hostel. "This is where I do most of my projects."

As the car turned down the steep bank to the Nobuhle Hostel some two dozen children ranging in ages from three to twelve came running, shouting and laughing and waving, towards the car.

"*Umkhonto! Umkhonto! Umkhonto!*" they shouted in greeting.

Irving's face expressed sheer amazement.

I stopped the car in front of the pre-school facility that Friends of Alexandra had built and pointed it out to Irving, while the children crowded around the car. I gave the oldest girl, about twelve years old, a twenty rand note. "Here, Portia. Go and buy chips for everyone." The kids scampered away, yelling with delight.

As the four of us chatted I saw Ernest approaching. Ernest was the hostel *nduna* (overseer) and played a pivotal role for our non-profit organisation.

"*Umkhonto*," he said holding up his hand in salute.

"Hello Ernest"

"*Umkhonto* we need to have meeting for *bafana* (the boys)."

"Yes Ernest, can't do it today, as I have people with me. I'll come back during the week."

He nodded in understanding, shuffled his feet and looked embarrassed.

"What's the matter Ernest?"

"*Umkhonto*, I need airtime. Have no money."

I sighed. "How much?"

Ernest shrugged, his face expressing total despair.

"Here," I opened up my wallet and handed him a two hundred rand note, "buy your airtime."

He beamed with delight, as though he had won the lotto.

"*Ngiyabonga* (thank you) *Umkhonto, ngiyabonga kakhulu* (thank you very much)."

Ernest opened the door of the pre-school and the five of us, followed by some stragglers among the children who were starting to drift back, happily munching their chips and watching us with large enquiring eyes.

Irving looked around the tiny room.

"How many kids come here?"

"Fifty," I said. "Next door is our kitchen, so these kids get a square meal every day—a balanced diet of meat, fish and chicken and of course vegetables. We pay three teachers, so they are groomed for school when they are six or seven, in fact, look here."

I stopped at photos stuck to the wall with dirty sticky-tape, showing little children of six years old wearing academic gowns and mortar-boards.

"These are pictures of their graduation last year. These are the children leaving to go to proper school."

Irving looked at the photos. "Who are these big buggers in soccer kit in this pic?" Irving chuckled, "hell, they must have been slow learners if they were still in your pre-school."

I grinned. "Come on Irv, that's the under fifteen soccer team that Friends of Alexandra funds and runs. They're not from our pre-school. These boys started with nothing, and almost won the league this year. They are named after me—the Umkhonto Eleven."

Irving looked at me appraisingly. "Well done, Robbie, you're doing a good job. I'm impressed. I had no idea of the work you're doing. Yvonne would have loved to see this. You know that we are supporting that school down at Haga Haga, together with our friends—the Smythes—from England?"

I nodded. "Yes, I think you mentioned that before. Are you still involved?"

"Yep. I was hoping to get down there and see how they're doing, this trip, but don't think I'll have the time."

A short while later we left the hostel and Alexandra, heading for home.

"Let's go out and have an early meal, save you cooking, Margs," I said over my shoulder, "let's go to the Grill House in Rosebank."

"Good idea, Robbie. What a great day. Hell; that was really interesting. Glad we did the tour. Fantastic. Tell me Robbie," he frowned enquiringly, "was that your money you were dishing out there? But before you answer the question," he looked at me with one eyebrow arched, adding a question mark to the query that followed, "what happened?"

"What do you mean, 'what happened'?" I glanced at him.

"Well, when I knew you, as far as I can remember, your political views were a little to the right of Ghengis Khan." He waved his hand loosely, flopping at the end of his arm. "Now, I mean, look at you: helping the kids, your own charity. Shit. What happened?"

I concentrated on my driving and didn't answer, but could feel his gaze on me.

"Come on. I asked what happened?"

He wasn't going to let it go, I knew. He was like a fish gnawing at the bait, not letting up until the scrap was spent.

"Well, I suppose I did have a bit of a turnaround."

"What happened?" he asked again, a slightly impatient edge to his voice.

I grimaced. "Well, maybe you don't know this, but in 1993 this place was really burning. People were dying in the townships by the score. The violence was really, really bad. I mean, do you know that after Mandela came out of jail, fourteen thousand people died here, due to political violence?"

He looked surprised and shook his head.

"Well, on 10 April 1993, Margie and I were driving back from Haga Haga. We had been down for the Easter holidays. I had the radio on, listening to music, when there was a special announcement. The leader of the communists and the head of *Umkhonto we Sizwe*, who had only recently returned from exile, a man named Chris Hani, had been shot dead in his driveway after going out to buy the Sunday papers."

"Who by?"

"We didn't know at the time, but as it turned out he was shot by two white guys—Clive Derby-Lewis, and ..."

"Who was he, AWB? (*Afrikaner Weerstandsbeweging*). Wasn't he something to do with Rhodesian politics?"

I shook my head.

"No. He was a real right-winger. First, he had been a Nat, then after being elected to parliament he joined the Conservatives, real right-wing. The other one was a man named Janusz Walus, but we didn't know that then. Anyway, I said to Margie, at the time, that's it. H.K.G.K."

"HKGK?"

"*Hier Kom Groot Kak* (here comes a pile of crap)."

"Go on."

"Well, I said to Margie that the killing of Chris Hani would be the tipping point of the killings we were already experiencing; that the violence which had been going on in the townships would spread throughout South Africa, and that this whole country was going to go up in flames. That was when I decided to do something."

He snorted then asked, "What were you going to do?"

"At first I wasn't too sure. But on the drive home I had a lot of time to think. I remembered hearing about a group of volunteers who were trying to stop the violence. Set up by big business with the backing of the government and all the political parties. They called them Peace Monitors and I decided to contact them and volunteer to help."

"And so? That was it?"

"No, not quite as simple as that. When we arrived home that afternoon, I managed to find their number and called them. I don't remember how I found their number, but I did. Anyhow, some guy answered and after I explained to him that I wanted to volunteer, to help, he took down some basic details and told me he would call if they needed me."

"Sort of 'don't call us, we'll call you'?"

"Yes, exactly. It didn't quite work out like that though. A few hours later, that same day, he phoned back. His name was Peter Harris and he was one of the blokes in charge of the Peace Monitors. I was quite surprised to get the call. He introduced himself and then asked me whether, by any chance, I had a radio operator's license. As you might remember, I used to fly; I had my own plane at one time and still had a radio operator's license. So I said yes, I had one. He nearly dropped the phone. I could hear the delight in his voice. 'We need someone to take control of all communications for the Peace Monitors at Chris Hani's funeral, as well as before the funeral. It means you'll have to come in tomorrow. Are you interested?' That was that. The next day I joined the Peace Monitors and in fact my first assignment was Chris Hani's funeral."

"Very interesting," he mused, "but I don't see how that led to you working in the townships and having your own charity and all that."

"Well, my involvement lasted for some time after the Hani funeral. It wasn't something I did every day. At that time I still had my fishing company, so on a daily basis that's where I worked. But whenever there was the likelihood of a clash between the ANC and Inkhata Freeedom Party members, I would get a call; then I'd have to drop everything, go to the township concerned, join the other Peace Monitors and try to defuse an explosive situation."

"You mean you went into the trouble spots? Wasn't it dangerous?"

"It was, I suppose; yes, we went into places like Kathlehong, Thokoza, Soweto."

"So that's what changed you? You saw some terrible things I suppose?"

I thought for a few seconds before answering. "Yes, we did, but strangely enough, it wasn't that. When I think about it, it was more the fact that life just carried on in our white suburbs. We fretted over the rugby and cricket scores, the gold price, the stock market. We talked about 'them' and 'us'. For us, very little changed, while people were dying in the townships, being shot at, being necklaced.* That was the issue. For white South Africans life carried on without missing a beat. That, I suppose, was the cause of my epiphany, if you can call it that. But when I look back that appears to have been the defining moment. From then on as they say, the rest is history."

Irving stroked his beard pensively, his thumb and forefinger rubbing each corner of his mouth.

"Shit Binckes. I'm impressed—not that it seems you were very successful if fourteen thousand people were killed. You obviously didn't stop the violence," he said with a wry grin.

"No, we didn't. But I genuinely believe the death toll would have been a great deal higher if the Peace Monitors hadn't existed. I think we played a role. Who knows how many others might have died?"

"Well, full marks for trying, Robbie, full marks. At least you got off your arse and did something, didn't you? Not like many of the other fat cat whites I know here. Well done." He was nodding his head up and down,

---

* Necklacing is a form of execution conducted by forcing a rubber car tyre, filled with petrol, over a victim's chest and arms, and setting it alight. It is a grue-some form of mob justice and was reserved for lynching suspected traitors (police informers) in South Africa in the 1980s and 1990s.

doing an impression of Enid Blyton's 'Noddy' as he spoke. "Did they give you a medal?"

"No, nothing like that." We drove in silence. "I did write to Mandela though, and asked him whether he would send me a letter acknowledging that we had made a contribution. It would have been nice for the kids to have, one day."

"You didn't!" he exclaimed. "What did Mandela say?"

"Nothing. I was fobbed off by his secretary a few times. Something along the lines of the heraldry people looking into it, along with other medals and awards for MK veterans and so on. So, we're still waiting," I laughed. "Anyway that was years ago, 1994 or 1995. Not important any more."

He glanced at me. "Still, would have been nice to have some recognition, wouldn't it? Now tell me about the money?"

"No. They didn't pay us or anything, Irv."

"I don't mean that. I mean the money that you spend in the townships Is it yours? If not where does it come from?"

"No, not at all, from the Friends of Alexandra," I replied.

"Well, where do you get funding from?"

"From clients. People like you who have done the tour with me and seen what you have."

"Really? They give you money?"

"Some do, not all. I've had some very generous clients, and others that give me a just few dollars. Every little bit helps. A lot of people feel more comfortable giving me money for the Friends of Alexandra, rather than giving me a tip. That's not the purpose of the tour but it does sometime create a spin-off."

"Tips? They tip you?"

"Sure they do, and some of them very well."

"Why did you buy that bloke airtime?"

"Ernest? He's the *nduna*, the head of the hostel. He's my liaison with people at the hostel and the initiator of the projects that I work on there. I have to talk to him quite often."

He pulled a face, nodded again, and looked thoughtful.

I didn't realize then that it was the most costly airtime I would ever buy. In time to come, I would understand that it had caused Irving to distance himself from the Friends of Alexandra, forever.

Chapter Three

IRVING'S PLAN

The Grill House was full, as usual, but we had called ahead and booked a table. On arriving the four of us were shown to one of the outside tables.

"Good evening. My name is Gift and I will be looking after you, tonight," said a friendly smiling face, presenting the menus with a flourish.

"Bring us a drink first, Gift, we're bloody thirsty," said Irving, "and let's have a look at that wine list. Mmm, they've got some damn good wines here." He nodded approvingly.

"And the prices aren't bad either," said Mike.

"Hey! Look at this. That's what we'll have, a bottle or two of Chocolate Block—a magnificent wine."

Gift beamed as he retrieved the menus and rushed off to fetch the wine.

"Margs," said Mike, "I know you prefer white, but just try this red that Irv has selected. You'll never drink Sauvignon Blanc again."

"Nice waiter," said Irving, "I bet he's Zimbabwean."

"Why do you say that?" asked Mike.

"Well, they 're much more pleasant than the blacks down south, aren't they?"

Irving was looking down at the food menu and didn't see the three of us exchange glances. Margie shrugged slightly, looking mildly perplexed; Mike and I were quietly irritated.

Gift returned and triumphantly presented a bottle of Chocolate Block.

"Well done, my man," said Irving, "and where are you from?" This said while Gift was carefully pouring our wine.

"Zimbabwe, sir."

"I thought so. I suppose there are some quite pleasant ones here, but the *Zimbo's* are the best."

I saw the waiter serving the table next to us send an icy glare Irving's way, but luckily Gift returned with the food menus and another flash of teeth, looking like a Great White coming in for the kill.

"We have a great special tonight," he offered.

We all looked at him expectantly.

"Fillet on the bone."

"What's that?" I asked.

"Wonderful cut," said Irving, "fillet on one side of the bone and sirloin on the other. That's what I'll have, Gift, make mine medium rare."

"I thought you were a sheep man," said Mike, "that's what you farm isn't it? What do you know about cattle?"

"I know a lot about animals. Yvonne and I had to learn and learn fast when we started farming. Over the years you rub shoulders with other farmers and people in the meat industry and you learn. I know as much about cuts of beef as I do about lamb and mutton. Have it, Robbie, you'll love it."

Persuaded by Gift and Irving, we all ordered fillet on the bone.

While we waited for our order Irving stretched back in his chair and looked directly at Michael. "So, young Binckes. What are you doing with yourself, now days?"

Michael explained about going to the Cayman Islands.

"I hope you aren't pissing around too long, my boy. How old are you now?"

"Forty," Michael replied.

"Shit. And now you are going off to 'jol' (have a good time) in the Caribbean? Hope your dad isn't paying?"

He glanced at me sidelong, gauging my reaction. Irving and Yvonne had never had children, as a choice. I had once asked Irving why they had no children and he replied that they didn't need anybody else; as a couple they were totally self-sufficient but mutually dependent. "To be honest Robbie," he had added, "we were both selfish. We didn't want to have to share each other with anyone else."

"Of course not, Irv!" Michael replied, a little vexed at the question. "It's years since I had to ask Dad for any help."

"Hey!" Irving grinned, changing the subject, "while we wait for our food let me tell you a great joke." He leaned forward with a chuckle while the three of us smiled in anticipation. Irving loved jokes. Having delivered the punchline about a Jew and the Taliban, he pushed back his chair and roared with laughter; I laughed so much I nearly choked and had to wipe my eyes with the back of my hand. The red wine, the company and the ambience blended into an evening of great fun. While Irving and Michael chatted I looked at him and thought how well he had adapted after Yvonne's death. He and Yvonne had been inseparable, and it was now only four months since she had died, alarmingly soon after having been diagnosed with ovarian cancer. Irving had obviously moved on, or so I thought.

Replete with fillet on the bone; three bottles of Chocolate Block; two Windhoeks for me, topped off with two Burgermeister shooters introduced to Irving by our family alias 'Christo van der Burgh', I eventually asked Gift for the bill.

He rolled his eyes, showing a great deal of white, in Irving's direction. "He has already paid, sir."

"Come on, Irv. You can't pay. Let's split it. Please?"

"Not at all, Robbie. I've had a great night and a lovely tour today. It's the least I can do."

So Irving paid for the entire and not inconsiderable bill. I thought what a cantankerous character he was on the one hand, and how he had a heart as big as an open field on the other.

We made our loud goodbyes to Michael, climbed into the chauffer-driven car we had ordered, so as not to have to drive after drinking, and made our way home laughing and talking, while one of their drivers followed us in my own car. All in all, it had been a thoroughly pleasant day and evening.

And then Irving told me he was going to kill himself.

⸜

We were sitting in the lounge at home, after his story about Sotheby's and how overnight he had become a millionaire, he with a glass of red wine in his hand and me with a can of Castle beer.

"What am I going to do?" he repeated my question. "Well, yes, I *have* decided what to do. I'm going to kill myself."

For a second or two the shock of his statement hung in the room, like a man on the gallows.

"Come on Irv, don't be bloody stupid. You can't be serious!" I blurted out, shocked and apprehensive.

"I am one hundred per cent serious. I am not joking. I have decided to kill myself."

I looked at him carefully. Irving Tucker had a history of playing practical jokes on his friends, so it would not have been a surprise if this was just another of his tricks. Out of the corner of my eye I noticed that he wriggled his toes in his sandals as he spoke. He smiled slightly and took a sip of red wine, watching me all the while. He ran the tip of his tongue over his lips as he savoured the flavour and smiled again. I wasn't sure if he was expressing delight at the quality of the wine or pleasure at my discomfort.

"Delicious. Very nice wine, Robbie."

I ignored his comment. I was still trying to recover from his announcement. Hell, I asked myself, how can he talk about wine when he has just told me that he is going to kill himself? As I watched him calmly sipping his wine and observing me, I realized Irving was absolutely serious. He really intended killing himself.

"Shit!" I said, shaking my head in disbelief, "I really hope you're joking, man." Again I shook my head, like a prize fighter after a haymaker punch. "Irv, come on man, you really can't be serious! I, we, all know that you miss Yvonne, but life goes on. It's only been a few months; give yourself time; you'll heal. You've got all that money; what are you going to do with that? You could do so much good, you have such a lot to offer." I realized I was babbling.

Irving didn't take his eyes off me and coolly sipped his wine. He pursed his lips briefly then said, "No, Robbie, I have decided and that's that."

"But why?" I pleaded. "Why such a drastic decision?"

"I've had a good life. Actually, a fantastic life. I don't want to have to start all over. I would rather decide when I go, before I end up in some kind of home with people I don't even know wiping my bum for me."

"Come on Irv, it doesn't have to be like that. Hell's teeth, you can't just go and kill yourself. I mean it's not as though you're miserable? You had a good time tonight, didn't you? Well, I thought you did; maybe I was wrong. Shit. Killing yourself, Irv, it's just not an option. Put it out of your head."

"You must understand, Robbie, that of course I had fun tonight and of course I will have fun on holiday. That's why I'm here. But this isn't my life. Life back at the farm, well, you wouldn't want to know. It's lonely."

"When are you going to do it, if you are so determined?"

"I haven't really decided. There's a lot that has to be done first. I have to put all my affairs in order."

"Jeez—you won't do it tonight under our roof will you?"

He laughed. "No, but you'll know when. I'll tell you, I promise."

"Irv, I think you must have gone mad. You need to get help, counselling, see someone, surely? I mean this is madness, if you're really serious?"

"Of course I'm serious. And I have been having counselling, talking to that friend, Helen, the one I told you about."

"Have you told her?"

"Ja, she knows."

"Who else? Does your friend Tony Taylor know?"

"He knows, but I don't think he believes me."

"Not sure I do. You can't be serious, with all that money. Shit! Why don't you go and do something with that money? Make a difference in the world. Go and work for hospice, you were impressed with them and what they did for Yvonne, weren't you?"

He nodded but didn't say anything.

"Anyway, I don't believe you. People who say they are going to kill themselves never do. If you were really going to do it, you wouldn't tell a soul, you would just go and do it. I mean, didn't you once have a friend who killed himself?"

He nodded again and sipped his wine.

"Well, there you are. Did he tell you before he did it?"

He shook his head. "No, can't say that he did. Robbie, believe what you like. I've told you I'm going to do it. If you don't believe me, well, I really don't care. It's not going to make any difference whether you do or not." His face flushed.

I could see I had irritated him so decided to back down. I still didn't believe him but decided to play along.

"There is so much good you could do Irv. You have your health *and* all that money. You could maybe help young boys in the city; there must be youngsters who have never had a chance, even in England. You could help them financially, set up an organisation like my Friends of Alexandra. Start a charity. Shit, there is so, so much." I was almost shouting as I warmed to the subject, trying desperately to convince him to change his mind.

"Easy, Robbie. I will do some good. I'm planning to leave money to people who deserve it."

Immediately, inevitably, I wondered who Irving felt deserved to receive his money. Maybe Margie and I would be lucky—maybe we would be included on the list of his 'deserving' friends?

"Like who? Do they know?" I asked.

"Well, the Johnsons for a start—your pal, Ray. They are battling a bit," he said with a wry smile, "but no, I haven't told any of the people who are going to benefit."

Reluctantly I realized that by telling me he had ruled me out as a beneficiary in his will. I felt an acute twinge of disappointment. With all that money to be shared out, surely some could come our way? This was followed immediately by thinking, hoping, that Irving couldn't, wouldn't, actually kill himself. Would he?

Chapter Four

LONDON 1962

I first met Irving John Tucker in London in 1961. He was a kid of eighteen, I was two years his senior.

It was the time of Elvis Presley, Ray Charles, Chubby Checker and 'Big Bad John', James Dean, pencil skirts, winklepicker shoes and drainpipe trousers known as 'stovies', West Side Story, Joe Loss, the Twist and the Union Castle mailboats. Earls Court had earned its long lasting name of 'Kangaroo Valley'. I was never too sure whether this was because of the number of Australian itinerants or the hopping from bed to bed on the part of the residents; and of course there was the Overseas Visitors Club (OVC) where a lot of the hopping occurred. Home to twenty thousand plus South Africans, a similar number of Aussies, New Zealanders, Canadians and whoever else felt like a jol.

In the early sixties South Africans could work and romp in London without work permits, restrictions, visas or the fear of AIDS. In those days of *apartheid* South Africa it was a great novelty to get a job in London that would have been filled by a black person back home. For us South Africans, the more manual the work, the more it was in demand.

Apart from the fact that those type of jobs were easy to get, we took mischievous pleasure in being able to write home to 'white South Africa', in those pre-email times, letters—carried by the Union Castle mailboats, which took three weeks to arrive and usually double that time for a response to return—along the following lines:

> Dear Mom
> Have landed a job as a porter carrying suitcases ... Or ... Have landed a job as a labourer on a building site. Or, for those fortunate enough to have landed the most sought after job of all—good money in tips and very little effort required—Have landed a job as a parking attendant ...

Back home, there would be howls of mirth and amazement when reading these letters. Only black people did those jobs in the 'old' Republic.

The OVC became our home away from home. It was a real turnkey operation before the word turnkey was ever used. It comprised a 'main club' and several separate buildings dotted around Earls Court. We had meals in one of the restaurants, served by fellow travellers, and drank till we fell over in one of the bars, all staffed by fellow club members. Our favourite bar was the Grotto which featured the Club's talking parrot, named Max, after the founder of the OVC. We slept in rented accommodation at the OVC; collected our mail from the 'main club' and eagerly tore the envelopes open—in the days before skype, cell phones, text messages and twitter—for news of home. We booked tours to Westendorff in Austria to ski, before we had earned the money to pay for them; and of course, we looked for work. Best of all though, in the days before AIDS, we chatted up 'birds' whenever we could; and if we got lucky, took them back to our small, single rooms which accommodated a bed, a wash basin and a cupboard, miraculously squashed into a tiny space between four walls, warmed by gas heaters (fed with coins) to keep alive the flickering flame of passion, and warmth, against those crisp, snow-covered days.

Three young South Africans, Max Wilson, Connie Dresden and Nick Tarsh, together founded the OVC, affectionately referred to as 'The Club'. These three entrepreneurs cleverly recognized the need of youngsters from commonwealth countries, who were pouring into London, to have a base where they could rub shoulders, and sometimes a great deal more, with like-minded young men and women. The OVC filled that gap and soon mushroomed in size and number of 'members'. To keep the tills ringing and enough bodies in the vast number of beds they provided, the three bright young pioneers chartered ships to bring Australians, New Zealanders and South Africans, in increasing numbers, to the UK. South Africans sailed on Union-Castle mail boats, while Aussies and Kiwis travelled on ships of the Empress line. These sailings, with good reason, soon earned the reputation of being the first of the 'Love Boats'. The two-week voyage from Cape Town to Southampton offered all the ingredients required for a romance.

The passengers were young men and women, straight out of school or university or the army, navy or air force (at that time most white South African males of school-leaving age, were conscripted into National Service), feeling the freedom of 'civvy' life for the first time away from home, pumped full of testosterone, sunshine on their backs, a bit of money in the pocket, mixed with a rush of adrenalin at the adventure ahead, provided the perfect mix for ensuring shipboard romance and animal sexuality. The money in the pockets, meant for survival on reaching London, and which had been saved so carefully for the adventure, usually disappeared on gin and tonics in a fraction of the time it had taken to save.

Of course, after two weeks at sea, the party was over. As the Union-Castle liner nudged its way through the fog into the port of Southampton, reality struck home. Watched with envy and silence by the kids, most of whom had already exhausted their meagre finances, the stewards (who had been made to jump through hoops for the past two weeks) climbed into their e-type Jaguars parked on the quayside. The e-types having been paid for by profits the stewards made by pulling a trick as old as the hills. After serving the first couple of G&Ts, they would dip their fingers in gin and then run them around the rim of a glass containing tonic and a slice of lemon, only. We got the taste of the gin, they got the profit. With, at most, a disdainful farewell wave of their hands, they roared off into the early morning mist for a week's leave—before exploiting their next batch of young innocents.

The Union-Castle ships were usually met by OVC management at Southampton while the Empress ships docked nearer London at Tilbury. The welcoming party would herd the six hundred and more passengers, like sheep dogs behind their flocks, onto ten or so passenger coaches. These coaches would transport the new arrivals in convoy into their new world of London, Earls Court and the OVC. Luggage was taken from the ships, packed into furniture removal trucks which had been chartered for the day, and transported to the OVC, to meet up with its owners a few hours later.

I had been in London for five months and was lucky enough to land a job as a porter at the OVC soon after arriving. It was my responsibility, among others, to employ 'casual' labour on the day the ships came in.

The club was abuzz that day. Great excitement at the thought of a new supply of 'talent' to brighten the scene. Resident gigolos like Hilton Whittaker alias Lergy, his good-looking face brown as a berry from the recent glare off the snow slopes of Westendorff, were swanning through the club as he waited; waves of Old Spice wafting in his wake, glancing around to see who was watching him. He wasn't the only one. A new ship arrival brought out all the Lotharios, like flying ants after a Highveld storm, as pomaded hair and seldom-worn 'best' outfits oozed around the club like sharks circling their prey.

I was studying the passenger and room lists, determining where the six hundred Australians and New Zealanders arriving that day, at Tilbury on an Empress liner, had been allocated accommodation in one of the OVC's twenty establishments.

"Do you need any more porters this afternoon, Rob?" enquired Tony Ferrie, the Club's newly appointed manager. Tony shared his lofty position with Lester Jolly. Both were South African and only a few years older than me. Lester had a personality that matched his name and Tony was a gentleman down to his toenails, who tried to help everybody who needed it.

"No, Tony. I'm okay, thanks."

Tony looked disappointed.

"Oh, look, there are a couple of guys who I always use for the arrival of the ships, see what you can do, will you? I've told them you will give them a casual job for this afternoon. There are three of them. The coach is leaving Tilbury at lunchtime. Lance Schroeder will phone just before they leave to give us his time of arrival … should be about three-thirty. I've told them to report to you here at two o' clock. See what you can do. Can't let them down now, can I?" Tony turned and walked away.

I shouted after him: "Okay Tony, but what are their names?"

"Tucker, Schneeberger and Starling," he called back over his shoulder, "and by the way, Starling is spastic. Thought you'd better know."

"What? What do you mean, spastic? How will he carry suitcases?" But Tony had gone.

A wall of Old Spice hit me as Lergy leaned over the counter in the reception area, resting his elbow on the counter and cupping his chin in his hand.

"Hi sport," he drawled, "what time are the coaches coming?"

"Come on Lergy, can't you wait? What's wrong with that lovely little blonde you were slobbering over the other night?"

"She's boring—and she's falling in love with me. That's always the time to say goodbye, in my book. I need a new adventure and that means fresh stock." He looked around with his sleepy 'come to bed eyes', searching for a new conquest.

I looked at my watch.

"Twelve o' clock now; they should be leaving shortly and the baggage vehicles should arrive here before the coaches. The luggage will probably be here at three-ish."

Lergy sighed, stood up straight, smoothed his brylcreemed, wavy, shiny, black hair with his right hand and, satisfied there was not a hair out of place, sauntered off in a swirl of aftershave, flashing a Colgate toothpaste smile at two young new arrivals, his bright, white, gleaming teeth highlighting his impressive tan. They had their backs to Lergy as he looked back at me, smiled, winked and held his thumb up as if to say, "They'll do in the interim."

I carried on with my work, head bent over the reception counter, studying the lists that matched people to their accommodation and luggage. I felt the presence of someone waiting to speak to me.

I looked up.

A strange apparition stood in front of me. Dressed in a safari type short-sleeved khaki shirt, old long khaki shorts held up by an old tie acting as a belt around his trim stomach, barefoot and smiling, was a bright-eyed, good-featured young man. His curly golden brown hair, fairly long, peeped out from under a large brown paper bag (the kind in which sugar was sold, back home) used now as a hat. He was dressed in the same way as black labourers, working on the docks back home.

"Hello my *baas* (boss)!" said the apparition, smiling broadly.

It was Irving John Tucker.

"I looking for work, *baas*. *Mnumzane* (Mr) Ferrie say we can have job carrying cases when people come. He tell me, find *Mnumzane* Robin." He pronounced 'work' as 'wok', imitating, rather poorly, the accent of those same black labourers when speaking English and not their native dialect.

Behind him I could see two grinning faces. My eyes had widened at the sight of the apparition; now I looked more closely at the other two. I realized that one had an inane grin and was holding his arm in front of his body at right angles to his torso; his fingers pointed to the ground, looking like a chicken's foot.

I looked back at the man in the paper hat who was watching me carefully.

"Well you've found me. I'm Robin. Don't tell me ... yes, I know, you must be ..." looking at the paper on which I had noted their names, "Tucker and Schneeberger and Starling. Shit! Have you been sent by Tony Ferrie?"

"Yes *baas*. He say we can have work," said the paper-hat.

Schneeberger was a young man of similar age, with curly black hair and a suntanned face, also showing evidence of a recent visit to the ski slopes of Westendorf.

I looked at the third grinning figure, the one with a hand like a chicken's foot, Starling, and noticed a thin dribble of spittle trickling from the corner of his lop-sided smile.

"You must be Starling?" I said unnecessarily, noticing that my voice quavered.

He convulsed and dribbled more spit. I took this to be an affirmative nod.

"Shit!" I said again, not really knowing what else to say.

"Don't worry *baas*. We good wokkers. We got plenty, plenty experience."

"I don't have much option now. Come on, we'd better go outside and wait for the furniture vans and luggage."

The three of them followed me, Mike Starling trailing behind. He dragged his right leg behind him as he walked and his head was permanently cocked, like a pet budgie, at a forty-five-degree angle, leaning towards his right shoulder.

A light drizzle was falling as we stood waiting for the arrival of the three baggage trucks. The trucks carried over fifteen hundred pieces of luggage that we were to match to the names of arrivals in each of the accommodation buildings. When the new occupants arrived teams of porters would deliver their luggage to their rooms. For casual porters it was the chance to earn tips and be the first to stake a claim to new, fresh, unsuspecting Aussie and Kiwi 'sheilas'. This was a perk of the job. But before that happened, my helpers and I would sort the luggage and allocate it to the respective buildings.

"Here they come," shouted Schneeberger, as the first brown furniture truck came into view. It was emblazoned with the words 'Parsons Removals' in large letters, beneath them, in smaller letters, was the slogan 'We move you to a better place'. The truck swished to a standstill on the wet road.

The four of us, assisted by another ten porters I had employed as casuals, set to off-loading the baggage. As they off-loaded they called out the name of the owner as it appeared on the luggage label, and I shouted back the accommodation allocated. In this way we would end with twenty different stacks of luggage for the twenty different buildings in which the guests would be housed.

Despite the cold drizzle it was hot work, but we managed to complete the task before the passenger coaches arrived. Down the length of the street outside the OVC, as far as one could see, the pavement was covered with over one thousand suitcases. Every type and size of suitcase imaginable was there.

"Well done, you guys."

The booming voice of the most envied man at the club rang out. It was that of Lance Schroeder, a fellow South African who had the glory job of meeting new arrivals off the ships and, as their guide, escorting them on the two-hour journey to the OVC. Lance was a natty dresser, sometimes wearing a pastel pink shirt, always a navy-blue blazer with a bright red handkerchief showing in the top pocket, a matching red tie, grey slacks and highly polished black shoes. When Lance smiled, which was often, his gold fillings showed, whispering 'success', and not very quietly.

Lance shot his cuffs, showing off a pair of gold (certainly not plated) cufflinks. "The passengers will be here in five minutes. Well done," he said looking around at the piles of luggage.

"Everything sorted?" he laughed at his own pun, flashing his gleaming fillings.

"Ja baas," shouted Irving, from where he was placing the last of the suitcases.

Lance looked at him in amazement. Irving had taken an empty cement bag from an adjacent building site, torn a hole in the bottom, slipped it over his head and was wearing it as a cape; his paper was now quite soggy from the drizzle. He was still barefoot and as he moved closer I saw Lance recoil slightly, as the rich aroma of Irving's sweat and damp paper reached his nostrils.

"Who are you?" he asked in amazement.

"Just an ordinary wokker, *baas*, doing some wok. Thank you *baas*, thank you *baas*," as he obsequiously rubbed his hands together, bowing his head in deference.

"Yes, well," said the sartorially elegant Schroeder, for once at a loss for words.

The situation was saved by the first of the coaches swinging round the corner into our street. All the porters were watching the coach expectantly. The first coach drew to a halt in front of the OVC with a squeak of brakes and a whoosh of air as the door was released. The convoy of Aussie-laden coaches pulled up behind.

We gazed up at the first coach. The windows were covered with condensation, making it difficult to see the interior. A few of the occupants had used their handkerchiefs or hands to clear the moisture on the inside of the windows and their faces were pressed enquiringly against the glass, keen to catch the first glimpse of their future Earls Court companions. Eager pairs of eyes looked out excitedly. Below them, on the pavement were piles and piles of their luggage, but their interest was captured by the sight of Mike Starling, Irving Tucker and Graham Schneeberger.

Each was dragging his right leg behind him, like a wounded crab; each had an arm extended in front like a Caliban claw; each head was tilted towards the right shoulder; and each had a thin trickle of saliva dribbling down his chin. Then all three, attempting to make an even worse impression, rolled their eyes back in their sockets and gazed up at the horrified new arrivals with only the whites of their eyes showing. Irving and Schneeberger were copying Mike Starling.

I could see the shocked expressions on the faces of the Aussies. One or two of them shook their heads in disbelief and sympathy.

The coach door opened but before I could climb the coach steps to make a short speech of welcome, Tucker, still in his shorts, cement sack and paper bag hat, dragged himself up the steps.

His face was contorted, spittle dripped, eyes rolled back, his leg dragged and he scrabbled at the handrails with clawed hands. He reached the top and pulled himself, shuffling, into the gangway to stand behind the driver, facing the passengers, swaying, as he rolled his eyes further back.

I looked back towards the pavement and saw Mike Starling, bent over, holding his stomach, his shoulders heaving; tears of laughter ran down his face and merged with his spittle as he watched Irving mimic his own disabilities.

The Aussies craned their necks, leaning into the aisle to get a better view of Irving standing behind the driver, facing them. There were whispered comments of 'Shame!' and 'Poor thing!'

Tucker stood facing them in his worker's attire, barefoot, swaying and dribbling. When he had the attention of everyone on the coach he pretended to laugh; the sound emerged as a ghoulish cackle. There was an appalled silence as one hundred and twenty eyes looked on in disbelief. His face contorted into a smile that looked like a death's head grin. He gazed at the shocked Aussies, rearranged his mouth and slurred: "Mai ... naaame is Irving Tucker ... that is ... T.U.C.K.E.R. with ... a T. Weeelcome toooo London and the OVC!"

Mike Starling collapsed on the pavement holding his belly and crying with laughter.

⁊

Over the next few months Irving became a regular feature at the OVC, always shadowed by the highly intelligent Mike Starling, the New Zealander who suffered from cerebral palsy. Mike and Irving shared accommodation and could be seen everywhere together. Mike worshipped Irving—probably because Irving took the piss out of him as much as he did everyone else. Despite having to help him dress at times, like tying the knot on a tie or tying his shoelaces for him, he treated Mike as if he had no affliction at all, allowing him not an inch for excuses—unlike the rest of us who generally treated Mike like Dresden china, making him feel different or pitiable. With Irving, Mike was a regular bloke.

The days of the week at the OVC built to a climax on Sundays at lunchtime—the Sunday lunchtime dance session in the basement, usually with a live band performing. The OVC was full of young hopefuls who had come to London to make it big in the entertainment world. Some of them succeeded and went on to hit the big-time, such as The Animals and Don Spencer and The Strangers. It was even rumoured that the Rolling Stones had played there.

From midday on a Sunday a procession of what appeared to be monks streaming into a monastery poured through the doors of the club, as young men and women in the 'visitors to London uniform' of grey, black or blue hooded duffle coats entered its doors, their breath puffing clouds of steam into the cold winter air. Many walked hands-in-pockets as they approached the club, feeling and counting their coins to see how many beers could be bought, and whether or not they could afford a drink for a female target, to improve the odds.

Irving had graduated from being employed as a casual porter to the somewhat glamorous position of barman in the dance floor bar on Sundays. He had cast aside his paper hat, cement bag and Zulu imitations to wear a black bowtie above a false-fronted white dress shirt (under which he wore a T-shirt) and a red jacket.

From 11h30 onwards the bar filled rapidly with like-minded young men and women. Duffle coats came off, showing young women in pretty, dainty, shirtwaist dresses that contrasted with the high leather boots coming into fashion, usually marking new arrivals intent on creating a favourable impression. The older hands (someone who had been in London for longer than six weeks) wore the badge of experience: ski pants from the slopes of Austria, or jeans worn with loose tops, the more daring ladies showing their voluptuous breasts, signalling their new found liberation in swinging London by going bra-less.

The buzz of conversation and the tinkle of laughter would grow louder. Soon the eyes of the predators and their prey would begin to smart from the cigarette smoke that swirled and rose from glowing cigarette tips as Texan and Lucky Strike cigarettes (which cost five shillings and five pence for twenty) were puffed away with wild abandon by both sexes. Most males held their cigarettes between the thumb and the forefinger in a poor man's imitation of James Dean; women left bright red lipstick marks on the ends of their cigarettes (which were usually balanced between the 'v' made by the index and middle fingers) after having been drawn from pursed bright red lips, head tilted back, creating a sophisticated stream of smoke blown gently upwards, floating and merging with the already smoke-filled room.

Noise and laughter grew in volume. More people entered until people were squashed against each other. The temperature of the room rose, matching that of hot young bodies. Beer flowed. Castle and Fosters lager competed for dominance and were swilled down, Fosters by the Aussies and Castle by the South Africans. Beer glasses were held to lips below eyes that swivelled and scanned the faces and figures of the women like bidders at a cattle auction. Sometimes the gazes of the hunter and the hunted would meet and 'lock-on' like homing missiles; the males would edge towards their target, moving shoulders side to side through the tightly packed mass of bodies.

Opening lines ranged from the standard 'How long have you been here?' to the equally uninspiring 'What are you doing with the first part of the rest of your life—this afternoon?' One really did not have to be too inventive; everyone was reading from the same page, and apart from a few who actually came to dance, everyone had the same goal: to meet someone attractive, to dance as a form of foreplay and then to spend Sunday afternoon engaged in sexual pleasure.

Tension and testosterone levels would spill over as the band arrived, usually late and in a flurry. They tuned their guitars, making whining sounds as if pieces of music had been specially composed to match the building sense of anticipation. Then they were ready. There was a slight lull in the hum of conversation and then the air would be split as the band belted out 'Let's Twist Again', resulting in the dance floor filling and bodies gyrating and twisting, like some fertility ritual. By three o' clock the dance floor would have thinned out as newly-met couples departed, arms around waists. Those remaining swayed to the slower rhythms of the romantic melodies played at the end of the session.

The less successful males hid their disappointment and clustered around the bar, talking to Irving and his colleagues, sinking more beers, pretending that they were more interested in drinking then chasing 'a bit of tail'. By four o' clock it was all over. The bar counters would be wiped down, broken glasses picked up and cigarette butts thrown into rubbish bins. Irving worked while the beds of Earls Court rocked.

A few months later, in 1962, Irving and I went our separate ways. I remained in England; Irving returned home to South Africa and found employment with Plastic and Metal Industries (PMI).

Chapter Five

JOBURG REUNION

I had grown up among the beautiful rolling hills and valleys of the Transkei, with a coastal strip unequalled for its spectacular scenery, and was educated at Umtata High School. The school song said it all: "To rolling hills and valleys, to homes beside the sea ..."

In the 1950s Umtata was a small town with a population of some 12,000 white people. It had only two schools—one English and one Afrikaans—although there was a very good school for blacks, St Johns College, situated in the 'location' outside town. There were a few tarred roads, no traffic lights and two cathedrals—Anglican and Roman Catholic—which, we argued, made Umtata a city, rather than a mere town.

I had endured a rather torrid childhood. The product of a broken home, I was shunted between boarding school and charitable aunts and uncles who were prepared to give me a home. Fortunately, throughout this turbulent period my grandparents were always there—a permanent backstop in my young life.

When I was twelve years old my father died as a result of an injury received when he was serving in North Africa in the Eighth Army during the Second World War. An enemy shell scored a direct hit on his anti-aircraft gun which exploded, causing his lung to burst. The recurring problems associated with a collapsed lung finally became too much for his heart, and it gave up the struggle in 1953.

I spent two years living with Doff and Tim, my uncle and aunt and their two children, Gillian and Mark, in Boksburg, in the province known then as the Transvaal (now Gauteng), but finished my schooling in Umtata.

On completion of my military training at the Naval Gymnasium I returned to Umtata, not too sure what I was going to do next. As an interim measure and to earn an income while I focused on playing rugby for the local club, Pirates, I worked as a salesman for Sparg's Wholesale, selling a variety of wares to the many traders whose shops dotted the hills of the Transkei. My years of never really belonging anywhere had made their impact. I was used to fending for myself and had developed an independent streak.

My mother, who lived with my stepfather in Bechuanaland (Botswana), expressed a desire that I should go to Rhodes University. As I would be responsible for paying my university fees from the small inheritance I had received from my father, the idea of expanding my mind by travelling abroad for a year or two seemed far more attractive.

So in November 1961 I set sail for England and joined the thousands of young men and women from 'the colonies' at the Overseas Visitors Club in Earls Court. During my time abroad I met and fell in love with an English girl, Jean, whom I met one night at the Hammersmith Palais.

Spurred on by the desire to improve my prospects and to gain experience before returning to South Africa, I set about applying for a position as a sales representative. Based on what I had seen while growing up in Umtata, this was the plum job. As schoolboys we used to admire the 'reps' in Umtata: fancy company cars, expense accounts and status. My rationale was that if I landed a job with one of the large international companies, this would provide me with a career launch pad for my return to South Africa.

Landing a position wasn't as easy as I had hoped. Eventually, after having been rejected three times by Quaker Oats Limited, by sheer persistence (another characteristic that I had honed by years of fending for myself), I was offered a position as a salesman, or as we preferred to call it, a representative. The offer came with a company car (a Morris Minor Estate), a good salary and excellent training. I became a member of an elite company of 'reps' who had to wear a trilby when calling on customers. Now married to Jean, I began to look the part. I wore tweed jackets with leather patches on the elbows, a trilby and even smoked a pipe—not that I enjoyed the taste or the burnt tongue which resulted, but to hell with that, it certainly added to my image.

After a succession of postings and promotions, which saw us live in Felixstowe, Norwich and Berkhamstead, I was headhunted and joined the Co-Operative Wholesale Society as a Training Consultant. My training and grounding with Quaker Oats Ltd had been invaluable and I felt that I had more than compensated for not going to Rhodes University. Jean and I moved to Manchester where I started my new career.

As I became more settled in my career and lifestyle, my time in England stretched far beyond my original plans. But the pull of Africa's sun and the country, its people and smells, became stronger and stronger. Finally, in 1969, I was again headhunted, this time by a large chain store group, and was offered employment in Johannesburg. My training and experience in England had paid off—I was going home.

By the end of 1970 I was back in Johannesburg. My one year of 'broadening my mind and gaining experience' in England had stretched to nine years. I brought home with me an English wife and two children, Samantha and Michael, and took up a position with a major retail chain, the OK Bazaars group, as its Promotions and Public Relations Manager.

❦

Early in the new year I was walking down the passage on the sixth floor of our offices when I heard a shout. I turned round to look at the source.

"Robbie! It can't be! Is that you? Shit! You old bugger, it is! What are you doing here? I thought you were still in the UK?"

It was Irving. He grabbed me and we hugged each other. More mature, still smiley eyes and now decorated with a golden beard.

"I was. Came back last November. Joined OK as their Promotions and PR Manager and here I am. And you? What are you doing here in the OK?"

"We supply plastic toys. I'm with PMI, you must know Dave Feinstein, the toy buyer here?"

I nodded. Dave was one of the most pleasant executives at the OK, and I said so.

Irving agreed: "Well, he's in the toy industry, isn't he? We're all nice fun loving blokes in the toy business. I've come to see him; we do quite a lot of business with Dave."

So Irving and I arranged to meet for lunch the following week, to catch up on the years since we had gone our separate ways.

The following Friday, and every last Friday of every second month from then on, we met for lunch at the LM restaurant, next to the railway lines in Noord Street, at the bottom of Hillbrow. It was a scruffy Portuguese restaurant, plastic tables, plastic tablecloths, but very real Mozambican prawns, the best outside the waters of Lourenço Marques (LM), and served thirty-six prawns at a time, accompanied by three bowls containing the hottest chilli sauce this side of hell, lemon-butter, and garlic, with bits of fresh garlic floating in the sauce. Eaten with the fingers and ladled with the sauces, nothing more than rice accompanied the prawns. We soon developed a tradition: the meal always started with a portion of 'flaming hot' peri-peri chicken livers—which would have made Nando's 'extra hot' taste bland—served with fresh crunchy Portuguese bread that soaked up the sauce and gravy, prolonging our hedonistic feast.

As I walked into the LM the following Friday, only one table in the restaurant was occupied, by three people—Irving and two women. Irv stood up and shook my hand.

"Robbie, I've brought us a couple of chicks to liven things up," he said with a laugh. I looked at the smiling women who remained seated and nodded in greeting. I sat down in the vacant chair between the women.

"I thought you said you were married?" I asked, looking at Irving.

"I am," he laughed, "this is my wife Yvonne. We won't make her stand up because you'll get a crick in your neck looking at her, and this is our friend, Lynne Johnson."

"Hello Robbie," the two women chorused in unison.

"I'm his wife, Yvonne," the dark-haired attractive woman said, pointing to herself. She spoke with a London accent. Even while seated I could see that she was a great deal taller than average.

"And the other one, Lynne, is for you Robbie." All three were looking at me and smiling broadly.

I looked at Lynne; she had an attractive face framed by brown hair. I felt my face flush and hoped my embarrassment didn't show.

'Oh … well … um …" I stuttered and stammered, not sure how to wriggle out of the situation.

All three roared with laughter.

"Only bullshitting you, Robbie. Lynne is the wife of a good friend of ours, Ray Johnson. She and Yvonne were shopping in town and I suggested they join us for lunch. I have to take them home at the end of the day and I'm certainly not going back to the office after lunch. Are you?"

I shook my head in answer.

"Well, I suggested they join us here," Irving paused as the waiter arrived with a tray of four bottles of Laurentina beer, opened and poured them into four ice-cold frosted beer glasses, "so you had better not try anything with her, otherwise Ray will be bloody pissed off."

"I can assure you I have no intention of pissing off her husband and certainly won't be trying anything."

Yvonne stood up. She was strikingly tall and wore a green scarf around her slim neck, a green skirt and green blouse. "He's teasing you Robbie, but he's not bullshitting you about my height, is he?"

She was right.

I looked up at her and noticed Irving looking at her at the same time. His eyes sparkled and his face wore an expression of complete devotion. A smile flickered at the edges of his mouth as he gazed, almost in awe, at the woman he so obviously adored.

They had met two years earlier when Irving was on holiday in the Cape and Yvonne was visiting from England, staying with a friend in Camps Bay. Fate destined that the two would choose the same hot summer day to go to the same beach—Camps Bay. Irving was lying on his towel covered in sun tan oil when, about thirty metres away, he noticed two women wearing bikinis. Despite being seated it was clear that one of them was extremely tall and lithe. She was wearing a summer straw hat with a blue ribbon around the crown. Irving watched; he had never seen a more beautiful woman. He tried to catch her eye but each time he looked in her direction she looked away. Desperate to make an impression he leaped to his feet, dusted off the sand, ran down to the water, splashed through the shallows and dived into the sea. When he looked back his heart sank; she was lying down and paying him no interest. After swimming for a few minutes he made up his mind to approach her directly, steeled himself to the task and began walking out of the sea. To his horror, he saw the leggy beauty packing away her towels and clothes in preparation for departure. "Damn!" he whispered to himself and speeded up, but without a backward glance the two women set off to the car park. Irving was too late.

The gods interceded. A gust of wind lifted the straw hat of the taller girl. She shrieked and tried to clutch it, to no avail. The straw hat, blue ribbon streaming behind, sailed through the air and then cartwheeled across the sand towards Irving. He seized the opportunity, and the hat; with pounding heart and hat in hand he jogged up to the two women. Close up he was even more entranced by the long-limbed, black-haired, brown-eyed, olive-skinned beauty.

She saw a smiling face with crinkly blue eyes under a mop of curly brown hair, atop a sun-tanned body a good few inches short of her own height.

Irving bowed in mock deference, sweeping the sand with the hat in an exaggerated gesture.

"I believe this is your hat ma'am?" he said, offering the hat to her. "My name is Irving and I would love to buy you a drink," he said rather breathlessly.

"Yes, it is mine," she said with a smile, "thank you very much. I think I should buy *you* a drink, for saving my hat for me."

That was it. They were married six months later. And Irving was still besotted. Here they were together and happiness radiated from them.

"Well, wearing that green outfit you remind me of 'the Jolly Green Giant'," I teased, relieved that we had moved off the subject of Lynne and me.

Yvonne laughed and sat down.

"Jolly green giant, Robbie?" she murmured in a pronounced London accent, smiling. "I like that. Yes, the jolly green giant."

And from that day on Yvonne was known to me as the Jolly Green Giant.

"Anyway, cheers!" Irving raised his glass in salute and clinked it against mine.

"Good to see you again, old friend," he smiled at me.

"Thanks Irv. Good to see you as well. We had some good times in London didn't we?"

We each drank a mouthful of the ice-cold beer and Irving smacked his lips.

"Let's order," he said, "call that Mozambican waiter over here."

Six bored waiters stood against the wall watching us.

"How do you know he's Mozambican?" asked Lynne.

"You can always tell, they're much blacker than our locals," said Irving confidently.

We ordered our prawns and a bottle of Gateaux Portuguese wine with which to wash them down, and another to lubricate our throats as the conversation flowed. Irving related the story of Mike Starling and the OVC. He had us in stitches. The waiters watched in amazement, smiling when he leapt to his feet and demonstrated how he had copied Mike Starling that day in London. With the next bottle of wine our laughter became louder, and after another our jokes and wisecracks became hilarious, or so we thought. All the while, apart from the interlude of Irving's one man show, the bored waiters, having given up all hope of any other customers, stood with their backs to the wall and watched us getting more and more drunk.

"What's the time?" Irving asked nobody in particular.

"Don't you have a watch?" I asked.

"Never wear one. People think you have money if you flash a watch."

"Come on Irv, don't be ridiculous." I held my wrist towards him so he could see the time on my watch.

"Wow! It's five-thirty already."

I jumped up. "I left my car on Queen Elizabeth Bridge—they tow them away if they're there after four!"

"Leave it Robbie, you're much too late. It's either gone already or, if it hasn't, it'll be waiting when you get there. Have another drink. Four Irishes," he shouted to the waiters.

Lynne looked alarmed.

"No Irving. I really should go home. Ray will be home any minute now."

"Phone the bugger, tell him you are having a bit of fun for a change. Anyway you can't go till I take you, hey?"

Lynne's face was shining from the effects of the alcohol and although she had freshened her makeup her lipstick was crooked and slightly smeared above her top lip. Despite this she looked even more attractive than when we had first met, earlier.

"Okay," she shrugged, and said in a resigned tone, "I'll get hell when I get home if Ray is waiting for me. Still, it'll be worth it," she said, blushing and giggling.

Night was creeping up as the four of us staggered down the stairs and into the evening. Despite it being dusk, the light of day after the gloom of the LM was startlingly bright. I blinked, struggling with the glare.

48

"There's my car," I said, pointing. "Hell, that's a lucky break—it hasn't been towed away after all."

"Lucky sod," said Irving. "Lynne, why don't you drive with Robbie and Yvonne and I will follow."

"Great idea," we agreed, and set off for my car, the only vehicle parked on the Queen Elizabeth Bridge.

"Hey wait!" Irving exclaimed. "Here's an idea —why don't we jerk old Ray's chain? He's never met you Robbie, and he doesn't know that Lynne has been shopping with Yvonne. Why don't you bullshit him that you're an old friend of Lynne's, bumped into her and took her out for lunch? He won't know that Yvonne and I were there as well. We'll park around the corner while you give him a rev."

Lynne looked uncomfortable but said nothing to oppose the suggestion. Irving was already chortling at the idea of Ray's probable agitation.

"Oh go on Robbie—it'll really rattle his cage," urged Yvonne, cheerfully promoting Irving's mischief.

"Ja, but then we'll come round the corner and he'll see the joke," said Irving, "come on, let's go."

"Let's find a phone booth first. I must phone him; if he's at home he won't know where I am," said Lynne.

"Don't you give the game away, Lynne; don't tell him you've been with us. Just tell him you'll explain why you're so late when you get home."

She nodded. "Has anyone got five cents for the phone?"

I dug in my pocket and handed her some loose change. We found a nearby phone booth and watched as she opened the door, propped it open with her foot, and dialled. We couldn't hear what she was saying but Ray was evidently at home, waiting for her return. She hung up and joined us on the pavement, wrinkling her nose in disgust. "Whew! That phone booth stinks. Someone's peed in it."

"You were lucky to find a phone in it," I commented, "they've been ripped out of most of the booths in town."

"What did he say—you didn't tell him, did you?" quizzed Irving.

Lynne shook her head. "He didn't say much. I just said I'd been out for lunch. But he's not too happy that I wasn't home when he got back from work."

"Come on, let's go. See you at Lynne's. We'll wait around the corner till you've finished pulling old Ray's chain."

Irving was already chuckling in anticipation as he and Yvonne walked off, arms around each other for support, neither too steady on their feet.

Lynne and I climbed into my Chev Commander, a perk from the OK, and she directed me to her home in Malvern. By the time we pulled up outside the house it was already dark and I was beginning to have second thoughts.

"I hope your husband doesn't blow a fuse!"

"No, he'll see the joke after we tell him, he's got a great sense of humour—I hope." She bit her lip, glanced at me, but said nothing more.

I looked in my rear view mirror and was reassured to see Irving behind us. He cruised past in his Beetle and turned the corner. All the lights were on in the Johnson's house and as we climbed out of the car the front door opened. A fair-haired man stood at the top of the steps, silhouetted by the light behind him.

"Hi darling!" Lynne called as she climbed the steps, shakily, with me following, treading as steadily as possible under the circumstances.

"Where have you been? Look at the time. Shit, I was worried—" Ray broke off, seeing me walking behind Lynne, "—who's this?"

I smiled and held out my hand to shake his. He ignored me.

"It's okay, darling," as she tucked her arm under mine, "this is an old friend, Robbie."

"Robbie? Robbie who? From where?"

My smile now somewhat strained, I greeted him. "Hi Ray. Nice to meet you at last."

Ray was looking totally confused.

"Lynne and I go back years. We were very, very good friends, at one time weren't we Lynne?" I turned towards her for confirmation.

"Yes," she smiled, playing along, "yes, very good friends.'

"Well, I hadn't seen Lynne for years and we bumped into each other shopping this morning."

"Remember? I told you I was going shopping, darling."

He nodded. Tight-lipped he looked at me, clearly wanting an explanation.

"Well, after we had chatted we decided to have lunch. I remembered that Lynne loves prawns, hey Lynne? So off we went to the LM. Well, sorry about the hour, but we had such a good time together, time just flew, next thing it was getting dark. Anyway, here she is, safe and sound."

Ray looked as though he was going to explode. "Christ! Do you know what time it is now? Lunch! You can't have been having lunch all this time—all afternoon? Jeez. How can you do this Lynne?"

"Well," I said, "we certainly had a lot to talk about, didn't we Lynne."

"Come on darling, don't be a wet blanket, I'm home now." We were still standing at the top of the steps. "Why don't you invite Robbie in for a drink."

Ray glared at me. If his eyes had been pistols he would have scored a direct hit.

"You want to bring him into my home—well BUGGER THAT!"

Howls of laughter gusted from the pavement. Irving and Yvonne had crept up and witnessed the entire exchange. Irving opened the gate and he and Yvonne tottered up the steps, clutching their stomachs and roaring with mirth.

"What are *you* doing here?" Ray asked Irving.

"Ha ha! Ha ha! You fell for it, hey Ray? You really fell for it!" and Irving slapped him on the back.

Ray still hadn't realized that it was a practical joke and looked from one to the other in dazed bewilderment. The four of us cracked up and Irving clapped him on the back again.

"We all went for lunch, Ray. Robbie's bullshitting you. Come on Ray, where's your hospitality? Lost it with your sense of humour? Let's go inside and have a drink."

Irving led the way and flopped into a large armchair; still chuckling he wiped his eyes with the back of his hand. "You should have seen your face, Ray."

Ray smiled sheepishly. "You mean Ronnie, I mean Robbie, didn't go for lunch?" he asked hopefully.

Irving burst out laughing, again. "Yes he did, but we arranged the lunch. Lynne was with us. She and Yvonne had been shopping so they joined Robbie and me at the LM. We had a great time, a long lunch, now we're here. Lighten up Ray; give us all a drink!"

Ray's face fell. He looked daggers at me and has disliked me ever since.

Chapter Six

THE JOKER

Irving was born to Dan and Freda Tucker on 15 August, 1944. A typical Johannesburg middle class family, they lived in the suburb of Parkwood, and Dan worked as an auditor for one of the major international auditing companies. Irving attended Parktown Primary School and then completed standard eight at Parktown Boys' High. Dan and Freda realized then that he needed extra attention and sent him to Damelin to complete his matric. Despite his typical, middle class environment, Irving proved anything but typical. He was always different. Being five years younger than his brother, Brian, did not stop the youngest Tucker from taking control.

His achievements at school were unremarkable—he always did only just enough work to scrape through the exams. In this way he squeaked through his school career, never distinguishing but never disgracing himself either. However, on the school rugby field he soon earned a reputation as a fearless tackler, and from the first day he played until he finished school, his good-looking face was permanently marked by a succession of black eyes, scratches and bruises. The blemishes changed places but never disappeared entirely. It was as if he felt no pain and no fear.

His ingenuity and canniness were evident from an early age and would remain a feature throughout his life.

As a small boy Irving would walk from their home to the bus stop at Zoo Lake, a distance of a few kilometres, where he would meet his father coming home for lunch. Dan worked in the mornings in Braamfontein and sometimes returned to work from home in the afternoons. On one of these occasions, when Irving was eight years old, as they were walking home from the bus stop Dan heard the sound of coins jingling in Irving's pocket.

"What's that sound of money I hear from your pocket?" he asked.

"My pennies," Irving replied, sticking his hand into his pocket protectively.

"Where did you get pennies from?"

"School," was the reply, as he pushed his hand deeper into his pocket.

"Since when has the school been dishing out pennies?"

"No, it's not from the school. It's from the boys at school."

Dan stopped walking and looked at Irving in amusement.

"Why do the boys at school give you pennies?"

"No, Dad, they don't just give me pennies for nothing." Irving kicked a stone and then continued. "You see, if the boys in our class forget their pencils at home, the teacher makes you stay in after school. I know that all the boys hate staying in so I asked Mom to buy me six Venus HB pencils. I cut them in half and sharpened them, and now when the boys forget their pencils at home, before they get into trouble, I hire them one of my pencils, for a penny a day. That's why you can hear pennies in my pocket."

He looked at his father and smiled.

That night, Irving approached Dan.

"Have you got one pound?" he asked.

"I might have."

"Well, if you do, I have 240 pennies which I want to change for a one pound note. They're in this bag." He held a flour bag aloft which was crammed with coins.

Dan handed over the one pound note and placed the bag of coins on the table. Later that night he tipped the coins onto the table and idly began to count them.

"Hey, Irving, come here," he shouted, after counting for a while.

Irving came into the dining room.

"Yes Dad, you called me?"

"Yes. I've just counted the coins you gave me."

Irving watched his father, his face a blank sheet of paper.

"There are only 220 coins here. You've short-changed me. I gave you a quid."

"No, Dad. No mistake on my part. You must have lost some. I definitely gave you 240 coins. I'm sure. You should have counted them when I gave them to you, and asked me for a receipt. It's too late now. No, I am afraid you must have lost them." He turned and walked from the room.

Taken aback his father watched the departing figure, not sure whether he should feel pride at Irving's business logic or annoyed at having been tricked and lied to by an eight-year-old.

Some years later, in 1962, at the age of eighteen, Irving and the majority of white South African young men of similar age were called up to do compulsory military service. Irving was deployed to the South African Irish at a military training camp at Lenz, on the outskirts of the small town of Heidelberg, some seventy kilometres from Johannesburg. From day one it became apparent that Irving and the military were not designed for compatibility. Irving set out to beat the system and on completion of one year of service he could lay claim to the dubious distinction of being one of only a handful of soldiers who had never fired a weapon. He avoided every training session, target practice and combat drill in whatever way he could—by feigning sickness, claiming death in the family and simply by absconding.

He continued his business entrepreneurship while in the army.

Elder brother Brian received a phone call from Irving.

"Howzit Irv? How's the army going?"

"Don't ask. Full of bloody bullshit, man. Can't wait till it's over. Listen Brian, I need a favour? You know that Remington shop near your offices?"

"Yes, just below our floor. Of course I know the shop."

"Well, won't you nip down there and buy me an electric razor? They sell them there. The one I want, or should I say, must have, sells for twenty rand. You'll see the one I mean. Get it for me. I'll be coming in on the post van. I've managed to wangle a ride into town. I'll give you the money when I see you. Can you do it?"

"Of course I can do it. What on earth do you need a Remington electric razor for so urgently?"

"Thanks Brian. Don't let me down now. I'll explain when I see you tomorrow."

Brian purchased the razor and waited for Irving and his explanation.

The next day Irving arrived at Brian's office and anxiously enquired, "Did you get the razor?"

Brian pointed to the brand new Remington razor in its unopened box, lying on his desk. Irving picked up the box and examined the picture on the lid of the razor.

"Perfect. That's it. You are a lifesaver. Thanks Brian."

He stuck his hand in his pocket and pulled out a wad of notes. Quickly he counted out twenty-one rand notes. "There you go. Thanks a lot. I must dash."

"Not so fast. You can't go without telling me what this is all about," as Brian held the Remington on the desk, his palm covering the box.

"Aw, come on, Brian. You're going to make me late and I'll be in crap again."

Irving looked at Brian's determined expression and realized he was not going to relent without an explanation.

"Okay. I'll tell you." He heaved a sigh. "I told you about some of those rich Jewish kids we have in our regiment? Well one of them had a twenty-first last weekend and went home for the weekend and his party. Anyway, he arrived back on Sunday night and was showing off with his brand new gifts. One of the gifts was a Remington razor, which he proudly showed us. I told him that it was a bit of a waste for him as he only had bum fluff on his cheeks. Anyway, I had an idea when I saw this beautiful new razor and all the fuss the other guys were making, so I asked him if I could borrow it for a few days as he wouldn't be using it yet anyway. I didn't of course tell him what my plan was. Once he had agreed I went to see the regimental sergeant major and told him my plan."

"What was the plan?"

"To raffle the Remington Razor for one rand per ticket."

"You're joking. I bet the sergeant major hit the roof?"

"Not after I offered him one hundred rand to let me do it".

Brain looked at his brother in amazement.

"He let you? And you went ahead? Now you have to replace the razor and pay the sergeant major. You are going to be *really* out of pocket."

Irving grabbed the razor from Brian's hands and ran for the door.

"Ha ha! No, I won't. We sold seven hundred tickets—that's seven hundred rand. I just have to get this back to Solly Levine before he hears about it. Bye!" he called over his shoulder as he ran out the door.

⁓

Having completed his military training Irving did what so many of us did at the time—we left South Africa to travel abroad, to gain some real-life experience and, in the process and with the passage of time, a measure of maturity.

After returning from England Irving stayed with his parents in Parkwood for some time. The initial pleasure of having him home began to fade slightly, particularly as Irving seemed quite content to be living at home and made no effort to look for a job.

One Saturday morning as Dan and Freda were having breakfast, Irving staggered sleepily into the kitchen, yawning, hair tousled, clad in his pyjamas. Dan finally snapped: "This isn't a hotel, or some kind of free board and lodging establishment you know!"

Irving looked surprised but leaned across the table and took a piece of toast, which he lathered with a thick spread of butter, and topped this with marmalade. He bit into the toast with Dan and Freda watching him, and replied in a muffled voice, "I know that Dad," and carried on eating, crunching through the crust.

"Well, what are your plans, my boy? I bet you don't have any idea of what you are going to do, do you?

Irving blinked the sleep away and finally surfaced. He looked taken aback.

"Oh yes, I have. I've got plans."

"What sort of plans? You don't know even what you want to do, let alone what company you are going to work for."

"Oh yes I do," Irving was now fully awake and as sharp as a flick knife.

"What are you going to do and who are you going to work for?" Dan challenged.

"Here—I'll show you." He leaped to his feet and went into the hallway where the telephone was positioned on a small hall table. He returned carrying the Yellow Pages directory. He sat down at the table and began to page through the book like a dealer shuffling a pack of cards. The book fell open at the 'P' section. Dan watched Irving, bemused.

"Here", said Irving, "here," pointing at the page. "That's who I'm going to work for".

Dan's eyes followed Irving's finger. He was pointing at a display advert for Plastic & Metal Industries (PMI).

"What do you mean? Have you seen them? Have you had an interview or anything?"

Irving shook his head.

"No, not yet. But I will."

Dan grimaced.

"I don't believe it. You loll around the house all day. You've done nothing about getting an interview and now you say that's where you're going to work. I think you picked that company at random out of the Yellow Pages just to get me off your back."

"No, I didn't. That's who I want to work for. I'll phone them and make an appointment for an interview."

"Go on then. Phone them right now. Let me see how serious you are about getting a job."

"I will," said Irving, and he walked into the hall carrying the Yellow Pages with him.

They heard the sound of a number being dialled and then Irving's muffled voice. Dan and Freda exchanged glances

"Hello ... Plastic and Metal Industries?" Pause. "Can I speak to the Managing Director please?" Pause. "Sure, I'll hold on."

A gust of wind slammed shut the door between the kitchen and the hall. The sound of Irving's voice could still be heard but not the words.

After five minutes they heard the phone being put down and Irving walked back into the kitchen. They looked at him expectantly. He was wearing a broad grin.

"Well, that was lucky," he said. "The guy who answered the phone said that they don't normally work on Saturdays, he had just popped in to collect some papers, and then it turned out that the MD was also there."

He picked up another slice of toast and began to butter it.

"And so?"

"Well, he said he'd be there for another hour and that if I really wanted to work for PMI I should get my butt down there now. Not tomorrow or any other day, but now." He lathered marmalade onto the toast. "So I must dash and get ready, he'll interview me today." And Irving rushed from the room.

Fifteen minutes later, a spruced-up Irving, wearing collar and tie and carrying a blazer over his shoulder, hair combed, face shaved and smelling strongly of 'Old Spice' aftershave, wafted into the room.

His parents looked at him in disbelief.

"Are you serious? You got an interview? Well good luck … off you go."

Irving held out his hand.

"Can I have your car keys, please Dad?"

"Don't be silly. You aren't taking my car to attend an interview. Take a taxi."

Irving looked pleadingly at Dan.

"I can't do that, Dad."

"Why on earth not?"

"It will look as though I have too much money and they won't pay me enough to start."

So Irving took the car, had his interview and got the job with PMI.

∽

Following our renewed contact and several somewhat bibulous lunches at the LM Restaurant, Irving and I developed a robust friendship over the next few years. We enjoyed many wild dinner parties at their home, where wine flowed like the Jukskei River in the valley below and Yvonne excelled in the kitchen, preparing the most delicious and mouth-watering meals, and where we met most of Irving and Yvonne's friends.

The Tuckers had moved to Broederstroom. Irving had bought a fifty-two-acre piece of land, next to the Jukskei River, positioned between properties owned by Gordon Voster, the celebrated South African wildlife artist, and Jacques Malan, the equally celebrated sculptor, and his French wife.

Irving, with the help of Faraway, a labourer whom he had found living on his newly acquired land, set to and began to carve a future home out of Pelindaba rock, bricks and hard sweat. He chose the site of the house carefully, positioning it at the top of his piece of land which swept down to the Jukskei River bubbling over rocks below. The house was built in Irving's spare time, and sometimes his working hours, and he made liberal use of the VW Beetle provided by PMI, where he was responsible for several major accounts.

During the lengthy construction period a journey as a passenger in Irving's car was something to be avoided—unless you wished to share the space with bags of cement, window frames, lengths of planks, wooden doors and bricks. All these items were carried in the Beetle, travelling the thirty-plus kilometres between his work place and his future home. Having turned off the main road, the dirt road to the farm was washed out, rutted and rocky and made for a bone-shaking journey of eight kilometres before reaching the building site. No supplier of bricks, cement, window frames and doors would deliver to the site. As he saw it, Irving had no option but to use the PMI Beetle.

This practice was summarily halted after Gil Catton, Chief Executive at PMI, one day announced to a surprised Irving that he would like to accompany him on a few sales calls, to 'pump the flesh' with the trade. Irving's heart sank. Just twenty minutes earlier he had loaded the VW from the floor to the roof with bags of cement; bricks had been squeezed into every other available space, including the luggage compartment under the bonnet; various other bits of building materials were jammed into any remaining nooks and crannies. There was space for one person only, squeezed into the driver's seat behind the steering wheel; all the other seats had been removed to make space for building materials.

As Gil Catton and he walked to the Beetle, parked in front of the PMI building in Mayfair, Irving's mind raced. From a distance they could see the VW—like a hen sitting on her nest; low, very low on its springs; the Beetle sagged beneath the weight of building materials. As they drew closer to the car Irving feigned a reaction of total shock: "Look at that!" in a surprised tone, "some cheeky bastard has filled my car with building materials. I must have left it unlocked." But the game was up and 'Tucker's Building Materials Transport', as Irving referred to the beat up old VW, reverted to its primary role—that of transporting passengers.

The house and tennis court took Irving and Faraway a year to build. When he had completed the task we were invited frequently to play tennis on a Saturday afternoon. The tennis was always followed by one of the Tuckers' memorable dinner parties which usually ended in the early hours of the following Sunday morning. Sensibly, Yvonne would have retired to bed at a reasonable hour, leaving Irving and the guests laughing and joking and finally dossing down in the lounge, or wherever space could be found, to waken the next morning with the sour and furry taste of having drunk too much wine the night before.

⊰

Throughout his life Irving loved playing practical jokes on his friends and no-one was exempt from becoming a victim of his wicked sense of humour. One of the friends that we met at the Tuckers' home was a colleague of Irving's, Tom Crisp, who had recently fallen prey to one of Irving's many practical jokes.

Johannesburg had been hit by a 'flu epidemic and Irving began to show the symptoms of the early stages of the illness. His face felt hot, his throat itched and his croaky voice told the story. On the morning that Irving woke with these symptoms he considered staying at home but decided to go to work. Soon after arriving at the office he realized his mistake: he felt lousy and should have stayed in bed at the farm. He decided to go home and do exactly that. He packed a few papers in his brief case, climbed into the Beetle, and drove home. Yvonne was at work in Randburg where she was employed as a chemist's assistant, earning the name among us all of 'Nurse Vonnie—the Jolly Green Giant'. Irving made himself a hot toddy of water, plenty of brandy, lemon and honey, and crawled into bed.

As he was dozing off he remembered that he had come home without telling anybody at the office where he was going and why. Groggily he climbed out of bed, walked to the phone and dialled the office number. For some reason the call wasn't answered by the switchboard and went straight through to the desk of Tom Crisp, the Production Manager.

"Tom Crisp here."

"Hello Tom," Irving croaked.

"Can I help you?"

Irving realized that Tom had not recognized his voice.

"Hello? Tom? Tom Crisp, you say?"

"Yes, that's right, Tom Crisp. How can I help you?"

"Well Tom, my name is Thompson, and I'm phoning from Anglo American."

Tom's ears pricked up.

"Yes, Mister Thompson?"

"Well Tom, we are interested in buying twenty thousand plastic bread baskets for our mines."

"Bread baskets? We don't make any bread baskets Mister Thompson."

'Yes of course you do. We've tested them underground."

Trying to gain a clue as to what Thompson was talking about, Tom asked, "Please describe the bread basket that you tested?"

"Well, it's about three foot in diameter and about eighteen inches deep. The sides have holes to let the air come through."

"Oh yes, yes, we do have those. You mean laundry baskets?"

"No, we use them as bread baskets to take bread underground to the miners."

Tom digested this for a few seconds in silence, then ventured: "May I ask why you use laundry baskets for bread?"

"They're perfect for taking bread down to the miners; the holes are big enough to allow the air through, to ventilate the bread and keep it fresh, but small enough to stop the cockroaches underground from crawling into the breadbaskets."

Tom's mind was whirling. "I see ... how many did you say you wanted?"

"Twenty thousand. And Mister Crisp, they must be white."

Tom's heartbeat speeded up as he made a quick mental calculation. At five rand each the order was worth one hundred thousand rand—at full profit margin. It would take a month of production; the machines would have to be stopped; blue dye replaced with white; the order for the OK Bazaars would have to wait. But it would be worth it; this was not the usual order where they had to discount for the big retailers and shave margins. This was twenty thousand units at full margin.

The factory had been battling to get the production of blue laundry baskets right. They had just succeeded, and Irving knew this.

"When do you want them, Mr Thompson?"

"I want you to start delivering tomorrow, and then deliver in batches as they are finished."

"Mr Thompson, please give me your number. I'll check this out and call you back, but I'm sure it will be fine."

Irving gave Tom his home number, which Tom, in his excitement, didn't recognize.

"Thank you, Mr Thompson. I'm going to check this out with Mr Catton, our Managing Director. I'll call you back shortly."

"Thank you, Tom. I look forward to your call," said Irving, hoarsely, holding back his chuckles.

Tom rang his production clerk and asked, "Can we run white laundry baskets? How are you off for polyethylene?"

"No problem," was the answer.

"Hold fire," said Tom, "I'm just going to get the go ahead from Catton."

Tom ran from his office to Gil Catton's office. He paused at the open door and knocked. Catton looked up and saw his excited expression. He put down his pen.

"Come in Tom. What are you looking so pleased about?"

"You won't believe it Mr Catton—I've just had an order for twenty thousand white laundry baskets from Anglo American; they have to be in white and they want us to start delivering tomorrow. I have to phone them back to tell them whether we can do it."

"What on earth do they want twenty thousand laundry baskets for?" said Catton with a frown.

"They use them for bread baskets on the gold mines. They take the bread in them underground to the miners."

Catton's frown deepened and he looked puzzled.

Tom explained, repeating Irving's words: "The holes in the sides are big enough to ventilate the bread but small enough to prevent the cockroaches from climbing through the holes and getting at the bread."

Gil Catton looked at Tom in disbelief.

"Shit! They must have enormous cockroaches underground if those holes stop them from getting in?!"

There was silence for a few seconds as Tom thought. "Have you ever been underground?" he asked.

"No. Can't say I have," said Catton.

"Cockroaches … underground … they're enormous. As big as this!" said Tom, holding his palms face-to-face but about six inches apart, demonstrating the size of a giant cockroach. Catton looked amazed and grimaced.

"That big? Really? Well, you had better get onto it, Tom. Well done. That's a nice order."

After telling the switchboard operator to hold all calls Tom sent for the production clerk to discuss the new requirements.

Irving lay in bed and despite his flu he chuckled at the trick he was playing. After half hour he thought, "Time to tell Tom the truth." He dialled PMI's number.

"Plastic and Metal Industries?" Sue answered, from the switchboard.

"Sue, it's Irving. Can I speak to Tom?"

"No, sorry Irv, he's in a meeting and he's not to be disturbed."

Irv's stomach lurched and he felt the start of mounting panic.

"Oh shit. Why, what's going on?"

"Oh, they don't tell me, but it's something about a big, big order."

"Are you serious? Please ring him and tell him to phone me, give him my number. Tell him it's urgent. Oh shit! You'd better hurry!"

Irving waited anxiously for Tom to call, fearing that Tom had already stopped the production run of blue laundry baskets for the OK order, and that work was even now underway to drain the blue dye and replace it with white dye, to make twenty thousand bread baskets, in white, for Anglo American. He fretted that all traces of blue dye would have been removed by the time Tom received the message to call Irving's number and lay in bed, wide awake, waiting nervously for the phone to ring. Finally, two hours later, it rang.

Irving leaped out of bed and grabbed the phone.

"Hello?"

"Mr Thompson. It's Tom Crisp here. Mr Thompson we can do the order—"

Irving interrupted: "Tom, it's Irving."

Tom still did not recognize Irving's voice. "—Thank you Mr Thompson, I mean Irving."

"Tom it's me! Me—Irving Tucker!"

There was dead silence for a few seconds as the truth, like smoke oozing under a closed door, started seeping into Tom's brain.

"Tucker. Tucker! I don't believe it! Oh no! What the fuck have you done? Fuck you Tucker! FUCK you!"

Tom slammed down the phone and buried his face in his hands.

Chapter Seven

PACKING FOR PERTH

Five years after my return from England, Irving dropped his bombshell. Just before Christmas in 1975, at one of those fun-filled days of tennis in the afternoon, followed by dinner, wine and companionship in the evening, Irving, through a fog of smoke and alcohol, said to me, "Robbie. I think we're going to bugger off."

"What do you mean, 'bugger off'?"

He took a sip of his wine and looked at me, long and hard, head tilted to one side.

"Come, let's walk outside and chat." He strode outside and breathed deeply in the soft evening air. "Lovely out here isn't it?"

I nodded.

"Ja, out here you don't get any of that city pollution that you buggers breathe in all day, do you?" Then he continued from where he had interrupted himself. "There's big crap coming, here. Do you know what's going on in Soweto at the schools?"

"What?"

"Big *kak* (crap) my boy." He sipped his wine. "Big, big, *kak*."

I shrugged dismissively. "We've heard it all before."

The light was rapidly fading as the evening darkness stole it away. We were standing outside the house, wine glasses in hand. As the darkness thickened the night sounds of Africa filled the space around us. The shriek of a Fish Eagle floated up from the Jukskei River.

Irving cupped his hand to his ear, grinned. "Hear that? Fish Eagle. He's got a nest down below."

Again the eerie and plaintive cry reached us.

"Lovely hey, Robbie? Bloody Fish Eagle. Isn't that great? Hell, I love this place."

He sipped his wine thoughtfully, listening to the night, staring into the darkness.

Crickets chirped, toads and frogs that had made their way up to the farmhouse from the river below, croaked and squawked, as if waiting for a conductor to take charge and marry their sounds into some rousing composition. In the distance the shouts of Faraway and his family calling to one another floated to our ears. The cackle of a hadeda shattered the sounds of the frog orchestra. A chill ran down my spine and I shivered.

"Cold?"

"No, someone just walked over my grave."

Irving laughed. "No, I don't think we have a future here. We're thinking of putting the farm on the market."

"Serious?" I asked. "I think you're wrong. We'll get over it. We always do."

"Do you know that less than ten per cent of the kids who finish primary school this year will be able to go to high school in Soweto in 1976, next year? That's a recipe for disaster." He shook his head. "No, I'm afraid not, not this time." He had been pacing slowly around the *stoep* (veranda) where we stood. He stopped walking and became more animated.

"You see those hills there?" he indicated by pointing in the dark towards the Magaliesberg mountains, lying twenty kilometres to the north.

"Not really," I said, smiling in the dark.

"Well, my boy, at this moment it's not only the pot in Soweto that's starting to bubble before it boils. That's nothing to what is going to happen here. Next time you look at the Magaliesberg, picture those hills with Chinese troops, all carrying AK-47s, pouring over them towards Johannesburg. That's the shit that's going to happen here. The commies are going to take over, and it'll be the Chinese who do it."

"Think so?" I asked, not convinced.

"Bloody sure. That's why we're going to pull out."

He sounded serious.

"I can't believe that, Irv. You're as South African as a *veldskoen* (traditional South African outdoor shoe). In any event where will you go? There's nowhere that can give you this lifestyle. I suppose you would go to Aussie?"

"Not sure really. Maybe back to the UK. Yvonne's brother lives in London and she has family there."

"Somehow, despite her accent, I never think of the Jolly Green Giant as a pom."

"Her father was a refugee from Germany during the war. Their name is Hess. German Jews. He had to flee the Nazis, from Berlin, and went to London. Been there ever since. Had to leave most of what he owned behind him in Berlin. Still I think he recovered and did well for himself in the UK. Not as well off as he would have been, if he had remained in Berlin. Then again, the Nazis would probably have bumped him off. Shit! Great pity. I wouldn't have to work even one more day if he had managed to get all his paintings and things out. He was worth quite a few bob. He got some of his stuff out, but certainly not the greater part. Do you know that Yvonne and I are interested in art? I suppose it really stems from her father. Despite her dad leaving most of it behind, Yvonne grew up in a really privileged household. Private school and all that you know."

The last sentence was spoken as if he had a hot potato in his mouth, in an exaggerated British upper-class accent. "Hell! I would never have had to lift a finger." He sighed regretfully. "They call Yvonne and her sort 'Sloane Rangers' in London, you know?"

I nodded. "Ja, I know what you mean."

Sloane Rangers usually lived in the vicinity of Sloane Square, a wealthy area in London. They were single, moneyed, svelte and well-groomed and were looking for a husband, but one with a lot of money or a title.

"Well, Yvonne got it wrong when she met you, didn't she Irv?

He made as if he was going to punch me in the ribs and laughed.

"You've been a good mate, Robbie. Do you remember my mate Garth that you met in London?"

I thought for a few seconds.

"Yes. Tall guy. You shared a room with him before Mike Starling?"

He nodded.

"Ja, well, we stayed friends when we came back, but he tried to con us into a business deal. That was the end of our friendship. You can't use friendship you know, Robbie? It's too precious. He tried to use friendship to get us to join one of those pyramid selling operations—Golden Products or something. We thought he had invited us to dinner one night at the Carlton Hotel, when in fact all he was doing was getting us to attend a sales pitch by Golden Products. We've not seen him or his wife to this day. The moral of the story is, don't ever use friendship for personal gain. It's too precious."

We were walking inside to join the others when he stopped and turned to me with a worried expression on his face.

"Only problem is, I don't know what will happen to Faraway when we sell the farm. We can't just leave him. He's like our family, you know?"

"Take him with you," I joked.

Irving snorted. "Faraway? To England or Aussie? You must be kidding!"

And then he said, "Also our friends." He grabbed me by the arm and looked at me earnestly, his face close to mine. "Remember your friends. They are the most important asset you have. Friendship is forever. We will miss you and our friends if—I should say 'when'—when we go."

⁓

So they sold the farm and Irving and Yvonne left South Africa, Faraway and their friends, in February 1976, to start a new life in England. They bought a farm near the tiny village of Oswestry, near the Welsh border.

Having learned from his experience at Broederstroom, Irving immediately began building another farmhouse while he and Yvonne lived in a caravan parked near the construction site on their new farm. This time there was no Faraway to assist him. For the next few years the Tuckers kept themselves busy, learning to be sheep farmers, and we kept in touch with each other by letter and the occasional international telephone call.

In the mid-1980s, on one of my overseas visits to England, I hired a car and motored down to the quaint village of Oswestry, to pay a visit to Irving and Yvonne on their farm. From the village it was a short drive through the countryside, on winding lanes bordered by high, snow-covered hedges, and I had plenty of time to reflect on my friendship with Irving and Yvonne.

I realized how much I had missed the two of them since they had left South Africa: our lunches at the LM; the tennis parties on the farm, always followed by wild dinners and plenty of drink, surrounded by his friends. I had lost contact with most of the people in their circle after Irving's departure—he had been the glue that held us together. I even admitted to myself that I missed his practical jokes and sense of humour. I wondered what had happened to Faraway: Irving wouldn't have just left him in the lurch; did he give him money to live off when he left? I shook my head as I drove. No, Irving wouldn't just abandon Faraway. He always cared about people. Even when he was bombastic and sarcastic he never meant to offend or cause hurt.

In fact, the more I thought about it, the more I realized that Irving had a heart big enough to keep at least five men alive and well. He was generous to a fault. One moment he would cut you down with a tongue as sharp as a pair of scissors, the next he would be buying you gifts and flowers; although that seemed to have slowed down a bit since he and Yvonne had married. Maybe she controlled the purse strings now.

It would be odd seeing them again in such English surroundings. Yvonne of course was English, to see her striding around in the snow in her 'wellies' would be quite natural. But Irving? A man who loved Africa far more than the average person? I still thought of his emigration as a complete waste.

The English dark of winter was rapidly approaching when I finally found their isolated farmhouse. Their nearest neighbours, also sheep farmers, lived some fifteen minutes' drive away. As I approached the newly-built farmhouse, its lights already ablaze, the wheels of my hired car crunched on the surface of crisp freshly fallen snow.

Outside the house Yvonne was standing on the back of a trailer hitched to a tractor with its engine running, puffing out black clouds of diesel smoke. Every now and then Yvonne disappeared into the smoke billowing around her in the still, crisp air. She was wearing green gum boots and green working overalls and looked every inch the Jolly Green Giant, pushing and tugging bales of hay off the trailer, where they flopped into the crunchy white snow like yellow parcels on a white tablecloth. A flock of sheep stood watching with hopeful eyes at the sight of food. As the bales thumped into the soft snow, the sheep came closer and began to nibble at the hay. She saw me approaching and waved an arm in greeting.

"Hello Robbie!" she shouted from some distance away. "Good to see you. Sorry. Have to do this now! Have to get food to the sheep. We've had so much snow, poor little buggers have got no food. Go into the house and say hello to Irv. You'll find him inside."

I opened the door without knocking. Irving was sitting in front of a roaring log fire, feet resting on a coffee table, watching television. Next to him lay a German sheepdog, tongue lolling out of its mouth. Surprised by my entry, Irving leaped to his feet, knocking over the coffee table as he did so.

"Shit!" he said looking at the coffee table and bending to right it. "I mean, hello! Sorry Robbie. Wasn't expecting you yet." He stood up, squeezed my shoulder and pumped my arm as he shook my hand. "Good to see you, good to see you. Come in. Hey! Terrific to see you. Hell, I've missed you, you bugger."

His face was one big smile.

"Let's have a drink. It's a special occasion, I'll open a bottle of KWV wine."

He disappeared from the lounge. I looked around me. The house, or what I could see of it, had recently been completed. It was solidly built with large spacious rooms, including the comfortably furnished lounge where I stood. The number of paintings on the walls immediately struck me. I peered at them and, despite not knowing a great deal about art, could see that this was no ordinary collection. Some of the artists I recognized, like Gordon Vorster, but some of the names I had never heard of before. I was standing looking at an abstract painting when Irving came back carrying two full glasses of red wine and an open bottle of KWV wine tucked under his arm. I looked around as he came into the room.

"You like that one, Robbie?"

"Not really, to be honest. I prefer those by Gordon Vorster. I'm sure this is very good but it's not my cup of tea."

"I'll have to give you a few lessons on art next time we come out," he said with a laugh.

"To be honest Irv, I knew that you liked art, but I didn't know you had such a big collection."

"Yes. I have always been interested in art. Used to go down to the Johannesburg Art Gallery, often, when I was at school. Then of course Yvonne was always keen; so since our marriage, and because we share a common love of art, our collection has grown. Actually we have far too many pieces," he said, looking around the room. "Yvonne will be with us just now. She just has to finish feeding the sheep; they've not had food because of the snow so we have to take hay to them."

"I know, I saw her," as I took a glass from him and sipped. "Mmm, nice wine. I saw the Jolly Green Giant, hard at it. How can you sit here while she does all the work, you lazy bugger?"

He laughed. "Yvonne is the farmer. Bloody good too. My oath, you should have seen her when we first arrived. Her brother, Michael, was helping to build the road up to the farmhouse-to-be, and we were living in a caravan at the back. It had been raining and there was her brother, Michael, up to his knees in muck and mud, laying drains next to the road, when Yvonne comes striding out of the caravan, walking all upright in that Grenadier Guards sort of way she has, over the first field towards Michael and his workers. I'll never forget the expression on his face. She really looked the part. *Ja*," he said, nodding, "except that she was wearing a designer leather coat, high fashion leather boots and swinging a designer handbag. Michael's mouth dropped open, and so did those of his workers, I can tell you."

I laughed at this image of Yvonne the Farmer.

"Well, she certainly isn't wearing designer gear today, I can assure you. Unless its designer overalls and wellies, which, knowing Yvonne, it probably is. What do you do while she's farming?"

"Robbie, Robbie! There's a lot of important work to be done—like plan the national budget, watch world affairs on telly so that I can make the right decisions for the country, read the papers about how the bloody Nats are screwing up your country—"

"My country? It's yours as well."

He shook his head then drank from his glass.

"—No, Robbie, that's where you're wrong. Not my country. Not at all. I'm English."

I burst out laughing. "English? Listen to your accent man. You're as South African as I am."

A gust of wind blew the door open. I had not closed it properly behind me and a blast of cold air hit us. Irving slammed the door closed.

"Jeez, Irv, I don't know how you can live here in this freezing cold weather. Didn't you love the sunshine? Don't you miss it?"

"I did. You get used to the cold. It's sort of refreshing. Anyway there was too much going on there that I didn't like."

The door was thrown open again, this time by Yvonne, assisted by the icy wind; it crashed against the wall.

"Whew! It's cold out there," said Yvonne, as she slammed the door closed and then stomped off snowflakes stuck to her boots like icing sugar.

"What are you doing for dinner?" asked Irving.

"Roast lamb?" she said, looking at me questioningly.

I nodded. "As long as it's not one of your pet lambs?"

"Don't be silly, Robbie. They are all our pet lambs, actually."

Yvonne made her way to the kitchen and I could hear pots being rattled, fridge doors opening and closing, and finally the oven door banging shut. Her shout reached us: "Hope you're not too hungry?" in her London 'received pronunciation' accent. "Be about an hour and a half."

"That's fine," Irving shouted back, "we can open another bottle of wine. Come on Robbie, drink up, let's open another."

We did— and over dinner of delicious lamb and fresh, home grown, organic vegetables (everything we eat is organic, Robbie. Don't you watch your health?) cooked by Yvonne who, I was reminded, was a *cordon bleu* chef, the talk was all about South Africa and the fun we used to have at Broederstroom.

"Don't you miss it?" I asked.

"Only our friends like you Robbie. Apart from that not really, hey, Yvonne?" Irving looked across to her for confirmation.

"Not at all Robbie. We have a very good life here on the farm."

"Yes. But the sun? And the open spaces?"

She laughed. "We have as much open space as we can manage right here. I've got my horses and we love sheep farming. As you can see, we're still building our home. Irving is going to add a conservatory over there," she indicated with a movement of her head towards the wall, "no Robbie, I don't miss it at all."

Irving looked down at the table for a few seconds. "No, I don't think that's quite right, Yvonne, we love the bush and we do miss that, but other than that and our friends, nothing else really."

"Ah," Yvonne sighed, "the bush. Yes, we both love the bush. You're right Irv. I do love the bush and I do miss it."

"Well, your friends miss you guys as well. That's always the hardest, parting with one's friends."

"We *do* miss them, but we've also made quite a few friends in the farming community here. They were so good to us when we first arrived—"

"They still are," interrupted Yvonne.

"—Yes, yes, they are. But back then they really took us under their wings. I mean, Yvonne and I knew bugger all about farming sheep."

"How did you cope?"

"Well, like I say, our friends helped us. They helped us buy our initial flock and guided us in raising them."

"Plus Irving and I read everything there was to read about sheep until we could teach our neighbours a thing or two, I can tell you."

"Well, that lamb we've just had for dinner was delicious, if that's anything to go by," I said, wiping my mouth and taking another sip of wine.

"Well, I take the lamb to be slaughtered at a special abattoir I've found. They kill the lambs very gently."

"Ha ha!" I laughed. "How can you kill something gently?"

"Seriously Robbie. If you kill the lamb in a humane way, the muscles don't tighten up at the time of death and the lamb is tender. Didn't you know that?"

"You've obviously learned well. What about your friends back home? Tony Taylor, Ian Strachan? All the blokes I used to see at your place at Broederstroom. What's the name of that guy from the estate agency who always fell asleep at dinner parties? How are they all getting on? I've lost touch with them since you left."

"You mean Billie Mathews? We still hear from him; he's still selling houses, and probably still falling asleep at dinner parties!" Irving laughed at the memory. "Doing well, I think. Of course Tony Taylor is doing very, very well. He's a director of Woolworths and on all sorts of boards. He has a new wife, lovely lady, Anne. We see quite a lot of Tony when he comes over on business. Always comes down and spends a few days here. Then during the year, here in the UK, I buy Afrikaner books for him. Did you know that he's a big collector?"

I shook my head.

"And what about old Ray whatshisname?"

Irving threw his head back and roared with laughter.

"You mean Johnson? He and Lynne moved to Australia. I think he disliked you so much after that joke you pulled on him he couldn't stay in Joburg."

"*I* pulled on him?" stressing the 'I'.

"Well, okay, *we* pulled on him."

"Although he always blamed you for it, Robbie," Yvonne interjected, "he disliked you after that, you know. If ever your name was mentioned he would change the subject or walk away."

"That's a bit unfair, isn't it? I mean, nothing happened between Lynne and me."

"*Ja*, but he doesn't know that does he?"

"What do you mean? You didn't ever set him straight?"

"No, I like to keep a joke going for as long as possible." He leaned back in his chair, hands clasped behind his head. "So, life is good here. We go up to London to see the shows whenever we feel like it. When there's a good rugger match on at 'Twickers' Yvonne's brother gets me tickets. Michael, her brother, is one of the big shots at the Richmond Rugby Club."

"You've never met Michael, have you Robbie? You weren't there when he came out to Broederstroom?" asked Yvonne.

"No, I don't remember meeting him. Didn't even know you had a brother."

"We don't see him that much. He's a bit difficult." She changed the subject, "We can always come out to SA you know, Robbie. In fact I have family who have a place in Plett and they've said we can stay there anytime we choose."

"You mean with the 'rich and famous'?" I asked, with a smile.

"Absolutely Robbie! I'm surprised you haven't got a place there as well."

"You must be joking!"

"But what about you?" Irving asked. "How's your promotion business going?"

"Very good. In fact we've had an offer to buy from a listed company in Cape Town, which I'm probably going to accept. Give me a few bob in the bank."

"That's great, Robbie, let's drink to that," said Irving, filling all three glasses with red wine.

"Well, here's to us all getting together again, soon, when we come out there," said Irving, raising his glass and clinking it against mine and then Yvonne's.

"Cheers!" we said and drank the wine.

Chapter Eight

HAGA HAGA

It wasn't long after my visit to Oswestry that Irving and Yvonne began what became an annual pilgrimage to Plettenberg Bay, 'the home of the rich and famous', where Yvonne's cousin had offered them a place to stay.

A pattern soon developed. They would come out from the UK every December for about four weeks. After arriving in Johannesburg and staying with me at Fourways, they would move on to Tony Taylor's farm and a safari in the bush, then end their holiday with a few weeks at Plettenberg Bay. Their stays with us were always marked by raucous laughter, fun, braais (barbecues) and jokes. I loved it when they came out and so did they. But each year Irving became more and more jingoistic about England, and this continued into the early nineties when I remarried.

On their first visit after I had married Margie they skipped Johannesburg and I caught up with them in Cape Town. We got together after I had paid my monthly visit to my Cape-based seafood shops, located in the Hyperama stores. Hyperama was a large chain of giant stores and I was the leased operator of the seafood departments, under the name of the 'Gansbaai Fishing Company'. I was flying back to Johannesburg that evening but had arranged to meet Irving and Yvonne for lunch at Blues, a trendy restaurant in Camps Bay. As usual, it had been a year since we had last seen each other.

They were seated at the table when I walked in.

"Hello Robbie!"

I gave the Jolly Green Giant a hug and a kiss.

Irving shook me by the hand and clapped me on the shoulder. He grinned broadly.

"Hello Robbie. Good to see you. Shit! What's that smell?" he wrinkled his nose in disgust.

"I can smell it as well. Shit, something must be off; must be fish." Yvonne screwed up her face and looked for the offending object on the white table cloth.

I had spent the morning counting stock in the freezers of the Gansbaai Fishing shops in the Hyperama stores in Parow and Blue Route. I knew that my clothes, inevitably, would have absorbed the smell from the freezers but I had hoped it wouldn't be too noticeable. I laughed and bent my head to my shoulder, sniffing at my tennis shirt.

"It's me. I'm the source of the smell! I've been in the fish shops all morning, some of us have to work you know."

"Hell Robbie! That's terrible. Do you always stink like this?'

"Shhh. Everyone's looking at us."

Embarrassed, I glanced around at the full and now almost silent restaurant, the background music now in the foreground. All eyes were on us, and then, as if at a signal, the buzz of conversation and the clatter of crockery and cutlery and eating resumed.

We sat down and ordered our food and a good bottle of red wine.

"Shit! It's good to see you again. I really miss you and the good times we had together," Irving said with a smile.

For the next hour we caught up with each other's news and then Irving said, "We went to see my *boet* [brother] this morning."

"Oh yes? I had forgotten you have a brother. What's his name again? I remember meeting him one day in Johannesburg some years ago, after you had left. He came up to me in a car park in Fourways."

"*Ja*, Brian."

"How is he?'

They exchanged glances.

"Same as ever, same as ever," he took a large swig of his wine.

"You don't talk about him much, do you?"

"No, we don't, Robbie," said Yvonne, "Irving and Brian are not that close. They've never really been very close."

Irving flashed a sideways glance at Yvonne.

"*Ag*! He's not that bad. Actually it's mainly because of our age difference that we were never that close; also he was sent away to boarding school at Potch, while I stayed in Joburg. So apart from school holidays we didn't really see each other much. It's more his wife. She's a nice lady but ... you know ... she's RC." As if that explained the universe.

"RC? What's RC?"

Yvonne burst out laughing. "Don't be such an arse, Robbie," she leaned towards me and said, in a loud voice, "Roman Catholic."

Again the restaurant went quiet and people looked across at us.

"Shhh Yvonne! There might be some around."

I joined in the laughter that followed, not wanting to ask what was wrong with being a Roman Catholic.

A waitress arrived to take our order, wearing hipsters and showing her bare belly.

"I think I'll have the oxtail," I said.

"Are you mad, Robbie?" they looked at each other and then at me, in obvious amazement.

"Why?"

"Shit man. That's from the arsehole of an ox! You don't want to eat that. Try something else."

I laughed. "No, I'll take my chances thank you. I love oxtail. Don't you two ever eat it?"

"Not bloody likely," Irving said with a grimace.

Over our meal Irving and Yvonne told me that the holiday home that they had visited in Plettenburg Bay for a number of years was no longer available.

"So, that looks like the end of our holidays out here every year," said Yvonne.

"Bummer," I said, "but you can always stay at my house in Haga Haga, if you like. I've just built it and as long as you don't want it while I'm there, it's yours to use, every year."

"That's fantastic. Thank you so much Robbie. Will it be okay to stay for a month? We usually come out at this time of the year, say early January. How does that suit you?"

I nodded. "That'll be fine. I really don't mind how long you stay, it would be quite nice to have someone in the house. Oh, just remembered, my stepfather sometimes stays out there to take a break from East London. But that's no problem, it'll be fine."

∽

For the next fifteen years Irving and Yvonne holidayed, for a month each year, at my house in Haga Haga, near the sleepy coastal town of East London. Each year their routine was the same. They would arrive in early January, pick up a hired car at the airport and stay with us in Johannesburg for a night or two, during which time they would visit other friends in and around Johannesburg. Then they would fly to East London and, after shopping for groceries at the local Pick n Pay, they usually got a lift out to Haga Haga with my uncle, Mike Thompson. Mike had built a house next door to mine and lived there permanently, although he worked in East London. If Mike was unavailable they would persuade Tony Taylor's brother, who lived in East London, to drive them the sixty-eight kilometres, much of the journey on rutted and washed away dirt roads, to Haga Haga. The car would arrive weighed down on its springs after their shopping spree, loaded with a month's supply of groceries packed on top of their three suitcases, one of which carried old clothes for the 'Africans' in Haga Haga. On top of the suitcases were boxes of groceries, and on top of the groceries were boxes of meat, fruit and vegetables—enough of everything for their month-long stay.

After Haga Haga they would spend time on safari in Botswana, or visit the Karoo, staying on Tony Taylor's farm. Most times they stayed in telephone contact with me and they usually spent their last night in SA with us in Johannesburg, before flying back to the cold, wet and wintry UK. Occasionally, if they couldn't make the visit to Johannesburg, I would meet them at the airport for a farewell drink before they flew home.

For the first few years we were quite envious of the relationship that Irving and Yvonne established with the locals at Haga Haga. When we spent time there we fished and 'chilled'. Irving and Yvonne, on the other hand, seemed to have been swept into a social whirl of visits and dinner parties with the locals, particularly the farming community, most of whom we— after some years of visiting Haga Haga—had yet to meet.

"You mean you don't know Buck Wright? Come on Robbie, you must be kidding. How long have you been going there? Surely you know him? He's got a farm over near Marsh Strand?" This would be followed by a forced laugh, and they would both look from Margie to me, wearing expressions of incredulous disbelief. This response left me feeling like a schoolboy unable to answer a teacher's question correctly, and it made both Margie and I feel distinctly inferior as visitors to Haga Haga. We were both envious and impressed by the locals' acceptance of the Tuckers.

But after about five years we noticed a souring of these relationships.

On our visits we would occasionally interrupt our 'chilling' and fishing and make the trip up the hill to Ninky Noo's—a little pub on the golf course run by Neil Arnold— to say hello and enjoy a few beers. I had known Neil for many years, having first met him when he was General Manager of the Transkei Wild Coast Hotels, operated by the Transkei Development Corporation. At the time I was their public relations consultant. I always enjoyed seeing this colourful character and hearing about his latest plans. On one of our holidays in Haga Haga, almost a year after the Tuckers had last been there, Margie and I walked up the hill to say hello to Neil.

"Well, if isn't Binckes and his lovely wife? How are you, my boy?" said Neil with a large smile, flashing a new set of false teeth. For a couple of years he had been toothless, much to the consternation of the locals.

"How are you my dear?" He took Margie's hand as if she was royalty, and kissed her on the cheek. Neil always saw himself as the answer to any maiden's prayer.

"Still drinking Castle?"

I nodded.

He slid the beer can across the counter.

"I'll put it on the tab. So what's news, Binckeses?"

"Not much. Life goes on."

"I suppose you heard about my visitors a few months ago?" Neil asked, with an enquiring lift to his brow.

I shook my head.

"Well this bloody great helicopter arrived. No notice ... no nothing. It was Sol Kerzner's helicopter. [Sol Kerzner is a South African hotel magnate and billionaire businessman. His company owns and operates casinos and resorts in exotic locations around the world.] "Ja," Neil continued, "he and a whole gang of his suits arrived here one day. He's interested in buying a stake in my development."

Neil took a damp cloth and wiped the counter, moving the cloth in circles as he spoke.

"You're kidding?" I said.

"No, I'm not."

"Well, are you going to sell to him?

"Not on your nellie, my boy." He took aim at the sink and threw the damp cloth into it as if it was Sol Kerzner himself. "I told him to get fucked. He thought he was dealing with a country bumpkin, but he got a surprise, didn't he?" He gave me a knowing smile and a wink.

I didn't quite understand what had surprised Sol Kerzner, known as the 'Sun King', but nodded my agreement anyway.

I soaked up the ambience of the homely little bar as I drank the cold Castle straight from the can. It felt good to be home. Looking around I noticed a portable set of traffic lights propped against the wall of the bar, similar to those used at road works, allowing one lane of traffic at a time. The lights looked out of place.

I nodded towards them. "What are they for Neil?"

"Ha ha! Those? Well, I had a bit of fun with those didn't I?

I sipped my beer and waited, knowing I was going to hear all about it anyway.

"Your pal, Tucker, he's something else, isn't he? Anyway he loved the story. I told him when he was last here in January, causing shit as usual with the locals. Anyway that's another story. I put the traffic lights outside on the road leading to the village."

Ninky Noo was about two kilometres from the village itself. The dirt road, which joined the main East London to Umtata road, ran past the pub only twenty metres from the window, and was easily visible from the interior.

"Ja, Rob. Picture the scene. Here's this bloody family, dog tired after driving ten, eleven hours from Johannesburg for their holiday. It's nine o clock at night, pitch dark, it's their first visit and they're unfamiliar with the road. They're all exhausted and it's pissing with rain as well. The kids have been crying and fighting for the last two hours and they can't wait to arrive at their destination. They are approaching the end of the trip and you can practically hear the father saying 'we're almost there now, only a couple of kilometres to go' can't you? But, my boy, they haven't counted on old Arnold here, have they?"

I shook my head, swigged my beer and guessed at what was to come.

"I put those traffic lights just outside the window, on the road, where we could all see them. I can control them from here." He indicated a control box on the wall. "It's Friday night, the bar is packed ..." I looked around—there were three people in the bar, including Margie and me "... I had the lights on green for 'Go' when we see from a looooong way away the lights of this car approaching. As they draw near to the traffic light, obviously relieved that they're green and they're not going to be delayed, I hit the controls!" He slammed his flat hand onto the wooden bar counter surface with a slap. "And wham! The lights change to red. He has to stop suddenly. There they are outside the window, in the middle of nowhere, stuck at a red light." He chortled at the memory of the dark shapes, discernible through fogged-up windows, sitting waiting while the Eastern Cape rain teemed down.

"They sit there and wait, while we are all in here, watching them and pissing ourselves laughing."

"That's priceless," I said.

"Hang on my boy. Not over yet. So what do we do? Well, while we carry on drinking in here, we leave the lights on red and they have to sit it out in the car. Of course they all think the lights are 'legit'." He indicated inverted commas with his forefingers in the air around the word 'legit'. "They wait and wait—and wait. You could hear the kids shouting and fighting and the father swearing at them from here. Eveeeeeentually I hit the switch, change the lights to green and they can carry on with their journey."

"How long did you make them wait?"

"*Ag*, not long. Fifteen, twenty minutes," he said with a mischievous grin. "Mind you, when the bloke came in here a few nights later, for a drink, and saw me carrying out the same joke on someone else, he realized what I had done to him and he wanted to *moer* (thrash) me!"

I laughed as I visualized the scene and then returned to Neil's earlier comment.

"So tell me why my friend Tucker pissed off the locals last time he was here?"

"What do you mean 'last time'? He pisses off someone, if not everyone, every time he comes here. He was fine in the beginning but after a few visits he started his bloody nonsense. Tell you what, I don't take his crap. He doesn't mess with me anymore. In fact they don't come in here that much, anymore, after what happened."

He pulled at a ring-top; the can made a comforting *shook* sound and he slid another Castle across the bar to me.

"Tell me, how long has he lived in the UK? You would think he was a pom or something, the way he always puts us down."

"He's lived there a long time, since the seventies. Why, what did he do?"

"Well, some of the blokes in the bar one night were talking about our cabinet ministers, if I can call them that," he grimaced. "One of the chaps went on about how they were all bloody useless and how they couldn't run a bath let alone a country and how most of them slept through all the proceedings in parliament and didn't even know what was going on. Shit. Most of them I wouldn't employ as my maid or garden boy. The women are the worst and we have a lot of them up there." He indicated with his head in a direction I presumed was Pretoria.

"So what did Tucker say that got everyone's knickers in a knot?" trying to bring him back to my question.

"Not a great deal that night. Remember this was the time before last that he was here. He said a few things that night about us being racist and all that. Racist? Shit. I speak Xhosa better than most of the local blacks."

To make his point he broke into fluent Xhosa: "*Sathana ukhutshwa ngomnye* (straight talk breaks no friendship). I grew up with the buggers. Some of my best friends are blacks."

I looked at his face to see if he was trying to be funny. He wasn't.

"Rob, I don't need to tell you that? You know it, don't you? You grew up in the Transkei with the *munts* [South African and Zimbabwean slang, a derogatory term for a black African]. You know what they're like? Racist? Us? What bullshit. Our blacks down here know their places and get treated with a great deal of respect and dignity around here. It's the youngsters that are the trouble. You've got all those uppity ones up there in Gauteng." He looked at me as if I was from another planet and it was all my fault that we had 'uppity ones' at all.

"Yes, yes," I said, "but you still haven't told me what he did to irritate everyone?"

"I'm coming to that." Another ring-top was pulled. The familiar *shook* signalled a fresh can opening. He slid the Castle across the counter and continued.

"Well, he annoyed a few people that night but it was the following year, last January that he reeeeeally pissed us off. We were all down at Chapel at the tennis club, on a Friday night, and in walks Tucker. He had just arrived. I think Mike Thompson gave him a lift out. We all say hello and are friendly, some of the *okes* (blokes) mutter a bit when he walks in, but generally he gets a good welcome. Someone buys him a glass of wine. You know he drinks wine instead of beer?" he asked, one eyebrow raised enquiringly, a note of bewilderment in his voice—as if this was the result of Irving having made his home in England rather than South Africa. "Anyway, he's been in the bar about ten minutes when suddenly he announces in a loud voice so that everyone can hear, 'Hey everyone. I've got a present for you'. Everyone stops talking and looks at Tucker. He's carrying a roll of paper in his hand with a rubber band around it, you know, like a rolled-up map?"

I nodded.

"So then he says to the whole bar, 'Some of you blokes were at Ninky Noo's last year going on about how useless the black government is, and you got irritated when I called you a bunch of racists'. I can tell you the boys were all ears now, some of them even stopped drinking. He takes the rubber band off the rolled-up paper and holds it up for everyone to see. He says, 'you see, you buggers—this is what *your* bloody Foreign Minister was doing at the United Nations—and he's a whitey! You've got no right to criticize black people'. He then holds up the blown-up photo he'd unrolled."

"Of what? What was in the photograph?" I urged.

"A fucking picture of Pik Botha asleep at the United Nations!" (Pik Botha was the Foreign Minister under the old apartheid government.)

"He must have had dozens made," I chuckled, "he left one at our home in Johannesburg on his last visit, and now that I think about it, he said he had brought them for 'those Eastern Cape types' and that 'they were in for a surprise'. I didn't know the background. He might just as well have used them as his Xmas cards—he seems to have left them all over the place."

"You're not kidding. The next evening he stuck one up on the bar in Ninky Noo's—in fact I still have it here." He opened a drawer and rummaged around among some papers. "Here it is," he exclaimed triumphantly, brandishing a torn half of a photograph of Pik Botha with eyes closed, clearly in a deep sleep. "I tore the bloody thing in half. Anyway the boys at Chapel weren't too impressed, as you can imagine."

Chapter Nine

HAGA HAGA SOURS—LOVE–HATE RELATIONSHIPS

Shook. Another ring-top was pulled open, another Castle slid across the counter. I felt I needed every beer, listening to Neil's stories. He turned to Margie.

"What will you have my dear? Same again?" Margie nodded. Neil poured some more Sauvignon Blanc into her glass and, using tongs, dropped in two blocks of ice.

"*Ag*, Neil. They should have given him a break. He was just taking the piss, he loves jokes like that."

"Maybe, maybe not. I mean if that was all, then fine, but it wasn't."

My heart sank. Tucker had obviously burned his bridges in Haga Haga.

"Why? What else did he do?"

"The next week at Chapel, nobody refers to the picture of Pik or anything like that and we're all having a *lekker* (nice) drink together. Irving is there. I think he's quite thick-skinned. Someone at the bar starts talking about how the rocks in front of the hotel have been stripped of all the *perlemoen* (abalone) and mussels by the local blacks. 'They come down onto the rocks at spring tide with fucking *mielie* (maize) sacks and take the *perlemoen* and mussels,' he says. And Irving bursts out laughing."

"What was he laughing at?"

"Well, he howls with laughter. Sort of a forced laugh, and sarcastic, if you know what I mean? And everyone in the bar looks at him. Then he says, looking around, 'You bunch of racists. You only care about conservation when black people are doing the poaching'. Everyone just looks at him. Then someone says, 'What do you mean?' Irving replies, 'I caught one of you *okes* nicking *perlemoen* the other day'. I can tell you everyone looked horrified. But there was no stopping Irving. Someone shouted: 'Who?' 'Mike Thompson's son-in-law, Michael Schroeter, that's who' says Irving. Then he says, 'It's okay for you bastards to poach, but not for the blacks. You're all a bunch of racists'. With that he finishes his drink, slams his glass down on the bar, throws a hundred buck note onto the counter to cover his drinks and walks out. That was the last time he came to Chapel."

"What?!" I exclaimed. "Mike Schroeter would never poach *perlemoen*. That I can guarantee. Certainly not. Hell, you know how hot Mike Thompson is on conservation? He even checks how many mussels *I've* taken off the rocks—that I haven't exceeded my quota—and I'm his brother! Well not really his brother, his nephew!" I corrected myself.

"You ask anyone here about it. In front of the whole bar he accuses Schroeter of poaching. You'd better ask Mike Thompson about it. Are you going to see him?"

I nodded my head, biting my lip, deeply disappointed at what I had just heard. I drained my beer and put down the empty can.

"Come, Margs. Time we went home." I didn't want to hear any more.

Shook another can opened and a Castle slid across the counter.

'No, you can't go yet. There's more. Surely Phil Conlon told you about the World Cup?"

I sat down again on the bar stool, not too keen on hearing more but curious as to what else Irving could have done. I swigged my beer.

"Tell us about the World Cup. Shit. I'm not surprised that he's not top of the pops in Haga Haga."

"Speak of the devil—hello Phil."

Phil Conlon, otherwise known as 'Mudguard' because of his bald head, came in and slammed the door behind him. When I had first met him and asked why he was called 'Mudguard' Neil had answered, saying, "Because he's shiny on the top with a lot of shit underneath." The name had stuck. Phil looked and was the typical Eastern Cape farmer. Open, friendly, suntanned features, khaki shirt, khaki shorts down to the knees, long brown socks and brown shoes. His face lit up when he saw us and he smiled, peering over his spectacles.

"Rob. Margie," he said, nodding a greeting, "Castle please Neil?"

"Well, now that you're here, Phil, you can tell the Binckeses about their mate, after the World Cup." He opened a can for Phil—*shook*—and pushed it across the counter to him.

"Is that so?" said Phil, turning to me, beer in his hand, "you mean that bugger Tucker?"

Neil had disappeared into the back to fetch something and shouted out, "Did you know that Newton was British?"

"Newton who?" I shouted back.

"Newton, Newton, you know, Newton and the law of gravity? He was always telling us that 'Newton, the man who discovered the law of gravity, was British'."

I laughed. Irving had said exactly the same thing to me.

"Haven't you heard what he did?" Phil asked.

"Well, Neil's just been telling us some of the things."

"*Ja*, but has he told you about the World Cup?"

I shook my head.

"Well, you know how he was always going on about England and putting South Africa down? I always took it as a bit of a joke, you know, I didn't think he was serious. But he was insufferable during the bloody World Cup, when we got beaten. Then of course, to top it, England won the damn thing. Well, he must have come prepared because the next day, I'm walking down the road, past your place, and I don't know what made me look up, but I did. You know that upstairs window that overlooks the road?"

I nodded.

"Well I'm damned if he hasn't got a giant bloody poster, life size, of Johnny Wilkinson, against that upstairs window. You know the one?"

I nodded again.

"He's put it there just to piss us all off."

"Bloody cheek," said Neil, shaking his head.

"He was just teasing you blokes," I said.

Phil chuckled and shook his head. "Ja, I think so. Well, that may be so. But I got the bugger back, I did. I waited till I saw that they had gone down to the beach and of course they left the house open. I nipped in, went upstairs and turned bloody Johnny Wilkinson upside down on his bloody head! That bloody Tucker, he's a good guy but shit, he can piss people off, can't he?" He laughed at the thought and sipped his beer. "Anyway, I would have loved to have seen his face when he discovered what I had done. He never mentioned it, you know. I think he went back to bloody England a few days later."

"Good riddance," said Neil.

"You know that they've got involved with the school up the road here, don't you?" Phil asked. Not waiting for a reply he continued. "I don't know how it all started but during one of their trips here, a few years ago, someone took them to the local little school up the road, it's on the Marsh Strand road. Anyway when they went back to England he got some of his pals to chip in and now they send money every year to help the school. Look, I don't know how much it is but ..."

Neil chipped in, "I believe it's about twenty to thirty grand."

"Ja, well, whatever it is, he didn't have to do that you know. I mean he's helping the bloody locals, you know what I mean?"

"Helping them what?" said Neil. "Bloody waste of money as far as I'm concerned. Pissing good money down the drain if you ask me."

'No man, you can't say that, Neil. I mean, his heart is in the right place."

"Well, what happened to the money last year?" asked Neil.

"No, I don't know. I think they were building toilets or something. Anyway, I don't want to get involved. All I know is that he does send loot over here. Plus they always bring clothes when they come. They're not a bad couple. In fact we're going to visit them when we go on a trip to the UK next year with the Browns." Phil paused and peered over his spectacles while he sipped his beer.

Neil snorted his disgust at this announcement.

We finished our drinks, said good night and made our way home.

The next day we drove into East London to buy fresh vegetables and to see the man I call my brother, who is really my uncle, Mike Thompson, and his wife Ann.

'What is this that Ninky Noo was telling me about Irving and Michael Schroeter?' I asked Mike. Michael Schroeter was married to Mike's daughter, Julie.

Mike gave a wry chuckle.

"Apparently he accused Michael of poaching *perlemoen*. Michael had actually taken the *perlemoen* from Yellow Sands when he was visiting his mother and then he came to see us. He was down on the rocks cleaning the *perlemoen* when Irving saw him. Plus he had a permit for the number that he had taken. Irving didn't say much to Michael on the day but we hear that he brought it up at Chapel. In front of the whole of Chapel he accused Michael of poaching. Not only does Michael want to kill him but Julie is furious about it. I wouldn't like to be in his shoes if Julie gets hold of him. She sent him an email in England challenging him: 'How could you? After all we have done for you'. As you know, like driving them out to your place when they come down, and all that. How could he be so unkind as to falsely accuse Michael in front of all the locals at Chapel?"

"What response did she get from Irving?"

"I can't really remember now. Something along the lines of 'you are all so quick to blame the blacks for poaching but meanwhile the whites are twice as bad'. You'll have to ask Julie. I don't think he ever apologized, though."

Margie and I both wondered what would happen when Irving and Yvonne returned to Haga Haga at the end of that year. But we never got to find out. That same year, due to poor business decisions I had made, we were forced to sell the house at Haga Haga, and that was the end of vacations for the Tuckers on the Eastern Cape coast.

✑

The Tuckers' annual visits to South Africa continued, but with a readjustment of their programme. Most times they still visited us in Johannesburg for a couple of nights, and spent time with Tony and Anne Taylor on their farm in the Karoo, or their farm near Louis Trichardt; sometimes they visited the Maythams at their guest lodge, also near Louis Trichardt. Whenever they were with us they popped out to visit their old friends, the Malans, in Broederstroom, and they always made a pilgrimage to pay their respects and give money to Irving's loyal old helper, Faraway. Faraway was retired and still lived on their old property. They left sufficient money each year to ensure that Faraway and his family had food and clothes until their next visit, in a year's time. And each year they arrived loaded with suitcases crammed full of clothes, which they always managed, somehow, to send down to Haga Haga, to be distributed to the local people who lived near the village.

In between visits our contact was sporadic and consisted mainly of emails from Irving. Most of the emails Irving sent included extracts from the English media which showed South Africa in a bad light. For example:

> From: IYTUCKER@aol.com [mailto: IYTUCKER@aol.com]
> Sent: Saturday, March 17, 2007 9:52 PM
> Subject: SAME SCRIPT DIFFERENT CAST
>
> March 17 2007 at 03:57 PM
> By Chris Otton
>
> Their prose did much to expose the moral bankruptcy of *apartheid* to the outside world, but the literary elite of white South Africa has now turned ferociously on the Rainbow Nation's new rulers.
> Following the departure of Nobel laureate J.M. Coetzee to Australia, authors such as Andre Brink, Rian Malan and Christopher Hope have delivered searing indictments of the state of the nation, sickened by what they see as an inexorable decline towards corruption and lawlessness.
> Brink, whose novels such as *A Dry White Season* brought him regular opprobrium from the *apartheid* rulers, has also burnt his bridges with their replacements in the corridors of power.
> He has described two cabinet members—Health Minister Manto Tshabalala-Msimang and Safety Minister Charles Nqakula—as "monsters", despairing at what he regards as indifference to HIV and AIDS and the rising tide of crime. In an interview, Brink has acknowledged that crime has long been a problem, but said the situation had now reached breaking point.
> "The cumulative effect has just reached a point where one cannot

take it anymore, and where the attitude of the authorities goes beyond all acceptable limits," he said.

"The attitude of Nqakula (who told parliament that those "whingeing" about crime should emigrate) has made it clear that the government simply does not take it seriously enough and, in fact, is in itself reason for despair."

Brink was also outraged at the decision of a number of senior ANC officials, including the speaker of parliament, to give former chief whip Tony Yengeni a hero's send-off when he went to jail to serve a corruption sentence.

"Faced with such blatant disregard for the law, and for the suffering of the people, we now have to speak out. To remain silent would make us complicit with evil."

Malan's memoir of growing up in the apartheid years, *My Traitor's Heart*, painted a devastating picture of the brutalities of the previous regime and, only two years ago, he was hailing the first "free" country as a veritable "paradise".

But in the latest edition of Britain's *The Spectator* magazine, Malan concludes the country is now sliding towards decay.

"We thought our table was fairly solid and that we would sit at it indefinitely, quaffing that old Rainbow Nation Ambrosia," he writes.

"Now, almost overnight, we have come to the dismaying realisation that much around us is rotten."

Malan identified what he calls the purging of whites from the ranks of civil service as the root cause of the decay.

"There won't be a civil war. Whites are finished. According to a recent study, one in six of us has left since the ANC took over and those who remain know their place."

Malan and Brink insist they will not be driven out of their native land.

Coetzee, however, has already voted with his feet, becoming an Australian citizen earlier in 2007. The famously taciturn author, a two-times winner of the Booker prize, has not gone into detail about his reasons for setting up a new home in Adelaide. But in a rare interview with Australian television after his move, Coetzee said: "Leaving a country is, in some respects, like the break-up of a marriage. It is an intimate matter."

Coetzee's 1999 masterpiece *Disgrace* centres around [sic] the rape of a white academic's daughter, speaking to the fears of many about sexual violence.

Writing about ANC deputy president Jacob Zuma's recent rape trial, Hope despaired at the "general feeling of helplessness in the face of the seemingly insatiable energy in and among South Africans for violence in all forms."

Hope's 1981 satirical debut novel, *A Separate Development*, was banned in South Africa. He now lives in self-imposed exile in France.

Nadine Gordimer, another Nobel laureate who has written extensively about the pre- and post-*apartheid* eras, said it was simplistic to reject the new South Africa wholesale.

"My own view is complex and I really prefer to write it down," she said. "There are things that are remarkably good and things that are very worrying."

Sapa-AFP

Other mails from Irving included comments about Julius Malema, the firebrand and rocket-out-of-control leader of the ANC Youth League (at the time); newspaper articles on South Africa's unwillingness to censure the ever-growing threat of Mugabe in Zimbabwe; and our poor performance on the sports fields, whether it was cricket in the summer, or rugby in the winter. The articles were always negative about South Africa, never positive. On the few occasions that one of our sports teams performed well, there was a stony silence and an absence of the 'you have mail' signal on my laptop.

Despite this we always looked forward to seeing the Tuckers. Irving's humour and joking and warmth and friendliness outweighed his negativity towards South Africa. I could accept it. On the balance sheet, as far as I was concerned, we had positive assets of friendship—although not everyone agreed with me. No amount of protesting from me about the bias of the articles or the other side of the story, could dent, even in a small way, Irving's view that South Africa was sliding towards doom and disaster.

Chapter Ten

YVONNE'S LAST VISIT

In January of 2009 the Tuckers returned to South Africa again, having emailed photos of their farm covered in snow and stressing how much they were looking forward to the sunshine. This time the pattern of their visit changed: They did not visit us in Johannesburg and went straight to Tony Taylor's farm near Louis Trichardt, but telephoned while there.

It was Yvonne on the line: "Hi Robbie," she said in her London accent.

"It's the Jolly Green Giant" I called out to Margie when I recognized Yvonne's voice.

"We've had a bit of a scare," Yvonne said after the greetings were made. 'Irv had a nasty kind of turn, the other day." I could hear from her tone that she was serious.

"Why, what happened?"

"Well he's fine now, but they think he had a very mild stroke. He sort of became disoriented for a while. Anyway we took him to a friend of Tony's, up here. He's a bloody good doctor, and prescribed some medication for him and Irv's now one hundred per cent. Look Robbie, we won't make it to Johannesburg to see you this time. We are going straight from the farm to the airport next Tuesday, drop off the car and then catch the plane."

"Oh that's a shame. So we won't get to see you?"

"Well, what about coming to the airport and meeting us before we catch the flight? We could have a drink in the bar."

So next Tuesday I finished a tour and drove to the airport to find Irving and Yvonne waiting for me in the Mugg & Bean. They both stood to greet me, smiling broadly. Yvonne gave me a big hug and Irving beamed as he shook my hand and gave me a self-conscious half-hug.

"Good to see you both," I said, "you're looking well and if your suntans are anything to go by, you've had a great holiday. No trace of any stroke, hey Irv?"

"No. I was bloody lucky, if it was a stroke. Anyway I'm fit as a fiddle now."

"I'm the one with a problem," Yvonne said with a laugh. "I've developed a bad back and will be seeing the doctor as soon as we get home."

At the time none of us realized the seriousness of her 'bad back'. This was the last time I would see Yvonne.

We sat down at the table, ordered wine for them and a beer for me, and caught up with the news of the past years.

"You know that Yvonne's a magistrate now?" asked Irving, unable to keep the pride out of his voice, clearly as besotted as ever with his wife.

'You're kidding? A magistrate. Hey, Yvonne! That's like making the poacher the game keeper, isn't it?'

She laughed. "I know but—"

Irving interrupted. "She's bloody good as well, let me tell you, Robbie, bloody good."

"Well done, Yvonne! Imagine that, the Jolly Green Giant sentencing people to death."

They both laughed.

"No, nothing like that. Anyway we're not barbaric, we don't have the death penalty in England. No, it's kind of smaller cases."

"All the same, it's a great achievement Yvonne," I said, smiling at her.

Yvonne was a highly intelligent person, a lover of art, literature, classical music and theatre—something of an intellectual snob, truth be told.

"Well, I found all this time on my hands once I sold all my horses."

"Why did you do that? Sell your horses, I mean?"

"I had fallen so many times and with my arthritis it wasn't a joke anymore."

"You must have been so sad to have to do that. You loved your horses and riding, didn't you?"

She nodded and sipped her wine. "Yes. I did Robbie, but that chapter's over. Time to move on," she said pragmatically, in line with her character. "And what about you?" Yvonne asked, a note of concern in her voice. "How are you and Margie getting on?"

"Fine thanks, we're both well."

"Robbie, don't be an arse. We know you're well. We mean financially?"

Margie and I had experienced a major financial disaster a few years earlier, which had led to me turning my hobby—history—into a job. I had qualified as a tour guide and had successfully built a tour business, taking overseas visitors on day tours and introducing them to the diverse cultures and history of this country. It was a job that I loved but found quite demanding, physically and mentally.

"Oh that," I laughed, "no, we're okay now, thanks."

I could feel them studying my face closely, as if hoping to see our bank balance, or the size of our overdraft, stamped on my forehead.

"Are you coping, financially?" Irving asked.

"Ja, well, we're not getting rich, but tour guiding pays the bills and I now have quite a nice little business. I get a fair bit of corporate work, as well. So yes, all in all, I would say we're okay."

"What about all the legal shit from those two partners of yours. Is that still on the go?"

Yvonne asked. "What bastards they were, hey Robbie?"

I could feel my blood pressure begin to soar as I thought of the two partners who had out-manoeuvred me and my other partners.

"What really happened there, Robbie? I mean, we came and saw your shop, it was great. Then we heard you had folded?"

"*Ag*, it's a long, unpleasant story. Suffice to say we not only lost all our money but also some of our friends. Let it be a lesson—don't ever go into business with friends."

I could see that I hadn't satisfied them with my answer, so I explained: "Two Johannesburg businessmen, Grenville Wilson and Barry Engelbrecht, approached us wanting to open a second branch of our business, RB's Theatre of Food, as a franchise in the shopping complex owned by Barry. But the existing partners and I were not keen on a franchise. As an alternative, we suggested that we open a second store, in which they would have shares. But we lacked the finances to make an investment of that magnitude, so I suggested that they put up the capital to open the second store, in the shopping centre, in exchange for shares in the overall company. A slice of a bigger cake, as it were … what a big mistake that was".

"To open a second store?"

"No—to take in new partners. We were so keen to build the second store we overlooked the fact that the site was not ideal. More importantly, when it came to signing the agreement with our new partners, we were so hasty we did not pick up that, should the business fail, the two new shareholders, Wilson and Engelbrecht, could claim their investment back, should we not have complied in every way with the terms of the agreement. The second shop failed, primarily due to its location, but the two new shareholders prevented us from closing it because it was located in the shopping complex owned by Engelbrecht. Friction and acrimony broke out among all the shareholders, but mostly between me and the two new investors. Scapegoats were sought and I was the target. Despite being the major shareholder, I left the business and six months later it went into liquidation. The banks called in their sureties, claimed their investment monies back and, after they had taken practically all we had, the two new shareholders claimed their investment back, and initiated legal proceedings against the five original shareholders. It was a terrible time and a very costly mistake. It meant that I had to find a way to earn a living, at the age of 59. That's when I turned my hobby into a career, qualified as a tour guide and the rest, as they say, is history."

"Wow! Quite a story, Robbie," said Yvonne.

"Did you fight the court action?" asked Irving.

I chortled. "That's funny, yes we did, or at least we started. What happened next just illustrates how friendships go sour when businesses go wrong."

"Tell us," Irving glanced at Yvonne, "we've still got plenty of time."

"Well, do you remember that Margie worked for one of the largest law firms in the country?"

They both nodded.

"We didn't have the kind of money that defending an action like that would cost, with senior counsel and so on; so Margie spoke to one of the partners, one of their best lawyers, and he offered to take our case on a *pro bono* basis."

"Great!" said Irving, smiling broadly.

"Yes, it was very good of him. He agreed to act for me and the four original investors against Wilson and Engelbrecht, for as long as we were all in agreement. But if one of us 'broke ranks' he would not be able to continue."

"Don't tell me! Someone did?"

I nodded.

"Yes. One of our friends, Johnny Meller, who was very influenced by Grenville Wilson's track record as a businessman, began to believe Wilson's accusations against Michael and me. In a meeting with the lawyers he intimated that the two of us, father and son, might have been stealing from the business."

"What?" Yvonne shrieked. "That's ridiculous! You were the major shareholder."

"Ridiculous or not, that was the end. The lawyer had to wash his hands of the case as we no longer presented a united front."

Irving shook his head. "I don't understand. Wasn't it in ... whatshisname's ... Mellies's ... interests to have the lawyers act for all of you?"

I corrected him. "Meller."

"Yes, yes, Meller. Wasn't it in his interests?"

"Yes it was, but as soon as the lawyers realized there was dissension among us, they could no longer act for all the shareholders."

"How stupid," said Yvonne, "so you had to settle?"

"Yes we did. But of course Margie and I had no money with which to settle; so Meller and one of the other shareholders, who had the money, settled the whole thing just to make it go away. And to finish the story, Meller really put in the boot. In meetings held with the original shareholders, to discuss an offer of settlement, we discovered that he had sent copies of emails which we had sent him, to our opponents, keeping them informed of everything we were discussing."

"Oh no! I don't believe it, I really don't," said Yvonne, looking horrified.

I grimaced.

"Hang on', said Irving, "didn't you say that Meller paid?"

I nodded.

"But then, he was acting against himself when he was giving the other two information, wasn't he?"

"Yes, he was."

"Fucking unbelievable, still don't understand it." Irving shook his head. "He shot himself in the foot."

"And us in the back," I laughed, "but that's the whole story. That's how we lost our money—and some of our friends."

"Whew," Irving exhaled.

There was silence. Then Irving spoke.

"So you settled?"

I nodded. "Yes we did, or at least the two partners with money did. At that stage Margie and I had nothing left after the banks had come after us. We put in all that we could and the others coughed up the balance which was the bulk of it. Not without quite a lot of pain and of course the souring of relationships and friendships. Not pleasant to lose friends. Anyway, that's all over now. Leaves a bitter taste, but there you are."

"Nice guys," Yvonne said caustically, referring to Wilson and Engelbrecht.

"Not really, Yvonne, just a lot smarter than we were. They set us up, so that if the business failed they could claim their money back. We walked into a sucker punch. Actually, in a strange way, I should thank Wilson and Engelbrecht."

"You've got to be joking Robbie! Thank them? Shit. I know what I would do to them," said Irving, "why thank them for taking you to the cleaners?"

"Well, look at it this way. If I hadn't lost our money I wouldn't have started guiding, or studying history. I wouldn't have learned so much about my own country; I wouldn't have started writing books; I wouldn't be doing something that I love passionately; I wouldn't have met fantastic people visiting South Africa—and I wouldn't have started an NGO in Alexandra township."

They looked at each other.

"Well, that's admirable Robbie, still ..." Yvonne tailed off.

"Bastards!" said Irving, with feeling. "Does the tour guiding provide you with enough money?"

I shrugged my shoulders. "For now it does, yes. Not sure about the future though."

"Yes, Robbie, we understand. It's fine for now, but are you building up any reserves? What are you going to do for money when you retire?" Irving asked.

"Retire, reshmire!" I snorted, 'I'm not looking at retiring at the moment."

"No, that's not what we mean. Of course you can carry on working—but for how long? We've seen how hard you have to work, and just so that you know, we admire you immensely."

"Hell yes," Yvonne agreed, "we both think you are amazing Robbie. A lot of people would have thrown in the towel when they lost their money, but you have gone out and created a whole new career and way of life, haven't you? We think what you've achieved is wonderful and what you do in the township—I mean how many of your friends do what you do?". Her English accent sounded as BBC as ever. "But Robbie, you aren't getting any younger are you?"

"Well, I'll just have to keep on working, won't I? Till I drop."

They exchanged glances, looking at a loss for words for a few seconds as we each, in our own ways, contemplated old age with no money.

"We worry about you and Margie, you know. Are you sure you're okay, financially, at the moment?" said Irving.

"For the moment we are fine."

"What are you going to do when you can't work any longer, though?" Irving was like a dog with a bone.

I laughed. "Let's cross that bridge when we come to it. We're fine at the moment, as long as I keep working. Maybe I'll make a fortune doing tours for visitors here for the World Cup next year. We'll see."

I didn't let them see that the conversation struck a sensitive chord. What *were* we going to do when I had to stop working? It wasn't a new question, but one that I shoved into a back corner of my mind whenever it came up, hoping it would just disappear. It never did of course. It was always there. I didn't like to be reminded of it because I hadn't yet found an answer.

"So when will you guys be out again?" I said, trying to change the course of the conversation.

"Same as always Robbie," Yvonne said, "this time next year."

She was wrong, of course. Yvonne would be dead within eight months.

Chapter Eleven

YVONNE'S STRUGGLE

One evening in May the following year our landline phone rang and I heard Margie's muffled voice as she answered the hall extension.

"It's Irv on the line, darling," she shouted.

I picked up the study extension, hearing the click as Margie put down the hall phone and returned to the kitchen where she was cooking supper.

"Hello? Robbie?"

"Hi Irv. How're you doing? Good to hear your voice, even though you're starting to sound a bit like those poms you love so much."

He laughed. "I'm fine, but Yvonne hasn't been too well since we came home. Remember she told you she had back problems when we saw you at the airport? They think she has gallstones or something. Anyway, not too serious. She's going in for some checks in a few days' time. Listen. What are you doing in January when we come out next year, in 2010?"

"I'll have to check dates in my diary, Irv. You know I get tours booked months in advance, and if I have a tour then that date is cast in stone … why do you ask?"

"Yvonne and I are looking at paying to watch an elephant being collared, in the Timbavati, on our next trip out there. You know how we both feel about wild life conservation. We were wondering if you guys would be keen to join us for a few days. Should be quite a lot of fun. We're just playing around with the idea but wanted to know whether you would be interested?"

I had never seen an elephant collaring and immediately jumped at the possible opportunity.

"Sure. Definitely interested, but I need to know dates so that I can check whether I have a tour booked at that time."

He promised to come back to me once plans were more definite and then hung up.

"What's he say?" shouted Margie from the kitchen, when she heard me put the phone down.

"Wants us to come to the Timbavati with them in January. They're paying to see an elephant being collared," I shouted back.

"That's nice," floated up to the study.

I walked down to the kitchen so as not to have to shout.

"Yvonne's not well. He says she has gallstones."

Margie pulled a face. "That's *not* nice."

I stole a piece of avocado from the salad she was preparing and popped it in my mouth, licking the bits off my fingers.

"Well, he didn't seem too bothered. Says she is going for tests in June," I said, through a mouthful of crouton which I had added to the stolen avocado.

"Don't do that Rob, that's supper."

"I'm sure she'll be fine. She looked okay to me last time I saw her. Anyway she and Irv live on organic foods and eat healthily all the time. Mind you, that's probably why her back is troubling her. Anyway, I'm sure things will be fine."

⤕

"It's Irv again" said Margie holding out the phone to me as I came down the stairs.

"Howzit Irv?"

"Hi Robbie."

His voice sounded flat.

"What's news Irv? Have you got those dates for the elephant collaring?"

"What? Oh that, not yet. Robbie, we've got a bit of bad news I'm afraid."

I felt all humour leave me like a beach at low tide.

"I've phoned to tell you that Yvonne had those tests," his voice quavered, "well, she does have gallstones—"

"I'm sorry to hear that Irv. Still, I'm sure she'll be okay," I said reassuringly.

"—I haven't finished ..." I kept silent, wondering what was to come "...she also has ovarian cancer." I heard the choke in his voice as he said it.

My stomach lurched—I felt as though I had been slapped in the face.

"Jeez. That's terrible. I ... we ... we're so sorry," I was stumbling over my words.

Hearing the shock in my voice Margie came and stood next to me, hoping to pick up the cause of my concern. She looked at my face and mouthed: "What's wrong?"

I shook my head and asked, for Margie's benefit as much as from my concern, "Cancer? Yvonne? Gee, I'm so sorry. Shit. That's a bummer, Irv."

"*Ja*," he said, and when he spoke he had his emotions under control. "It's quite bad, Robbie. They say that the cancer has spread and it's already at what they call stage three, or maybe even four."

"What does that mean?" I asked.

"I'm not sure. All I know is that it's either bad, or very bad."

"Jeez, Irv. I don't know what to say. She'll be okay though, won't she? I mean, with chemo and all that … nowadays they can treat cancer, can't they?"

"We don't really know. They're going to do a biopsy next week, and also drain fluid from her stomach. She's in a lot of pain at the moment, but once they've done that she'll be more comfortable; and after the biopsy we'll have a better idea of how bad it is. They think they'll have to operate, but they hope first to start with chemo and then operate."

"Well Irv, keep us posted. Our thoughts are with you. How's Yvonne taking it?"

"Nurse Vonnie? The Jolly Green Giant? She's telling the doctors what's wrong, you know her. She's on the computer as we speak, banging out a medical bulletin by email to all our friends."

The next morning, Saturday 13 June, I checked my emails. Yvonne's message was there, confirming what Irving had told me, and telling us that because of her illness, there was little chance of the two of them coming to South Africa on their annual holiday at the end of the year. However, despite the medical details, Yvonne sounded confident that she would come through it all okay.

> I am sorry to say I was given some very bad news today, after a long day at the hospital. I have ovarian cancer that has already spread to the uterus and to the bowel. Or possibly I have uterine cancer that has spread to the ovaries and bowel. They are not sure yet which is the primary, but it is most likely to be ovarian as the primary, as that is how it behaves. It sends very misleading symptoms. The fact that it has spread to the bowel is what has caused the gall bladder symptoms. I do obviously have a gallstone, but it was not just that that was upsetting the gall bladder.
>
> It is apparently at Stage Three (bad) or possibly Stage Four (very bad), they will only know late next week after they have done a biopsy and had the histology back. At the same time as doing the biopsy they will drain the fluid (several gallons I think) off my abdomen, which should get rid of a lot of the pain. Until it builds up again. Interestingly I have now had three doctors who were convinced my swollen abdomen was wind and not fluid. As soon as I heard it was fluid I knew it was going to be bad.
>
> I then start chemo, and they hope after three cycles they will be able to do an op and get a lot of the crud out. Then three more cycles of chemo. They don't want to do an op to start as even if they do a

perfect hysterectomy they cannot get the lesions or whatever they are on the bowel, and in order to get better I *have* to respond well to chemo. The three cycles of chemo should reduce the tumour(s) enough to make an easier op.

So that's the rest of this year stuffed. It may also mean no South Africa next year.

We have obviously been poleaxed by this. I can barely believe it. I am now focusing on what we do, what happens next, the best way of dealing with everything and believing that I will get through it.

Love

Yvonne

❧

A week later we received another update from Yvonne after she had spent four days in hospital having the fluid drained from her abdomen. They had drained ten and a half litres of fluid out of her and hadn't got it all. They were still waiting for the results of the biopsy, but she was home and expecting to hear the full diagnosis at the beginning of July.

Subject: Yvonne Update

Thank you all very, very much for your good wishes and interest and thoughts.

The latest update is, after four days in hospital draining off 10.5 litres, or 22 pints, of fluid, (can you believe it), a ghastly process that made me quite sick and ill, I am out now. Did not manage to get pain relief and nausea adequately sorted out at home the first night, so quite bad, but am much better now, on new anti-nausea drug and back on the morphine. Have still got football in front of my tummy so they haven't got it all. Now have to hope it doesn't come back at the same speed it came on first.

Next bit of news may come at the end of the week when they get the results of the biopsy. Until they have all that in, they cannot decide anything, which they are due to do on Friday at the multi-disciplinary meeting. I will probably only hear properly at my first appointment with the oncologist which is the following Friday, 3 July.

Will keep you posted!

Love

Yvonne

❧

"It's Irving, Rob," Margie called up the stairs to the study where I was working.

By now I had become used to regular calls from England as Irving updated us on Yvonne's condition.

It was 26 June, only two weeks since Yvonne had been diagnosed with cancer.

"Hello Irv. How's Yvonne?"

"Well she's battling with the fluid build-up. It looks like they will have to drain it again."

'I'm sorry to hear that."

"Well, ja. I just phoned to say hi and to tell you that you've hit the big time."

"Who? Me? Why do you say that?"

"You know I get all the South African papers? There's a piece called 'The Best of Johannesburg'. They give all the best restaurants and so on, and can you believe it, they recommend that people take a tour with you? They call you a walking encyclopaedia! Well done, Robbie, well done! I'll send you the cutting so that you can read the piece yourself."

"Well thanks, Irv. It's nice of you to call. I am sure you have other things on your mind right now. How is Yvonne?"

There was silence at the other end of the line.

"Irv? Irv? Are you there? I asked how Yvonne is?"

I heard him clear his throat; when he spoke his voice trembled.

"She's battling, Robbie. Lots of pain and seems to be having a tough time. Anyway, we are hoping that the oncologist will have some good news in a few days' time."

"And you, Irv? How are you coping on your own?"

Again a silence, then a cough and clearing of his throat. This time when he spoke there was no disguising his anguish.

"Jeez, Robbie, I'm lost. Yvonne is everything to me. Without her around I'm not a whole person. Robbie, I'm frightened I'm going to lose her. If she goes ... I ... I really don't know what I'll do. I can't even bear to think about the possibility."

"Come on Irv. I'm sure that it's not going to happen. We'll just have to see, won't we?"

I heard him blow his nose loudly on the other end of the line.

"Our thoughts are with you both, Irv."

"I know Robbie, I know. Bye."

I walked into the kitchen. Margie studied my face.

"Bad news?" she asked. "Yvonne?"

I nodded. "*Ja.* Irv broke down on the phone. Says he's lost without her and scared of losing her."

"Oh dear. How awful."

∽

The next email arrived the day after Yvonne had seen the oncologist. The news was not good.

From: IYTUCKER@aol.com [mailto: IYTUCKER@aol.com]
Sent: Saturday, July 04, 2009 7:31
To: robin@spearofthenation.co.za
Subject: (no subject)

Well, as you all know I saw my oncologist on Friday, who by the way I liked very much. Subsequent to that, they had had their multi-disciplinary meeting to discuss my Case Management. To cut a long story short, I'm going in for an endoscopy on Tuesday because they still do not know for certain whether my primary is ovary or stomach, which will determine the chemo drug I will be prescribed. I am also—finally—booked in to start my chemo this coming Thursday, which is good news. They will give me some form of chemo whatever the outcome of the endoscopy. It will therefore either be purely for ovary, or two drugs which cover both ovary and stomach. If chemo goes well, then the next stage would be, if possible, surgery. However, the fact that I have got so bad so quickly indicates this is a very aggressive cancer, and I may not respond well.

Many, many thanks for all your emails, messages of goodwill and lovely thoughts, and I or Irving will let you know my news as I go along.

Much love

Yvonne

∽

At the beginning of July they started giving Yvonne chemo but it was all to no avail. By the end of July she was too ill for chemo and had been transferred to a hospice. The end came quickly after that. Irving took over the role of sending email bulletins on her condition and she weakened steadily as the cancer ravaged her body.

From: IYTUCKER@aol.com [mailto: IYTUCKER@aol.com]
Sent: Thursday, July 30, 2009 9:19 PM
To: robin@spearofthenation.co.za
Subject: Yvonne 30th

Yvonne had a really bad turn the other night and was rushed by ambulance to hospital. She was due for her second chemo today but the oncologist said she was far too ill and they transferred her to the hospice. I spent the afternoon with her there getting her settled in and she is really in the best place. They got her pain and nausea under control within an hour as they quickly understood exactly what was required for Yvonne. They altered a lot of her drug regime and administer all drugs by injection either manually or via the pump (syringe driver) she is now fitted with.

Her food is wonderful with an extensive menu of stuff she likes and can eat, or they will make up anything she wants or get it in for her. The physio is going to give her a back massage tomorrow which she needs badly as she has seized up. She has been given her Walkman and she has chosen some books from their large library to listen to. All this and more, on only the first afternoon.

Even though the circumstances are terrible we are both so much happier now that she has effective control of her pain and nausea and is getting medical relief care specifically targeted for her cancer. The patient staff ratio seems very high indeed with permanent professional staff and volunteers all wanting to help. From first impressions we could not ask for more.

I would appreciate if you want to communicate you do it via email at the moment as I find discussing things on the phone quite difficult. Thank you all once again for your messages and love.

Irving

❧

Three days later on Monday 3 August 2009, fifty-two days after she had been diagnosed with cancer, Yvonne Tucker died.

"Hello?"

"Hello Irv." This time I had phoned him. It was the day after receiving the news, in a terse email from Irving, that Yvonne had died.

"How are you doing?" I asked quietly.

His voice sounded choked when he replied. "I'm okay, Robbie, thanks. Well, not really. I mean, I suppose I am. The neighbours and people have all been good. Sort of rallied around, bringing me food and stuff. *Ja*, they've been fantastic. I don't know when the funeral will be, but we will bury her here on the farm. No church or anything like that. You know neither of us were believers; so we'll do something simple on the farm. That's what she wanted. We discussed it all before she ... she ... died."

His voice broke and I could hear him blowing his nose. Then he continued. "Don't expect you to come over Robbie. Really. It's expensive. Tony Taylor has said that he'll come."

"No. I'm afraid I have tours booked, Irv, and also the cost. We won't be able to be there."

Yvonne's body was carried in a bamboo coffin on a crisp sunshine-filled morning on her Land Rover, (which she always called her 'Landy'), to her grave in the middle of the fields below the house they had built in the rolling hills of their farm, Bryn Uchaf, on the border between England and Wales.

Irving stood at the side of the freshly dug grave with a forced smile on his lips and tears trickling into his beard.

Irving is given a taste of Johannesburg via a Robin Binckes Tour ...

From left: Robin, Michael and Margie Binckes, with Irving Tucker, at the Hector Pieterson Museum, in Soweto, Johannesburg.

Graduation Day for children at the crèche managed by the Friends of Alexandra, in Alexandra, Johannesburg.

Mandisa, whose fees for private education are funded by the Friends of Alexandra.

The Great African Steps inside the Constitutional Court, Braamfontein, Johannesburg.

The first elephant collaring in February 2010 at Timbavati ...

The chartered helicopter performing an early morning search for the elephant to be collared.

The vet and rangers ensuring the comfort of the anaesthetized elephant, to be collared and named 'Yvonne'.

Irving lookin on as 'Yvonne' is collared.

View from the verandah of Robin's and Margie's seaside house at Haga Haga.

Ninky Noo's Pub at Haga Haga.

A classroom in the rural farm school at Haga Haga.

Sunset at Haga Haga.

The second elephant collaring in January 2011 at Timbavati ...

'Irving' the Elephant, drugged.

'Irving' the Elephant, collared and fully recovered.

Irving Tucker and Robin Binckes.

The quintessential 'Tucker with a T'

Irving sharing a joke with friends in a restaurant ...

Preparing sundowners on a game drive ...   ... braaiing in the bush.

The following photos were taken by Robin Binckes in February 2014, three years after Irving's death, when he journeyed to Irving's farm, outside the village of Oswestry, described by Irving as "the centre of the bloody universe".

From left: Emyr Jones, Andrew and Claire Belk and Steve Eisenstein, in front of Bryn Uchaf, the house that Irving built.

The country surrounding Oswestry and Irving's and Yvonne's farm, on the border between Shropshire and Wales.

The view from Bryn Uchaf.

Yvonne's grave at Bryn Uchaf.

The treasures of Oswestry, whose virtues and claims to fame were enthusiastically expounded by Irving ...

The memorial to Wilfrid Owen, one of the war poets.

The 25-pounder cannon, a relic from the Second World War.

Bellam House School in Oswestry, which dates back to the 14th century.

The Broadwalk in Oswestry, under which are buried 500 victims of the Great Plague of 1665–6.

According to Irving, this is "the largest organic fruit and vegetable shop in all England".

David Davies, the undertaker in Oswestry, "the best undertaker in the world".

One of Irving's final jokes? From 'Tucker with a T' to his great friends in Oswestry—Steve and Helen—the bequest of a pile of wood, described by Irving as "a very good vintage".

Chapter Twelve

"I'VE LOST HALF OF MYSELF"

The next few weeks were hard for Irving as he adapted to a life on his own. Neighbours rallied around and delivered meals in containers, specially cooked so that he could freeze them, to eat as needed after heating them in the microwave.

In September, during one of our telephone conversations, which had become quite frequent, Irving sounded particularly low and confessed to battling to control his grief.

"Robbie, I had no idea of the physical pain that I was going to feel." His voice cracked and I could feel him trying to get his emotions under control.

"I cry almost all the time. Anything that reminds me of her smells, sights, even my thoughts can spark it off and reduce me to tears in a second. I feel like a baby."

"Don't worry Irv, it's to be expected. Shouldn't you maybe go for counselling though? Talk to someone … it might help, you know? On the other hand of course it's early days isn't it?"

I could hear that he was crying. There was a silence. Then he spoke. His voice was still trembling and seemed to have lost its timbre, but it appeared that he had brought himself under control.

"I've been talking a lot to Helen, a friend of ours. She was a nurse and is now a counsellor. She's been a big help. She knew us both and how close we were and how we lived each other's lives, so I have been very lucky to have Helen. She's a big help. It would be difficult to explain to someone who didn't know us and how close we were."

"Ja, I suppose so. I do know that you two did everything together."

"No, Robbie, it was far, far more than that. Do you know that in the forty years that Yvonne and I were married, apart from five years in South Africa when she worked for a chemist and I worked for PMI, we have been with each other twenty-four hours of every day, for three hundred and sixty-five days a year? And neither of us would have had it any other way. No, Robbie, we weren't close, we were *one*. She was part of me. We were one person and now half of me is gone."

There was silence, then I heard a choked sob.

"It's because of our closeness that we never had kids you know? We were self-sufficient and selfishly did not want to share one another with children. Christ Robbie, I feel, I feel as if half of me is dead, and it's so fucking painful."

"I can't imagine what it must be like," was all I could think of to say. And I really couldn't.

"Look it's really shit here now. I've never felt so alone."

"But you've still got your friends, Irv."

The comment almost echoed it sounded so hollow. There was silence for a few seconds.

"Your old friends and mine, the Johnsons, you remember, your mate Ray, whose wife you tried to seduce? Well they've asked me to go to France and spend a bit of time there. So I'm going for four days in October."

'Irv, you know I never tried to seduce her—and I thought they were living in Australia?'

"They were, but they moved to France a couple of years ago and live there. Old Ray is quite the Frenchman now; beret, plays *boulle*, not sure if he smokes Gauloises though."

His voice sounded stronger, like a runner getting a second wind. I tried to keep him off the subject of being alone.

'What does he do for money ... did he do so well in Aussie?'

"Not at all. No, he paints and considers himself a writer. I've read his novel, set in Australia. It's really crap and I told him so as well."

I laughed. The tremor had disappeared from his voice so I continued with this new subject.

"Well, here is your opportunity to do the same with me. I'm writing an historical novel on the Great Trek; seeing as you have a lot of spare time on your hands, would you like to have a look at what I've written so far?"

"Sure I will, but Yvonne was the reader. It'll take me ages. I'm not a great reader, not very good with writing and emails and things. I manage, but that's why Yvonne handled most issues with numbers and stuff. Haven't you seen my spelling in my emails? Anyway send me what you've written and I'll give you my views. So I've decided to go to France in October. Not sure it's the right thing to do. Although going there and staying with your mates, the Johnsons, will be a break. I'm really looking forward to coming out to SA at the beginning of next year, even though it's going to be so different without Yvonne. We have so many memories of our life and holidays out there. It'll be six months since ... since ..." his voice tailed off.

"Well, presumably you will be coming to stay with us?"

"Yes, for sure. I want to go up to see Tony Taylor. I might send your book to him when I've had a look at it; he knows a lot about all that history. You know that we were going to collar an elephant for conservation, don't you? Well, I'm investigating doing it anyway, only now it will be in memory of Yvonne, bit different hey?"

The tremor in his voice was back and I could feel tears of sympathy welling up in my eyes. I was glad that he couldn't see me. I cleared my throat.

"Yes, Irv. I suppose everything is different now, isn't it?"

"You're not kidding. Anyway, send your book. It can't be worse than Johnson's. What about you and Margie coming up to Tanda Tula in the Timbavati Private Nature Reserve for a few days in January, if I go up there? Think about it. When I have final dates I'll let you know. If you can't come I definitely want to catch a Binckes tour when I come to Johannesburg. I'm told they are not to be missed."

Irving called a few weeks later.

"What are you doing in the first week of February next year?" His voice sounded almost normal and controlled.

"Irv, we always go to our timeshare at Sabie River Bungalows in early February. Why?"

"Oh hell! That's exactly when I wanted you both to come up to the Timbavati. Remember I told you about the elephant collaring? Well, it's going ahead. I'm sponsoring it in memory of Yvonne." At the mention of her name his voice faltered.

"Look Irv, maybe we could join you for a night or two."

He had recovered his composure. "I've got some friends coming to stay at Rock Fig Lodge in the Timbavati. See what you can do about joining us? Would love to have you with me for a few days. It would be fun."

I promised to do my best.

Chapter Thirteen

SABIE BREAK

At the time, for much of the time, my thoughts were frequently preoccupied with Irving's intended suicide. I continually recalled the night in January 2009 when Irving had arrived with us, straight from his flight, and the next day I had taken him on tour with Michael and Margie, enjoyed a lovely dinner at the Grill House—and after that he had told me he was going to kill himself.

I was dumbfounded then, and still couldn't believe it now. I had realized Irving was determined and had felt completely helpless. Although I was sure that he meant it, part of me didn't believe he would go through with it.

I shook my head in disbelief ... re-living that awful conversation ...

❧

... "Irv, what can I say? Is there anything any of us can do to stop you?"

He smiled wistfully. "No 'fraid not, Robbie. My mind's made up. Anyway, it's late now. Time for bed ... let's go."

He stood up, stretched his arms above his head, opened his mouth and yawned.

"It's been a good day. Thanks a lot Robbie, and sorry I burdened you with my crap."

"Don't be silly Irv. That's what friends are for, as the song goes. Shit. Can't believe it. Killing yourself?"

The combination of wine and beer and his announcement made everything hazy and unreal.

The light in our bedroom was off and Margie's deep breathing indicated that she was asleep.

I sat on the edge of the bed and clumsily dropped a shoe onto the carpet with a thump.

Margie stirred.

"Whassa time?"

"Half-past two in the morning," I whispered, not sure why as she was now half awake.

"He's going to kill himself."

"What?" still half asleep.

"Irving ... he's going to kill himself."

I saw Margie's dark shape sit bolt upright in bed.

"Don't be silly. Did he tell you that? Surely he's not serious?"

I nodded in the dark.

"That's not all. He's just sold a painting for twenty million rand ... he's got all that money and still he plans to kill himself."

"Twenty million and he wants to kill himself? Surely not. Do you think he will?'

Again I nodded in the dark. We sat in silence, contemplating Irving's decision. Eventually Margie slid down in the bed and pulled the covers around her face.

I heard a muffled, "How awful ... what a waste ... and all that money. I'm sure he won't ... he can't ... can he?"

She was asleep.

I lay awake in bed that night, racked to the core by Irving's revelation of his intended suicide. I certainly didn't want him to die, but found myself wondering what he was going to do with his money—if he killed himself. Wouldn't it be fantastic if he left some of it to us? He couldn't take it with him and if ever anyone really needed financial help it was the Binckeses. I felt horribly guilty at the thought. Finally I managed to switch off my distress, and guilt, and fell asleep. But I dreamt all night about what I would do with twenty million.

The next day Irving was to leave us on his annual journey to visit his SA friends. I wondered, after what he had told me the night before, if his visit was to say goodbye to them. We were in the kitchen finishing a light breakfast. Irving was drinking a cup of tea.

"I hope our conversation last night was a bad dream, and didn't really happen?" I asked, smiling weakly.

"Not at all, Robbie. It definitely happened; it's all true."

"Irv, I can't believe you are serious. Look, if you are talking about, about this kind of thing," in the cold, sober light of day I couldn't bring myself to say the words 'killing yourself', "you need to get help. Go for counselling, there are lots of people who could help you."

"I don't need help, I can assure you. I am of perfectly sound mind and I've decided. Quite simple really."

He looked slightly irritated and glanced at the clock. Irving never wore a watch.

"Listen, must go now. Try to get up to Timbavati for the elephant collaring, will you? We'll talk on the phone before then."

"Problem is we'll be at Sabie with our other friends from England, Rob and Monica Simpson."

"So bring them with you. Anyway we'll talk before then. Cheers Robbie, I'm off."

He shook my hand, opened the front door and stepped outside, calling over his shoulder, "We'll talk on the phone in the next few weeks, Robbie. Thanks to you and Margs for yesterday. It was fun. Cheers for now."

I heard the front door bang behind him. Irving had gone ...

⌘

Emerging from my recollection of that awful night, I found myself shaking my head in disbelief—and dismay. I was also beginning to feel a mild sense of panic.

A few weeks after Irving's invitation to the elephant collaring, and knowing that he was already ensconced at Rock Fig Lodge in the Timbavati, Margie and I left for our timeshare at the Sabie River Bungalows, near Hazyview. We travelled in a leisurely fashion, stopping for breakfast at Millys, about two hundred kilometres into our journey, arriving at the bungalows in the early afternoon. I was busy unloading the car when my cell phone rang. It was Irving.

"Robbie? Irving here."

"Hi Irv. How are you? Still around are you?"

He laughed. "Of course. Listen we're having a fantastic time. You and Margie *have* to come for the elephant collaring next Wednesday. I need to tell them, you know, for numbers. Come on Robbie, it'll be quite an experience for you. You can drive up early in the morning, and bring your friends."

"Okay Irv, listen, we've just arrived. We haven't even seen our friends yet, so we'll have a chat to them and give you a call. I'm sure we'll come, but I'll confirm later."

That evening, after a joyful reunion with our English friends, Rob and Monica, I called Irving.

"Irv, listen, we'll drive up in the morning—"

He interrupted me. "No, you won't be able to do that. I was talking to Michelle, the elephant lady, and there's a whole programme that starts the night before. A briefing and so on. Plus we have to start very early in the morning. Five o' clock. So you would have to leave Hazyview at about one in the morning. You'll have to drive up the day before the collaring."

I felt a pang of disappointment.

"Come up the night before. In fact you'll have to do that— we'll have to be at the airstrip at five in the morning and the gate doesn't open till later, so you have to come the night before. Are your friends coming too?"

"Well, they would like to, they've never seen a collaring and nor have we, but where will we stay?"

"Well, Rock Fig Lodge is full, but ..." I could hear from his voice that he was trying to find a solution, then he laughed, "Ag! Just come. Come up on Tuesday afternoon or whenever you can. Get here in time for the briefing and supper that evening. It'll be great. We'll make a plan, even if you have to doss on the floor. What does your friend do? He's not one of those uptight poms is he?"

I kept my voice neutral.

"He's a shrink. And I've told him about you. He wants to have you certified."

There was dead silence from Irving.

"Only kidding, man. He's a retired medical doctor, specialized in diabetes. Monica was born out here, like you, and grew up in Cape Town, but they live in the UK, like you. Rob worked out here for a couple of years when he first qualified. That's when I met them."

"Bastard," he said, "you had me going there for a minute. That's great. Bring them with you and we'll see you next Tuesday."

"One last thing, Irv. Do the others there know? What you told me?"

"Some do. Stop worrying about it, Robbie. See you Tuesday."

I was encouraged by his tone and his reassurance. Maybe he wasn't going to do it?

That night, in the warmth of the summer evening, sitting next to the braai at Sabie River Bungalows, looking out over the beautifully maintained golf course, the gentle smell of freshly mown grass from the fairway mingling with that of lamb chops sizzling on the fire, I told Rob and Monica about Irving's good fortune, and that he planned to kill himself.

They were appalled.

"He obviously isn't serious, is he Rob?" asked Rob Simpson. "He must be very depressed to be even talking like that, though."

"But I don't think he is depressed. Do you, Margie?"

I looked at Margie for confirmation. She shook her head and said, "You certainly wouldn't think so. You'll see when you meet him. He's a fun guy and certainly doesn't behave like someone who is planning to take his life. Judge for yourself next Tuesday, when we're up there."

"I can't believe it," said Rob, "I'm quite sure it won't happen. This is a cry for help."

I wanted to believe Rob, but wondered—doubted—that he was right.

The next week, on Tuesday, mid-morning, the four of us set off for the Timbavati, situated on the edge of the Kruger Park. The road we travelled took us through Bushbuck Ridge, a giant sprawling township of tin shacks, looking like chickenpox marks on the veld, spreading over both sides of the potholed road. Goats and sheep wandered across the road, dodging heavily overloaded taxis that frequently carried so much luggage and so many parcels that they had to be piled high on their roofs, there being no space inside.

I pointed at a taxi as we were overtaking it. "One of those was stopped in Joburg a while back—and one hundred and twelve people climbed out."

"Impossible!" stated Rob emphatically. He was sitting next to me while Margie and Monica chatted together in the back of the car.

"I have the newspaper cutting to prove it," I said.

We crested a rise in the road which sloped steeply downward.

"Look out!" shouted Rob, his right foot pushing hard against the floorboards, willing the brake pedal magically to appear on the passenger side of the car.

Two taxis straddled the whole road. Side by side they came up the hill towards us. The overtaking taxi, heavily laden with suitcases, boxes and a chicken coop on the roof, did not have the power to pass the other, so the two taxis occupied the full width of the road. There was no way past. I swung the wheel hard to the left, pulling off the road onto the grass verge. Stones clattered under the car. I felt the tail swing and almost lost control but at the last second the car righted itself. We jolted over the rough edge of the road, my hand pressed angrily on the hooter.

The two crawling taxis, still side by side, approached the blind rise behind us.

"Bastards," I muttered under my breath as I pulled back onto the road dodging potholes like landmines, some of them deep enough to permanently bend a rim.

"Whew! That was close," Rob exclaimed.

Monica and Margie hadn't even interrupted their conversation in the back.

A few kilometres further Rob muttered, "Oh oh."

He had seen two police cars ahead, at what appeared to be a roadblock.

"Maybe they won't stop us," I said hopefully.

A rotund traffic policewoman, as round as she was tall, who would have rolled like a ball if she didn't have legs, held up her right hand, signalling us to stop. She looked like a pincushion.

I pulled over, stopped at the side of the road and wound down the window. A policeman walked up and poked his head into the car.

"Good afternoon," he said, with a Colgate smile, "sir, you were speeding. I'm going to have to give you a fine."

"No, I wasn't. I was watching my speed. I was doing just over eighty kilometres per hour."

"Exactly right, sir. Eighty-four point three kilometres—in a sixty zone."

"Sixty! Oh no! I thought it was eighty," I groaned.

"That's a thousand rand fine," said the smiling teeth.

"Oh shit!"

He looked at me sympathetically. "Are you a pensioner?"

I nodded, hoping for some kind of concession.

"Well, a *madala* [old man] like you should drive like an old man, not like a Julius Malema."

We all laughed.

"How can I make my father pay a fine like this?" he asked, shrugging his shoulders helplessly, looking as though I was forcing him to do something too ghastly to contemplate.

I shrugged, put on my best patriarchal expression, and looked at him hopefully.

"Maybe if you can buy me lunch we can forget about it?" he offered quietly.

"How much is lunch?"

"Two maybe three ..."

"Hundred?"

He nodded, and pushed the clipboard with the traffic fine form at me.

I placed two one hundred rand notes on the clipboard. The clipboard did not move; it remained positioned under my nose. I added another one hundred rand note. That did the trick. Like a conjuror's act the notes disappeared—with one movement a practiced hand swopped them from the clipboard to a pocket, the toothy traffic officer withdrew his head and waved us onto the road to continue our journey.

As we pulled away I looked in my rear view mirror and saw him hand over part of the booty to the pincushion who, it turned out, also had a Colgate smile.

"Bloody corrupt buggers. Still, three hundred is better than a grand."

"I think he's done that before, don't you?" asked Rob, adding, "I wouldn't have paid him. You are just adding to corruption by paying him."

I nodded. "Yes, I have to agree with you. People like me who bribe the cop are just as guilty as those that ask for the bribe. I know that, but ..." I left the sentence incomplete.

For the rest of the journey Rob and I debated corruption and bribery in Africa. The only point we agreed on was that countries in Europe, and particularly Eastern Europe, were just as corrupt but in different ways.

Chapter Fourteen

ELEPHANT COLLARING

At about 16h30 we reached the main gate for the Timbavati reserve and followed the signs to Rock Fig Lodge. We bumped over the dirt road through lowveld bush and entered a clearing. Ahead of us was a safari vehicle with four adults and two children aboard. Irving stood next to the safari vehicle with a glass of wine in his hand, looking up at them and laughing. He turned around and grinned when he saw our vehicle.

"Hi Rob and Margie," sticking his head into the car, "you must be Rob and Monica?" looking from one to the other. "Welcome! You are more than welcome. I'm Irving. Quick you guys, you've arrived just in time. They're going on a game drive. Leave your things in the car and get on the landy. I'm sure you'd like to go?"

I glanced around at the others. They all seemed keen so we locked the car and walked over to join the group.

As we climbed onto the Land Rover, Irving, glass in hand, shouted to us, and waved in the direction of the others on the vehicle. "Introduce yourself to my friends—that's Murray Smythe and his wife Sally, from England, and in the back is a coolie doctor from Louis Trichardt, Casper, with his lovely wife Sarah, and their two boys, John and Owen. The Venters. Sarah and the boys, are lovely but you had better look out for the bloody coolie."

Casper Venter smiled a tired smile; he had heard it all before. Murray and Sally looked every inch the English couple and, for a few seconds, as I looked at Casper Venter's dark complexion, I thought that he was Indian. Then I noticed the reaction of his wife and children to Irving's comments, and realized that Irving was trying to be funny. We shook hands all round, introduced ourselves and set off on the game drive.

Within moments we were in a different world. The late afternoon sun was settling down on the horizon, bathing the bush in its soft light. Immediately outside the camp we stopped and watched a herd of twenty elephants amble across the track, trunks waving gently side to side as if in greeting. The silence of the bush smothered us, broken only by the 'tick-tick-tick' of the engine cooling. There was a hush in the Land Rover as we silently watched the prehistoric monsters lumber across the road in front of us.

"Wonderful animals aren't they?" asked Rob.

"Shhh! Look over there," hissed Scotch, our guide, pointing towards a clump of bushes twenty metres away. A female lion stood frozen in position, her front paw suspended in the air midway between steps, behind her crouched two lion cubs.

"She's teaching them to hunt," whispered Scotch.

"How old are the cubs?" asked Monica, also in a whisper.

"Nine months," said Scotch, still with the binoculars against his eyes, "look, look! They're stalking that impala."

We looked in the direction he was pointing. A lone female impala stood skittishly on its own, while a herd of about fifty impala grazed unconcernedly some ten metres away. The lioness had chosen the lone female impala for supper. Followed by the two cubs, she began quietly to move again, keeping a clump of bushes between the impala and herself.

"She's moving downwind," whispered Scotch, passing his binoculars over his shoulder to Rob Simpson.

We watched as the lioness and her two students slunk through the grass to a position downwind of the impala. The impala appeared jumpy. Her ears and tail flicked and she looked from side to side, but as yet had not seen the lion and her cubs. The rest of the herd carried on grazing, but a couple of male impala were looking nervously towards the clump of bushes where the lions waited.

The lone impala stood, looked around, and then decided to move. Like a delicate ballerina, head held high and neck stretched, she took three faltering steps—but the wrong way, towards the covering bush. At the same time one of the male impalas on the perimeter of the grazing herd barked out a warning cry. The herd, like leaping synchronized athletes, vaulted away from the lions.

There was a flurry of action and the lioness, in a flash of gold, burst out of the bushes and in bounding giant strides covered the twenty metres to her prey and leapt at the startled impala. She seemed mesmerized and had not moved more than two metres, despite her ability to jump ten metres in one leap.

Dust swirled as the impala, her eyes rolling back, was pulled to the ground, legs kicking and thrashing. The lioness and her two protégés snapped and snarled at the flailing legs, as the bleating impala struggled to escape. Growls and coughs and bleats of pain and terror suddenly filled the quiet of the evening. It was all over in less than a minute. A few final kicks and the impala lay dead. The lioness appeared to have donned a red beard as blood dripped from her mouth. Only then did the two cubs bite at the bleeding neck of the dead impala. Within minutes their faces too were covered with blood as they gnawed and chewed at the remains of the impala.

"Whew, that was quick." Everyone spoke at once. The two children were bouncing on the bench seats with excitement. "Wow! Daddy! Did you see that? We saw a 'kill'. Wasn't it fantastic?" said little John, the seven-year-old boy. His younger brother, Owen, was jumping up and down with excitement.

"Now you know why we call the impala the 'MacDonalds' of the bush—fast food!" said Scotch, with a laugh.

Three hours later, the headlights of the Land Rover cut ribbons of light through the bush as we returned to Rock Fig Lodge and clambered stiffly from the back of the Land Rover. Irving was there to meet us—wine glass in hand.

"How was it?" he asked.

"Terrific," said Rob and Monica, in unison, "we saw a lion kill."

"Really?" said Irving, looking at their faces to see if they were teasing him.

John and Owen were babbling with excitement. "We saw a kill Irv, we saw a kill! Yugh! You should have seen the blood," they shouted as they jumped down from the Land Rover.

Irving grinned and ruffled Owen's hair, taking care not to spill any wine.

"Oh yes? What did you see?"

"It was all over very fast. A lioness was teaching her cubs to hunt and she killed an impala. It took just a few seconds. I've never seen anything so fast," I said.

"Or brutal," said Margie.

"Yes, death comes fast in the bush. The weakest die, the strongest live. That's nature's way," said Irving, with a shrug. I looked at him and his eyes caught mine. I raised one eyebrow questioningly. Almost imperceptibly he nodded, a small smile twitching his lip. "Yes, it's the same for us, isn't it? The only thing is, we don't have the stronger people removing the weaker folk from society. Pity about that. Perhaps we should, then we wouldn't have sick and old people in ghastly old age homes, having complete strangers wiping their bums for them." He laughed humourlessly. "Ja, nature in the bush sorts it all out, doesn't it?"

Irving turned to Scotch in an obvious attempt to change the subject. "Did you see that family of leopards?"

He shook his head.

"Pity," said Irving, "we've been watching them all week. Wonderful sighting, wonderful. Listen you guys, I've booked you into Tanda Tula for the night. It's too cramped here. Michelle, the elephant lady is staying there as well."

My heart sank. I was embarrassed, and irritated. I had assured Rob and

Monica that we would be staying at Rock Fig Lodge and there would be no hotel costs involved—and I knew that Tanda Tula Lodge was well over two thousand rand per night, per person. Hell! I thought, it's going to be more than eight thousand rand for the four of us. Irving must have seen the worried expression on my face as I made the calculation.

"Oh, the accommodation at Tanda Tula is on me. So don't worry about anything, I've already sorted out the bill. Go up there, sort out your things and then come back for a beer or two and supper, which the girls are cooking right now. After supper Michelle—"

I interrupted, "The elephant lady?"

"—*Ja*," said Irving, "the elephant lady and her team will come down here to give us a briefing on what's going to happen tomorrow."

Rob interjected. "No Irving, I won't hear of that. We can't expect you to pay for our accommodation. I mean, you don't even know us, and you're already paying for the collaring and everything. You have been most generous to include us. No, thank you, but we'll pay our own accommodation."

"Don't be silly. I invited you here. You are friends of Rob and Margie and that's good enough for me. It's all paid for anyway, so there's no point arguing about it." He turned his back on Rob, indicating that the discussion was at an end.

"See you just now," and he walked into the lodge to replenish his empty glass.

I followed, taking advantage of him being out of earshot of Rob and Monica. He was pouring a glass of wine and looked at me over his shoulder as I approached. He smiled and went back to filling his glass.

"Want a glass, Robbie? Mmm," as he sipped, "lovely wine."

I shook my head.

"Irv, listen. You can't pay for all of us. We brought the Simpsons with us. It's far too much money—you are already paying for the collaring and hosting Margie and me."

He grinned and gripped my shoulder with his hand, his face close to mine.

"Don't worry about it, Robbie. Aren't we pals, have been for years? I'm just glad that I'm in a position to do it. It's my pleasure. As I said, friends of yours are friends of mine."

"You aren't still going to do it, are you?"

"What?" said Irving, looking puzzled. His face broke into a grin when he realized I was referring to his plan to kill himself.

"Oh that!" he laughed, "nothing's changed, Robbie. Of course, I told you what I was going to do, and I still am."

"Shit Irv. You really are serious?" A new thought struck me and I exclaimed, "Hey, you won't do it while we're all here, will you? Shit."

"No, I wouldn't do that to you and my friends, Robbie," he shook his head, "no, I still have some things to do back home, so you can relax. You won't find me with my brains scattered all over the room here."

I shuddered as a pictured the scene of Irving's head blown to bits, strewn all over the walls and pillows. For some reason I had always associated suicide with a shotgun and a mouth and a finger pulling a trigger. I pictured bits of brain and blood spattered across a room, feeling slightly ill at the thought.

"Is that how you're going to do it? Shoot yourself?" I asked, aghast.

"No, it's not. I'm not going to shoot myself."

I was sucked into a whirlpool of fascination by our weird conversation.

"Well, how are you going to do it?"

"Come on, Rob. Go and put your things down at Tanda Tula, and come back for supper and the talk. It won't be messy, Robbie, that's for sure."

I was like a dog with a bone—I couldn't let it go.

"You won't just do it, will you Irv? I mean, I would hate just to hear that you had gone and killed yourself. I would like to know … you know, to say goodbye. Anyway I don't think you're going to do it—you're just stringing us along."

"As I've said before, believe what you like. I'm certainly not doing it now. I'm not ready yet," he said. "You'll know when it's going to happen, but it'll be a while yet."

"You mean if you do, it will be after you've gone back to England?"

He nodded.

I heaved a sigh of relief and shook my head at the bizarre nature of the situation.

"Whew! Thank heavens. So we'll still see some more of you. That's good. Okay Irv, we're off. See you in about half an hour."

We returned after dropping our luggage at the upmarket Tanda Tula Lodge and joined the other guests on the veranda under a big fat sky full of twinkling stars. Irving, wine glass in hand, stood beaming as we walked up the steps.

'There you are. We're just about ready to eat. Gale and Anne have made us a wonderful meal. I appointed them as cooks because they're so damn good. They really are both bloody good cooks. *Cordon bleu*—like Yvonne."

We joined Tony Taylor and his wife Anne, one of the 'bloody good cooks', Alistair Maytham and his wife Gale, the other 'bloody good cook', Murray and Sally and the Venter family. The wine soon flowed, laughter pealed, crickets chirped and in the distance a chorus of frogs accompanied our merriment, under a sky which sparkled with dazzling stars like fireflies. There was a festive atmosphere and everyone joined in the laughter and joking.

I looked across at Irving. His face flickered in the light from the dancing orange flames of the fire in the *lapa* (a thatched roof supported on wooden poles) that roared near our table; the orange-yellow flames like darting fingers leaped into the sky. Every few minutes a burning log would change position and send sparks skywards in what looked like a sacrifice of fireflies. The distinctive smell of wood smoke added flavour to the moment. Occasionally a thicker cloud of smoke would be carried by the breeze in our direction and sting the eyes.

Irving smiled as he listened to the conversation around him, wearing an expression of contentment and satisfaction. As I watched him and thought of what he planned to do my eyes burned with tears, a reaction to both the wood smoke and my sadness.

"How did you get involved in this elephant collaring?" Rob asked Irving as we sat waiting for Michelle to arrive. We had all taken to calling her 'the elephant lady'.

"Last year, Yvonne, my wife ..." silence descended like a blanket; everyone was quiet, listening, "... we were here on holiday and Yvonne and I met Michelle from Save the Elephants. We got chatting and Yvonne in particular loved the idea of collaring an elephant. That's how it all started. Yvonne passed away ..." he paused and blinked rapidly, two or three times, his eyes shiny with tears. I looked round the table—he wasn't the only one blinking rapidly. "... in August. We were going to sponsor a collaring as we believe the work that Michelle and Save the Elephants are doing is important. So, after, after Yvonne died, I decided to go ahead with the idea. I'll leave it to Michelle to explain everything to you all, but the elephant is being collared in memory of Yvonne. In fact, the elephant is going to be called Yvonne after the collaring."

"That's great," I said, "the Jolly Green Giant would be pleased with that."

Irving gave me a small sad smile. "She would, wouldn't she?"

There was a sudden flurry of activity and Michelle and her entourage of vets, employees, game rangers and volunteers arrived. Space was made and chairs were arranged in a semi-circle. Dr Michelle Henley talked to us about the elephants and the work that Save the Elephants was doing across Africa.

It was started in Kenya by Dr Iain Douglas-Hamilton as a non-profit non-governmental organization, to help fight illegal elephant poaching and the trade in ivory. Since the 1989 ban on ivory trading, the organization has focused on research, education and communication. Today the transboundary programme operates in many southern African countries. Michelle, a professional research biologist with a PhD in Ecology, heads up the South African arm of STE. Their research is focussed on understanding the motivation behind elephant movements, from conservation areas such as the Kruger National Park to Zimbabwe in the north, Mozambique in the east, and the associated private nature reserves, an area which borders the Kruger National Park on its northwestern edge. STE collects data to establish elephant population dynamics, movements, and habitat use. This is done using advanced technology—GPS satellites and mobile phone collars on the elephants—which enables the research team to identify individual elephants and track their movements.

There was total silence while Michelle talked to us and explained clearly the procedure to be followed the next day. I thought how sad this must be for Irving. Yvonne had suggested that they sponsor the collaring of an elephant, which requires a significant amount of money, about forty thousand rand, and now she wasn't here to witness the event. I hoped that renaming the elephant in Yvonne's memory would provide some small solace for Irving.

"We have already identified and have been tracking the elephant that we will be collaring tomorrow. He is a bull elephant ..." I glanced at Irving but he seemed to have missed the irony of having a bull elephant named after Yvonne, "... and after the collaring we will be able to monitor and map, through signals transmitted from his collar, his movements for the next few years, until the power runs out in the batteries, when we will have to re-collar him. Having first been collared eight years ago, in August we re-collared a big bull elephant named Mac; he has a range that exceeds five thousand kilometres. This is the collar that we will be putting on the elephant tomorrow."

We all examined the giant leather collar that lay on the table in front of Michelle. "The collar is fitted with a GPS satellite tracking device which sends signals that enable us to monitor the elephant's movements. This collar weighs about twelve kilos," explained Michelle. "We have a very early start tomorrow, so I'm not going to keep you long. I do want to remind you that you are going to be near wild animals tomorrow, particularly elephants. Things can go wrong, so I want to stress that you are all to obey the instructions of the game rangers. They will be armed, to cover any eventuality, but your discipline and co-operation are critically important for the success of the operation."

I was thankful to hear the knock on the door, our wake-up call, at half-past-four the next morning. I had slept fitfully, tossing and turning, with images of Irving's brain-splattered bedroom filling my head, along with pictures of Yvonne who seemed to drift in and out of my dreams at will. The pitch-blackness of the early morning reality was a welcome relief.

The others were waiting when we arrived at the vehicle. We drove the short distance down the track to Rock Fig Lodge and joined the rest of the collaring party for coffee and rusks on the veranda.

"Hope there's some brandy or rum in this coffee?" asked Rob, grinning.

"No way," said Irving in a serious tone, "we are dealing with elephants, guns and the bush. Alcohol doesn't mix well with them. No alcohol I'm afraid."

"No, sorry, I was only joking, of course. I wouldn't have wanted any anyway." Rob looked embarrassed.

Our party, which now totalled twenty people, clambered into three Land Cruisers and we bumped our way through the dark on a rough dirt road to the airstrip. We were the first vehicle to arrive and stood around talking quietly. Funny, I thought, how everyone in the pre-morning light whispers to one another; an indication of their respect for the peace and tranquillity of the wild, I imagined. We waited for dawn to break, drinking more cups of coffee poured scalding hot from thermos flasks: the early morning, the bush and the thermos endowed the coffee with a special flavour; tendrils of steam wafted across the faces of the drinkers. The headlights of approaching vehicles criss-crossed the dark skies like searchlights, before levelling out and approaching us directly as they bumped up and down on the rutted, uneven track. Soon a fleet of Land Cruisers and Land Rovers which had transported the vets, game rangers and volunteers, was parked along the edge of the narrow tar runway.

The sky began to soften. Soon it was no longer necessary to use electric torches as outline shapes became people with faces and clothes. The world began to come alive with sounds. Bird calls, shouts in the distance from a kraal as a new day began, and even our conversations changed from whispers to normal speaking voices as if, with the rising sun, a command had been given. The outline of trees suddenly became filled in with greens and browns as the sun began to edge almost nervously above the horizon. A thin curve of orange slid higher into the sky until it looked like a giant fried egg, sunny-side-up, bathing the landscape in its gentle morning light.

"We're waiting for the chopper," explained Irving, and we all looked expectantly into the lightening sky. A small group gathered around Piet, the marksman, who was preparing his rifle for the darting. While we waited we watched the vets prepare the correct dosage of drug to be contained in a dart from the specially designed rifle, to be fired into the elephant's rump.

"We will be using a cocktail of drugs," explained the vet, "an opioid called A30-80 mixed with M99, a narcotic analgesic. We have to calculate the mixture and amount dependent upon the age, sex and body condition of the elephant. This elephant is a male adult bull and we estimate his weight to be four tons. We have added into the cocktail a drug called azaperone to reduce hypertension, and hyaluronidase to assist with absorption of the drug into the bloodstream. Everything is done to minimize the amount of trauma experienced by the elephant."

If all went well the elephant would be drugged, fall to the ground and the team would then have time not only to place the collar on him but also to take and record measurements of foot size, trunk size, tusks and other vital parts, for the purposes of research.

We stood, waiting and peering into the flushing sky, searching for the helicopter.

"There he comes," someone shouted. A gentle hum was heard before the tiny helicopter came into sight, looking like a buzzing insect. It swooped low over us, drowning all conversation, steadied, and then lowered itself gently onto the runaway. Clouds of dust swirled next to the runway as the rotors slowed and the engine idled.

Michelle and Piet climbed into the tiny three-seater helicopter. Piet sat alongside the pilot, rifle in hand. The door on the passenger side had been removed to enable him to get a clear view of the elephant for his shot.

"Glad I'm not Piet," said Irving. "He might fall out."

That's ironic, I thought.

The blades of the helicopter began slowly to rotate, picking up speed as they spun. Dust and leaves lifted into the air, hiding the helicopter from sight. Hesitatingly, it lifted above the dust, hovered, as if deciding where to go, and then its bubble glass nose dipped and the helicopter skimmed over the trees and bushes with centimetres to spare. We watched as it soared higher and then hovered over the bush a kilometre away from us.

"They've spotted the elephant," shouted Irving.

Like an angry bumble bee the helicopter dived almost to ground level and then ascended to about two hundred feet. Down again it plunged, then ascended. The pilot repeated this manoeuvre a number of times, all the while moving closer to the road.

"They're herding the elephant away from the group, towards us," shouted one of the rangers, "quick, onto the vehicles."

We scrambled onto the open Land Cruisers which then roared, bumping and rattling across the airfield, and turned onto the rough dirt road. All eyes were on the buzzing helicopter, now only about two hundred metres ahead of us, almost on the edge of the road. In convoy we began slowly to drive down the road in the direction of the helicopter. It was still yo-yoing up and down and moving from side to side—an aerial sheepdog, shepherding the elephant towards the road, in our direction. The elephant burst from the scrub onto the road and came towards us at a fast walking pace, trunk waving with irritation, ears like saloon doors lazily swinging from his giant head which swayed from side to side. Above him the helicopter, in short marshalling movements, engines roaring, turned and swooped and herded him along the road.

"Perfect! Perfect!" shouted Martin, "we've got a bet on—Piet gets a bottle of whisky if he can bring down the elephant on the road."

The helicopter hovered above and slightly behind the elephant, which had now broken into a lumbering trot along the road towards us.

Piet fired. The dart smacked into the rump of the elephant, immediately going to work. The elephant slowed down, walking towards us while the helicopter pestered him. We watched in awed silence as he lumbered closer. After a couple of minutes, the elephant's knees buckled and then, like a collapsing house, his giant grey mass folded and crumpled gently to the ground, unconscious before he hit the earth.

Engines screaming in protest all five vehicles roared up to the comatose elephant. Like midgets about to tie down the giant in *Gulliver's Travels*, we jumped off the vehicles and sprinted towards the massive inert hulk. There were shouts of alarm as a noise like a jet plane's *whooooosh* emanated from the trunk of the sleeping giant as he exhaled.

The practiced team of vets, helpers and rangers began taking all the necessary steps to ensure the elephant's safety, protection and comfort. His ear was immediately pulled over his eyes, to protect them from the direct rays of the now flaming sun; a monitoring device was clipped to the ear to measure his distress levels; a twig from a nearby tree was inserted into his trunk, ensuring that it was unobstructed and that the elephant would continue breathing. Then, just like the scene from *Gulliver's Travels*, Michelle and two assistants began buckling the giant collar around the neck of the elephant; other team members began to take measurements, pull samples of hair from his tail for later examination in a laboratory, and apply medication to some light wounds on his legs. They worked for fifteen minutes, the time punctuated by the *whooooosh* from the elephant's trunk as he exhaled every ten seconds. Buckets of water were poured over him to keep his body temperature down, and his pulse and breathing rate were monitored.

"Right! Everyone back to the vehicles," called out Michelle, "Irving's going to inject him with the antidote and he will begin to wake up in a few minutes."

Guided by the vet, Irving plunged the needle containing the antidote, a mixture of naltrexone with diprenorphine, into one of the blood vessels in the elephant's ear. When he had emptied the syringe he and the vet ran for the Land Cruiser and clambered up breathlessly. Engines revving, the vehicles reversed away from the elephant for thirty metres and then stopped.

All eyes were on the elephant. Nothing happened. After two minutes someone whispered, "He's starting to move."

The elephant lifted his head. Then, like an unfolding jack-in-the-box he began to clamber unsteadily to his feet. He stood in the road, swaying slightly, like a drunk man. Then he straightened up and casually sauntered off the road. His trunk explored the ground around him as he walked into the vegetation on the side of the road, sniffing along some branches and grabbing some twigs for a snack. He behaved as if what had just happened was the most ordinary event in his life and happened daily.

Spontaneous applause broke out from the occupants of the vehicles.

"How wonderful was that?" asked Irving, looking as if he had single-handedly carried out the collaring. "Wasn't that terrific? Yvonne would have loved that."

"Helluva thing really. Poor old elephant, hey?" I said.

Irving glanced at me and I could see that my comment had irritated him.

"Why 'poor' elephant? He hardly knew what was happening. There are no ill effects. Why call him 'poor'?"

"Ha ha!" I laughed. "Of course I feel sorry for him, Irv, so should you—it's like that old Johnny Cash song, you remember? 'A Boy called Sue'. Here he is, a great big macho male elephant, strolling through the bush on a lovely summer morning, not a care in the world. Nothing to do and the whole day to do it in, except maybe to go and sort out some female 'ellies'. Suddenly he hears a buzzing noise, then zap! A sting in his bum and that's all he remembers. When he wakes up, he's still a bull elephant but now he's wearing a pansy collar and his name is Yvonne. Of course you should feel sorry for him!"

Irving slapped his leg and roared: "Of course! 'A Boy called Sue'—a bull elephant called Yvonne." He led the shouts of laughter from the others.

We left Michelle and her team, collected our luggage from Tanda Tula and headed for Hoedspruit, thirty kilometres away, where we had all agreed to meet at the Station Restaurant for lunch before going our separate ways.

On the journey into Hoedspruit the four of us drove in silence, mulling over the morning's events. Then Rob spoke.

"That was a great experience, I'm so glad we were included. Thank you."

"Well, I'll take the thanks anyway, Rob, but of course it's Irving we have to thank," I replied.

"What a nice guy," said Monica from the back. "Of course, that's all nonsense about killing himself. Obviously nonsense. He's as happy as the rest of us. Great company and certainly not a depressive type, is he?"

I glanced up at her in the mirror.

"You don't think he's going to kill himself?"

She shook her head firmly. "Definitely not. He's been having you on."

Rob chuckled and punched me lightly on the thigh. "Ha ha! He had you old son."

I grimaced and caught Margie's eye in the mirror. I didn't laugh and neither did she.

"I hope you are right but I'm afraid you are wrong. I'm not so sure that he isn't going do it. One minute I convince myself that he's talking crap, the next I think he's definitely going to do it. He seems so certain when he talks about it. But I really hope you're right."

"Look," said Rob, "in my experience people who say they are going to kill themselves never do. I thought he might have been pulling your leg?" He looked at me questioningly.

I shook my head.

"No?" he continued, "well, I doubt it very much, Rob. He's too full of life to kill himself. He'd miss his wine too much!"

We all laughed.

"What do you say, Margie?" I looked in the mirror to see her expression.

"I agree with Rob," she said looking at Monica. "Sometimes I think he will, and at other times, like this morning when we watched him enjoying himself in the bush, I think he's definitely not going to do it. Of course, if he is serious, we have no idea when it will happen."

I told them of my conversation with Irving in the kitchen the night before.

"Well," said Rob, "he's certainly calm about it; he doesn't appear to be tortured in any way, does he?"

"No, he doesn't, but to be honest, I hardly slept last night. Couldn't stop thinking about him blowing his brains out. He might be calm, I'm not."

"He's not going to do that, is he?" Margie asked from the backseat. "Blow his brains out, I mean. How awful."

"No, he says not, but he wouldn't say how he is planning to do it."

"You said he works with animals, so perhaps he'll use something that he gives them?"

I shrugged. We were entering Hoedspruit and there was silence in the car as we all gazed out the windows and took in the town. The tyres crunched on the grey stone chips as we parked outside the Station Hotel.

A large table had been set up outside to accommodate us. The others were already seated at the table and had been joined by two friends from Johannesburg—Jacques Malan and his wife, Marie—who were going to spend a few days with Irving at Rock Fig Lodge. They had been neighbours of the Tuckers at their farm in Broederstroom.

During lunch Irving again entertained us all with his jokes and stories. He was the life and soul of the party. I noticed that Monica was scrutinising his face whenever he spoke, as if searching for a clue as to whether he was going to do what he said—kill himself.

I watched Irving and thought: What a waste of a life. He has everything going for him. He's only sixty-three, in good health, he loves life and he is now quite wealthy—and he wants to kill himself. The sight of him laughing and joking irritated me. He should be miserable if he's going to kill himself, I thought. Instead I was the one having nightmares and being stressed about it. Irving looked as though he didn't have a care in the world.

When lunch was over we stood to leave; after saying thank you and goodbye to everyone we walked to my car, accompanied by Irving. He put his arm around my shoulder as we strolled.

"Thanks Binckeses, for coming up. It was good of you. I'm so pleased you could make it. Pity it was so short. Next time you'll have to make it for longer."

"Next time? Next time? Is there going to be a next time?"

He smiled.

"Maybe, maybe not. I'll let you know."

"You've changed your mind, then?" I asked hopefully.

He shook his head and smiled. "Not at all, Robbie, but I promise to keep you posted."

He turned to Rob and Monica and held out his hand.

"Great meeting you," said Irving.

"Yes, likewise," said Rob, grasping his hand and shaking it. "I hope our paths cross again?" he said, looking Irving in the eye.

Irving smiled. "Yes. That would be very nice wouldn't it? Who knows? We both live in England, so perhaps ..."

He walked up to me, put both his hands on my shoulders and looked me in the eye.

"I suppose this is it, then?" I asked.

He gave a wry smile and said, "I thought you were talking about coming to Europe to stay in Rob and Monica's house in France, with your other doctor friends?"

I nodded. "We're just talking about it; we'd like to, but time, and money ... we'll have to see."

"But keep me in the loop. If you do, you'll have to come over and spend a few days with me on the farm. Thanks for the music, Robbie."

"What music?"

"You know, Robbie, 'Thank you for the Music', the old Abba song."

I nodded. My throat tightened.

He gave Margie and me a last hug and turned away, blinking rapidly.

We climbed into my car and headed back to Sabie to complete our holiday.

Chapter Fifteen

BRUSH WITH DEATH

I kept wondering whether he would actually do it. Surely someone who enjoyed life as much as Irving would not choose to end it? He loved the bush, the sunshine, the joking, good wine ... surely not? After all, he had nearly died once before and had fought desperately to survive. Would someone who had been on the edge of death, stared into the abyss, willingly take that step? I didn't think so.

Irving's earlier encounter with death began in 1968 when a spell of 'itchy feet' had caused him to persuade his boss, Gil Catton, that he needed an extended leave of absence to visit Australia, New Zealand and the East.

"At the same time, Mr Catton, I can call on some Japanese and Hong Kong plastic manufacturers and see what they are up to. Maybe I could bring back a few new ideas that would improve our business?"

Catton let him go.

Irving made his way to Cape Town and boarded a liner to Perth. The ship should have departed on 4 March but a fire on board delayed the sailing for four days. Irving should have recognized the omen and cancelled his journey.

He didn't.

After landing in Perth on 20 March he hitchhiked across Australia. He relished the wide open spaces and freedom and the relaxed and carefree lifestyle of the Australians. Perth, Canberra, Melbourne, Sydney, all were described in glowing terms in his letters home. In typical Irving fashion he relished every moment of his adventure, drinking in the scenery, the people and the differences.

On 7 April he flew to Wellington in New Zealand and caught the ferry to the South Island. He travelled again, hitchhiking whenever he could, marvelling at the spectacular beauty of the scenery in New Zealand. In a letter home he described Queenstown on the west coast as "the most beautiful town I have ever seen. It dinkum looks like something out of a fairytale". He loved the people and particularly liked the fact that he was never 'egged on' about South African politics. He loved New Zealand despite describing the government as "not far off bankruptcy".

After touring New Zealand he planned to return to Sydney and then travel to Melbourne, where he hoped to make good his promise to Catton to visit a few plastic manufacturing firms.

The sun was setting and the sky was gloomy as Irving, along with six hundred and nine other passengers, plus one hundred and twenty-three crew, boarded the ferry *Wahine* at Lyttelton on the South Island for the overnight journey to the North Island. The *Wahine* sailed out of the harbour at Lyttelton under dark skies and into slightly choppy seas stirred by a slight breeze at 20h40 on Good Friday, 9 April 1968. Irving found his cabin, dropped off his suitcase and made his way to the general lounge where, sitting at the bar, he enjoyed a glass of New Zealand wine.

The one-hundred-and-forty-nine-metre-long, eight-thousand-nine-hundred-and-forty-eight-ton *Wahine* was one of the largest ferries in the world. There was nothing to indicate that this journey should be any different to the sixty-six crossings between Lyttleton and Wellington she had made in the twenty months she had been in service. It had been a long day so Irving decided on an early night. As he left the bar he heard snatches of conversation between two of the bar staff.

"… cyclone …" said the first.

"Nah," was the dismissive reply from the second, "it's miles away."

Irving paid little attention and made his way to his cabin and bed.

During the night Irving slept fitfully. The sea had become angry and the ship was pitching and tossing in rough seas. He jerked awake as the ship creaked and rolled and looked at his watch. It was 04h48 in the morning.

Wind has come up … stabilizers are working overtime, he thought, as he dozed off again.

He awoke with a start and clutched at the side of his bunk to prevent being hurled out, as the ship lurched heavily to port, having been hit by a giant wave.

"Shit!" he said to the empty cabin.

He looked at his watch. The time was 06h10. Judging from the wild movements of the *Wahine*, they were ploughing their way through a bad storm. Irving could hear the wind howling outside as it battered the ship, which seemed to be wallowing. Before the *Wahine* could recover she was hit by a second wave. The captain, a Captain Robertson, had been battling to correct the drifting *Wahine* and the force of the second wave sent him flying twenty-two metres across the bridge. Bruised and bleeding he climbed to his feet and struggled to regain control of the ship. Below deck Irving and the other passengers were oblivious of the drama on the bridge or the seriousness of the situation. The *Wahine* was outside Wellington harbour alongside Pencarrow Head. Winds were gusting between 130 and 150 kilometres an hour. The passengers were unaware that the radar was no longer working and visibility had reduced to no more than 800 metres.

On the bridge Captain Robertson was fighting a losing battle—the helm would not respond in the giant seas. The *Wahine* rose and fell in the mountainous swells and troughs caused by the hurricane; the ship's giant propellers thrashed the water uselessly, grabbing for water as the ship plunged down like a dive bomber.

In desperation Captain Robertson decided to take the *Wahine* away from the harbour and head for the open seas. It was too late. The engine room was flooded. The engines stopped. Robertson had lost control of the ship. Driven by the winds the *Wahine* drifted stern first onto Barretts Reef, hitting the bar with a crash. The rocks ripped a hole in her bottom.

At 06h40 that morning Irving felt a slight jolt and a shudder run through the *Wahine* but he thought they had been hit by another giant wave. Nevertheless he decided to leave the cabin and make for the saloon and the company of other passengers who, he felt certain, would also have been awakened. He was pulling on his clothes when he heard the harsh clanging of the ship's alarm bells.

Shit! That sounds serious, he thought as he buttoned up his shirt.

Then followed an announcement.

"Ladies and gentleman, this is your captain speaking. We are aground on Barrett's Reef. There is no immediate danger. Please proceed to your cabins, collect your life-jackets and report to your muster stations."

Irving grabbed his life-jacket and opened the door. People pushed past him in the narrow gangway. He joined the flow of passengers strapping on life-jackets and heading for the lounge. A thought struck him—what if we sink? He turned round and fought his way against the tide of bodies back to his cabin. He grabbed his anorak and his wallet which contained his traveller's cheques and passport, shoved them into his anorak pocket and then rejoined the almost solid mass of humanity, noisily and excitely moving towards the lounge and assembly points as ordered.

Above the loud hum of conversation in the lounge Irving heard the sound of the giant chains and anchors clattering out of the bowels of the ship, as desperate efforts were made to stabilize the battered and helpless *Wahine*. The anchor chains had been lowered by an act of extreme bravery on the part of Chief Officer Luly and Bosun Hampson—they had risked their lives by venturing onto the foredeck in winds gusting at over 160 kilometres an hour. It took the two men twenty minutes to crawl their way across the exposed deck through the screaming gale to release the anchors.

In the main lounge the scene was like that from a movie of a World War II refugee ship. The lounge was over crowded with people. Many were elderly. Some were vomiting from sea-sickness caused by the violent motion of the

Wahine as the gale-force winds toyed with her, pitching and rolling her like a toy in a tub. Many of the elderly looked frightened, and the strong stench of vomit added to the misery. Irving felt rather than heard a new sound of *thump thump thump*. The pumps had been started in an attempt to keep the remaining underwater compartments dry. Four were already flooded. Water had also begun to enter the vehicle deck, although at that point no one was aware of this.

Irving sat in the main lounge trying to peer through the glass windows but the seas were pounding over the *Wahine* and the spray made it impossible to see. He had to rely on the rumours and speculation doing the rounds.

Despite the hammering seas and hurricane winds, inside the crowded main lounge some of the passengers—apart from those who were sick and elderly—joked and laughed nervously as the hours passed, waiting patiently to be told that everything was under control. All the seats were occupied; some of the passengers had removed their life-jackets to use them as pillows and lay resting on the crowded floor. After all, the *Wahine* was near the entrance to Wellington harbour. Not much could go wrong, so they thought.

One of the stewards burst into the lounge.

"One of the other ships or tugs is going to tow us into calmer waters!" he shouted through cupped hands.

There were a few cheers and some scattered applause.

A short while later the same steward, who had gone in search of information, returned.

"They've attached a line from the tug *Tarhui* to us. We'll be alright now!"

This time there was a better response: a loud cheer rose from the sardine-packed main lounge.

Ten minutes later the line parted with a snap like a pistol shot. Despite a few futile attempts it proved impossible to re-attach it to the doomed *Wahine*.

The fierce gale began to diminish slightly but massive waves continued to crash over the *Wahine*. The tide swung her side-on to the wind; she listed to starboard, providing some shelter on the starboard side. As the already heavy list to starboard increased, chairs, tables, glasses and crockery scudded across the floor of the main lounge and crashed into the starboard bulkhead, thudding and tinkling. The laughter and jokes had stopped. Conversation, when it happened, was in whispers. Many of the elderly wore expressions of outright fear while the babies present seemed to have absorbed the tension of the adults; their wailing splintered the hush in the lounge.

Fifteen minutes later, at 01h15, shouts of alarm rang out. The *Wahine* lurched further towards starboard and tilted at a crazy angle, so steep that it was difficult to remain seated without falling out of the chair. A crackle from the speakers high on the walls signalled an impending announcement. Everyone looked up hopefully.

The voice of Captain Robertson filled the room: "Abandon ship! Abandon ship! All passengers and crew. Abandon ship on the starboard side! Abandon ship on the starboard side! Women and children first! Abandon ship, I repeat, abandon ship on the starboard side!"

There were screams of terror and a rush for the doors as people scrambled to be first into the lifeboats. Unsure what 'starboard' meant, many passengers struggled up the elevated port side. When they arrived on the port deck they found that the lifeboats on that side could not possibly be launched. Realizing their mistake a number turned and scrabbled for the starboard side, sliding down the steeply tilted wet and slippery deck. Irving watched, helpless and horrified, as an elderly pair slipped, fell onto the steeply inclined deck, and skidded headfirst, screaming in terror, down the deck and into the steel side of the ship. They lay still while the water, streaked with red, washed over them.

Utterly appalled, Irving watched as people scrambled and fought to get into one of the four lifeboats on the starboard side. The wind and the spray tore at his clothes like hungry fingers; he had to screw up his eyes to see through the spray. He saw the first lifeboat, crammed with people, being lowered into the waves. No sooner had it been released than a giant wave swamped the vessel. Irving watched, aghast, as the boat overturned— men, women and children were flung into the sea. Some disappeared immediately beneath the waves, never to be seen again. Others clutched onto the boat and were swept away by the wind and tide, towards the eastern shore.

Having seen what was happening to the lifeboats, Irving decided not to attempt that particular escape. Unsure of his best course of action he looked feverishly for an alternative. The wind tore at his eyes so fiercely he felt they were going to be whipped from their sockets. Narrowing his eyes against the wind he could see, through the spray, other ships nearby. He decided his best option was to dive into the sea and hope to be picked up. He looked at the sea. The waters around the *Wahine* were dotted with wreckage; inflatable life rafts floated on the surface while swimmers desperately tried to reach them. People were holding onto pieces of wood and whatever else they could find, trying to stay afloat while the seas tore cruelly at them. Several of the liferafts were punctured; they and their occupants were rapidly swallowed by the voracious sea. Some survivors were dashed against rocks on the shoreline, and died. Others drifted, swept by the waves and the wind, toward a section of the shore not guarded by reefs and rocks. Many who were cast onto those shores later died of exposure, before rescuers could reach them.

Irving watched and waited. He saw that a number of the crew had gathered on the starboard side of the ship, near the stern, close to the water. As the *Wahine* settled further into the raging seas the crew leaned closer to the water. Irving felt the crew knew what they were doing and struggled across the slippery, tilting deck to join them. He stood there waiting, witnessing tragedy after tragedy. People in lifejackets were being whirled around like bobbing corks, being dashed against rocks; panicking and overturning their lifeboats ...

Irving looked at the ships standing by to assist and decided they presented the best option for survival. He caught a glimpse of the tug boat *Tarhui* nearby and tried to calculate the distance between the *Wahine* and her, but the enormous waves, some over ten metres high, made judgement difficult. He kept his eyes glued on the patch of grey sea where he thought he would next catch sight of her. When he saw her again, she was closer. This was his chance. He made sure his passport, wallet and traveller's cheques were inside his anorak inner pocket, checked his lifejacket and slipped his shoes off. With one last look to get his bearings on the tug Irving dived into the sea.

The impact of hitting the water and the freezing cold took his breath away. His lifejacket carried him to the surface, spluttering and coughing. He looked around for the tug, fighting a mounting panic when he couldn't see her—the towering waves locked him into a watery grey prison. He felt helpless; although he had been in the water less than a minute his fingers and feet were already numb. He struck out, trying to swim in the direction of where he thought the tug lay. A wave took him higher, as if on a roller coaster ride. He saw the *Tarhui*. She looked a great deal farther than when he had seen her from the deck of the *Wahine*

Terrified that she was moving away his strokes took on a new urgency; he swam desperately in the raging waters, buffeted by the waves and the wind. Then he saw the tug again. He was closer. He pulled at the water as hard as he could. The cold had entered his bones and he ached with the chill gnawing at him. He retched and coughed in the waves; his eyes stung from the salt water; the waves smacked him unmercifully in the face and he swallowed mouthfuls of sea. His wet clothes which, for a brief moment had provided some protection, now dragged at him and joined forces with the sea, intent on dragging him under.

He tried to shout but a mouthful of seawater and a coughing fit showed him the futility of the action; the wind whipped the sounds from his mouth and carried them away. He had been in the water for ten minutes, it felt like ten hours. His arms ached from exertion, felt as though they were being detached from his shoulders. His teeth chattered with the cold. He had lost all feeling in his hands and feet. Three thoughts flashed through Irving's brain: If I believed in God, now is the time to pray; and Shit! It's a long way from home to die; and Thank God for my life-jacket!

A wave like a giant hand lifted him high. He sailed up the wall of water and glimpsed the *Tarhui* again. She was closer. Plummeting down again, as if on a toboggan, he wallowed, floating in the valley of the giant waves, the wind tearing at him, the cold becoming unbearable, his strokes like a useless paddle flapping on the sea. Up again as the wave lifted him. He saw the *Tarhui*, metres away. His arms and legs were like lead; they felt like engine pistons that had not been greased for years. Exhausted, Irving stopped swimming and floated helplessly in the life jacket, head down. He could feel his life slipping away. He was so tired. One last try. He looked up. The steel hull of the *Tarhui* was only yards away. Vaguely he saw something snake out from the ship towards him. It took a second or two for him to realize a rope had landed a few metres from him. He was so cold he just looked at it; his mind as frozen as his body. The rope drifted tantalizingly close. He reached out for it—too far. He slid down a wave and was blown by the howling wind towards the rope, his arm stretching, his hand grasping. He had it! His fingers were too numb to feel the rope but he grabbed it with both hands and hung on, his hands like claws. He felt a jerk and then a steady drag as willing hands on the *Tarhui* pulled him towards the tug.

Irving was losing consciousness. His eyes were closed but he felt the reassuring hauling on the rope and the coursing of his body through the water. Then the movement stopped. He opened his eyes and looked at the steel hull of the *Tarhui* a few inches from his face. A wave lifted him and smashed him against the steel plates. He looked up. Faces looked down at him and he could see open mouths on the blur of faces. Their shouted instructions were stolen by the wind.

Irving hung onto the rope, grasping it with both arms like a passionate lover. It would have taken ten iron men to prise that rope from his clutches. Again he smashed against the steel, rising on a wave that almost dumped him on the deck of the *Tarhui*. Again his numb body clanged against the steel side of the ship. He felt the rope tighten in his hands. Hang on! he thought.

They were pulling him up. He spun like the weights on a mantelpiece clock as he rose up the side, one last numbing collision and he was pulled over the rails onto the heaving deck. He lay like a discarded dish cloth, spluttering, vomiting sea water, coughing.

"You alright mate?" yelled one of the men, cupping his hands round Irving's ear, against the howling wind.

"Never, (cough) felt (cough, splutter) better, sport," burped Irving. Then he vomited out half the Cook Straights.

Fifty-one people died that day.

Chapter Sixteen

RETURN TRIP PLANS

Irving returned to England a few days after our collaring experience in the bush. Life for us settled back to normal—except for the nagging concern about Irving's death. Reminders of our discussion popped up when I was least expecting them. I would be sharing a beer and a joke with friends and suddenly he would appear in my mind, like an uninvited guest. I would go to bed early but his brain-spattered bedroom appeared in my dreams so frequently that I felt I knew the room. I would be showering in the morning, my mind still sluggish from sleep, and find myself wondering if he had done the deed yet.

Eventually, I couldn't stand the worry any longer and decided to speak to the person we all knew Irving respected. It was quite funny really. Whenever Tony Taylor was around, Irving's personality changed—he would become sombre and serious, as though trying to impress Tony. I decided to give Tony a call and discuss the issue with him.

"Hello Robbie," he said, answering the phone after a couple of rings.

"Hi Tony," realizing that he had my number in his phone and had seen the caller ID, "how are you getting along?"

"Very good thanks. It was good seeing you up in the bush with Irving."

"Yes," I hesitated, "did you have a good time on the farm, after you left the bush?"

"Ja, you know what Tucker's like? Takes over, so we just leave it to him. He loves it up there."

"Yes, I know." I wasn't too sure how to broach the subject of Irving's suicide. "Did he chat to you at all while he was there, Tony? "

"Yes, of course, we chatted quite a lot. Why, what's up?'

"Did he ... was he ... I mean, did he say anything about killing himself?"

Tony laughed. "Oh that. Yes, he did try to talk about it. Listen, Tucker is not the suicide type, you know what I mean? Ja, he did say he was going to do something, but I didn't really talk about it. Waste of time talking crap like that."

"So you don't think he's serious?"

"No. Absolutely not. Tucker is a tough oke, you know? He wouldn't commit suicide."

I paused before I said, "I think he might, Tony. I think he is serious."

He laughed. "No, I don't think so. As I said, he's not the suicide type. He might have been a bit down at the time. Anyway, we're going over later in the year, with the Maythams, to stay with him. And he wouldn't be making plans to host us if he was going to bump himself off, would he? And he has our visit to look forward to."

"No, I suppose you're right. Perhaps you could speak to him about it, just to make sure?"

"No, I think it's best to just leave it. I'm sure that he won't do it. Waste of time talking about a load of rubbish."

"I suppose you're right," I said. But I wasn't thoroughly convinced. There was something about Irving's determination that worried me.

❧

I soon learned that the topic of Irving's suicide was a show-stopper, a popular dinner table subject.

"Have you heard about Rob's friend Irving who is going to kill himself?"

"Tell them about your friend, Rob."

After I had told the story there would be a flurry of comments; no one accepted that he was going to kill himself.

"It's a cry for help."

"Give him to me for a couple of hours. I deal with this kind of thing all the time, I'll sort him out," said a counsellor from Lifeline, while her friends nodded sagely and her husband said in a helpful manner, "You should put him in touch, you know. He obviously needs help from a professional. Anyway, he won't do it. They never do."

I shook my head. "You could be wrong. I think there's a very good chance he is going to do it. The debatable points are when and how?"

"Time is a great healer, you'll see. It's a lonely man's cry for help. They always threaten—to get attention. Those that do kill themselves don't threaten. You just come home and find the body."

I caught Margie's eye and gave a cynical smile and a shrug.

"This one is different. I have a funny feeling that he is deadly serious, excuse the pun." They laughed. "Well, if he won't get help, you should report him. Report him to the police and have him committed."

"Can't do that, he's my friend. Imagine if I did that? What would they do? Lock him up to stop him; put him in a straightjacket? Imagine that. No, if he does want to kill himself, the best we can do as friends is support him and try to discourage him, but at the end of the day, if that's what he wants to do, there's no way we can actually stop him. He's perfectly sane."

"I beg to differ," said the counsellor, "anyone who is seriously considering killing themselves has to be slightly insane. He is unhinged by his grief."

I shook my head, anxious to move the conversation along, away from Irving. I could see it was turning into a win-or-lose debate.

"Oh well, you're probably right. With all that money he would really be mad to kill himself, wouldn't he?'

There was a chorus of "Bloody right. Would you bump yourself off when you've just got twenty million in your bank account? Not likely!"

"What a waste," the recently divorced sixty-year-old woman with a low top, sagging breasts and no bra, said bitterly, "what a waste." She sounded like she meant it.

It must have been terrible for Irving, arriving back in England to an empty house in the middle of the English winter. He had picked up tick-bite fever while staying on Tony Taylor's farm and was feeling miserable anyway.

When I called him a few days after his return he told me it had taken two days to warm the house, and that he had left in thick snow and returned to thick snow, four weeks later. He sounded depressed about being back in England and spoke about the trip and the elephant collaring and how much he had enjoyed it. When he had finished talking about the collaring there was a slight pause.

"What about the other thing, Irv?"

"What other thing are you referring to?"

"Killing yourself."

He chuckled.

"That? Look, I appreciate your concern and comments, I really do. I'm certainly not telling you to fuck off with your advice, but please appreciate that we all see things from a different perspective. For you, killing yourself might not be an option; for me it's the right thing, the *only* thing. So if you want to know if I'm heeding your advice the answer is, definitely not. I'm going ahead with my plan."

I felt my face flush with irritation at his obstinacy.

He continued: "You're welcome to carry on giving me what you consider good advice, but you had better not be offended if I ignore it. By the way," he said, changing the subject, "I've been on the wagon since coming back. My body was so full of alcohol that I've been de-toxing since getting back to England. Had to get my body back into shape."

It was on the tip of my tongue to ask why—if he was going to kill himself. Seemed a bit of a waste of effort to me.

"Just to make you feel better, Robbie, I've been chatting a lot to our friend Helen. I told you about her, she's a sort of shrink and I must say I feel better after speaking to her."

"But you are still going ahead with your plan?"

"Absolutely, Robbie, absolutely. You have no idea what it's like to be alone. I miss Yvonne so much at times I ache."

There was nothing I could say.

We tried to stay in touch by phone as often as we could and usually he sounded as if he was coping.

In April I received an email from him in which he apologized for his silence, (his telephone calls had become far less frequent), and acknowledged that he had been feeling quite depressed. But his doctor had prescribed anti-depressants and he was feeling a great deal better. Worried that the depression would accelerate his act of suicide, I called him.

"How are you Irv?"

"Much better, thanks Robbie. Much better. Those anti-depressants from the doc have done the trick. And of course I'm still chatting to Helen, so I'm in a much better place than I was."

I felt an elephant being lifted off my shoulders—a huge feeling of relief.

"Terrific Irv. Glad you've seen sense. That's a relief."

"What?" he laughed. "What do you mean, 'seen sense'?"

"Well, sounds like you're still around," I said jokingly, "and that you're not going ahead with your plan."

"I never said anything about that, Robbie. I am still going ahead with my plan. Just that I'm not walking around feeling miserable. No, I am still on track with my decision, so put that idea out of your head."

The elephant sat down again, heavily, on my shoulders.

I was silent.

"Am I right in thinking that you are coming over soon, in the summer, to stay with your doctor friend in France?" he asked.

"I'm not sure about that, Irv. We want to, but we haven't planned anything. What with work commitments and the cost, I don't know that we'll make it this year."

"What about if I paid?"

"What do you mean? You mean to come and see us in France, if we go there?" I asked, taken aback.

"No, I mean, if I paid for you and Margie to come over to France and then come to the farm for a few days."

"I don't think we would have the time to do that Irv, so thanks anyway but—"

He interrupted. "That's okay. I'll pay for your trip to meet up with your friends in France, whether or not you are able to come over here to see me, courtesy of Frank Auerbach."

"Frank who?" I asked, then I remembered and laughed. "Oh, the artist. Why? Have you got more of his paintings?"

We both chuckled.

"That's really good of you Irv. We would love to come over."

"Well do it. The trip will be on me whether you come to England or not."

"Thanks Irv, thanks a lot. Thank you—I'll have to see if I can swing it."

A few weeks later he phoned again.

"When are you coming?" he asked.

I felt a stab of guilt; I had not made any plans to take up his offer.

"No Irv, not possible at the moment. I've committed to doing tours and I just don't have a week or ten days free until the end of the year."

"Oh well," he said, "that's a pity. But here's another invitation for the two of you, and I'm getting in early because I don't want you saying that you're too busy."

I waited.

"I've decided to take up my flight booking in January next year, to come out there. The Eisensteins—you know, the woman I've been telling you about, Helen Rooney? Well, her husband, Steve Eisenstein, is a South African and a surgeon, here in Oswestry. Bloody good one too. Helen's the counsellor. Anyway they came for coffee this afternoon and they are keen to go to Namibia in December or January, for a week, so I invited them to come to Zebenine in the Timbavati. As my guests. They jumped at the idea, so I phoned Murray Smythe and Sally, you remember them don't you? Well, he owns a school here and I invited them to join us. They all felt it would be great if you and Margie could come up as well. This time for a week, if I book you early enough."

"That's good of you Irv. Where's Zebenine?"

"Tanda Tula, where you came in February. Rock Fig Lodge. I'm going to book it again. Are you on?"

"Hang on Irv. Let me check dates right now so that I can block it off."

"No, we still have to firm up dates. Once I've done that I'll let you know."

"In principle though, are you coming?"

"Yes, we would love to. As long as you don't kill yourself!"

"I told you that I wouldn't do it around you, didn't I? Well, that's good news. I'll sort out dates and come back to you, so that you can block them off in your diary."

A few days later he sent me an email enquiring how the writing of my novel was going. I was writing a historical novel, with some spicy sex scenes which Irving described as '*boere* porn'. Irv wanted to show my writing to his friend Ray, who now lived in France, and who was going to be visiting with his wife Lynne, in a few days' time. Irv's parting shot: "I'll give his wife your deepest love." He promised to phone in a few days to finalize dates for Zebenine.

A few days later, in early June, the phone call came.

"It's Irving, Rob," Margie shouted up the stairs.

"At least he's still alive—he hasn't killed himself yet," I shouted back, picking up the extension in the study.

"Hello?"

"Hello. Is that Mr Binckes? This is Uncle Frank here."

"Who? Come on Irv, who's Uncle Frank?"

"Your bloody uncle, Frank Auerbach, the artist, man," he joked.

"Oh him! He's not my uncle, Irv, he's yours. Shit. I don't think he's an uncle anyway. More like a godfather!"

He laughed. "Look we're all on for Zebenine. The place has changed hands apparently. We can't have that guide, Scotch, that we had last year. Remember? He was damn good. Remember how impressed we were that he knew all the trees and insects as well? Apparently it's a whitey now. Anyway, I'm sure he'll be good. Steve and Helen will go to Namibia first, then fly to Joburg where Steve will spend a few days with his brother in Kempton Park. His brother's not very well, I think he has cancer. And Helen will come direct to Zebenine with me. Anyway, she's the one who's been helping me."

"You mean, counselling you?"

"Well, not really counselling ... she's just someone who knew us both. I've known them for thirty years and feel comfortable talking to her because she knew Yvonne as well. I don't think that Murray and Sally will make it, so it will be Steve and Helen, you guys and me, and the Taylors who'll probably come for a few days, as well as the Maythams. We'll have to see ... anyway it'll be a lot of fun. We're going to do another collaring."

"That's great Irv. It looks like the dates you sent us will work. We can come there for a week and then go on to our timeshare at Sabie, for another week. Do you want to join us at Sabie?"

"No, thanks very much, after the bush I plan on going up to Tony Taylor's farm and also to stay with the Maythams. Thanks anyway but that won't work. Oh, one more thing. Here's the bad news."

"What's that?"

"Well, you know my brother, Brian, and I never really got on, and even less with his wife. Well, last time I was in SA I felt that in view of ... of ... what I'm planning, I needed to put it all to bed, so I went down to see them, and we sort of sorted things out."

"But that's good news, isn't it?"

"I haven't finished giving you the bad news." I wondered what could be so bad? "He, they, don't have much money, so I invited them to Zebenine—which means they will overlap with you and Margie for two days. Sorry about that; I hope you don't mind?"

"Of course not, Irv. I've met your *boet* (brother). He seems quite a pleasant guy."

"*Ja* well. But the story isn't over, it gets worse. Brian has a son living in Las Vegas with his two kids, nine and eleven, and they are really hard up. So I invited the three of them also. None of them would be able to have a holiday like this without me paying for their air tickets and everything, and the kids have never been to Africa."

"Irv, that's fine with us. We are just so grateful to be included. It's your show, so obviously you can invite who you like. I'm sure they'll be good company."

"Maybe you won't find them as bad as I do. Anyway, sorry about that, but I hoped you'd be fine with it?"

"Of course we are. Hell, it's your family, it'll be fine. Do all the people who are coming to Zebenine know what you're planning?"

There was a silence for a few seconds.

"Yes, they do, except for my brother. He doesn't know."

"Are you bringing him up there to tell him?"

"No, no. I'm not sure. I don't think I'll tell him. Too complicated. I'll have to think about it."

"Hell's teeth Irv, it's your business, but if we and other people know about it, shouldn't you tell him? Who else actually knows?"

"Only a couple of people Robbie. No, I don't think I'm going to tell him. Maybe I'll have a chat to his son. He and I have always got on well.

It occurred to me that maybe the one person he was scared of telling was his brother.

"Anyway, the important thing is that you and Margie are okay with them coming?"

"Absolutely, Irv, absolutely."

"Anyway, perhaps you won't find them as grim as cynical me makes out, hey?"

"You said it, Irv. You are a cynic and I bet your brother is actually a good guy."

"Well, you'll have two days in the bush with him to decide, so we'll see. And you'll like the others who are coming. So that's all set then?" he asked.

"Definitely Irv, we're looking forward to it."

"Good. How are things going for the World Cup? From what we read here you have a lot of problems, don't you? There are even rumours that there are going to be strikes during the tournament? They had better lock that lunatic Malema away, don't you think? Every time he opens his mouth he scores an own goal. Anyway, although I hope it works, from what our papers here say it could all be a bloody disaster. Stadiums not ready, traffic problems ..."

I felt my face flush with anger, the palms of my hands were damp.

"That's actually total rubbish, Irv. Everything is going well here. All the stadiums are ready. You have never felt a vibe like we have here now and it's building every day. I can tell you, as a nation-building exercise, this is fantastic I wish you were here. You would be blown away. Your newspapers are something else."

"Hope you're right, my boy. Hope you're right."

For the next few weeks South Africa exploded with emotion as the World Cup unfolded around the country. Little did I know that the nation-building I had described to Irving had only just begun. Commencing with the spectacular opening concert held in the recently upgraded Orlando Stadium, featuring the Black Eyed Peas and Shakira, the World Cup stole everyone's hearts—*vuvuzelas* (a long horn blown by South African fans at soccer matches) and all. For four weeks people danced and sang in the streets, smiled and greeted visitors and strangers like long lost friends who, in turn, were overawed by the hospitality displayed. Cars hooted and the six colours of the flag fluttered proudly from aerials, wing mirrors and every possible office and house window. For four weeks men, women and children dressed in the jerseys and livery of our team, *Bafana Bafana*, even after the team was knocked out of the tournament. The country was carried along on a tidal wave of joy and goodwill. When the final whistle blew and the last spectator left the stadium empty after the closing ceremony, the gods must have looked down, smiled and nodded at a job well done.

The country melted back to normality, like ice cream on a hot summer day. Bleary-eyed, staggering, with a giant hangover, faded flags still attached to car wing mirrors, tattered flags on car aerials, a noticeable lack of trumpeting *vuvuzelas*, wearing normal work clothes again, we all slipped back into the real world. We had a couple of emails from Irving during that frenzied time, about his planned trip at the end of the year, one with a newspaper cutting from the English press about how the *vuvuzelas* were ruining the game of football, but we did not speak on the telephone. With all the visitors in Joburg I was busy with tours and of course, when not working, I was watching the tournament.

With the World Cup over Irving and I began to exchange emails again, firming up arrangements to join him at the end of January at Zebenine. I avoided the subject of his looming suicide, believing that he had moved on and that it was no longer going to happen. I felt the longer he delayed doing anything the less chance there was of it ever occurring.

It was September before we spoke again. After discussing plans and confirming that Margie and I would be joining the party at Zebenine, he said, "Listen, the Smythes are no longer coming. They can't make it, which is a pity. So I asked the Venters—you met them last time, didn't you?"

"Yes we did. But we were there for only one night so didn't really get to know them."

"Anyway, the Smythes will be in the USA so they can't come. And the Venters will also be overseas. So, the party will be Helen and Steve, our friends from Oswestry; my brother and his mob will overlap with you; and then the Maythams and Taylors will be there for a few days while you're still there. Did you know that they've just been over here?"

"Oh really?" Then I remembered my conversation with Tony Taylor earlier in the year. "That's right, Tony told me they were coming. How was it?"

"Terrific. It was really nice seeing them again. The farm is quite empty and lonely now that they've all gone back and I'm on my own again."

There was a few seconds silence as I thought of what to say.

"Well, that all sounds great to us, Irv. We really don't mind who is there, just happy that we are included and able to come. We don't know Steve and Helen but the others ... oh no, we don't really know your brother and his family, either. Still, whoever is there I am sure will be good company."

"Except maybe my brother? His son, Richard, and I get on well; I've always liked him. I told you that I'm paying for them, didn't I?"

"Yes, yes. That's good of you Irv. I met your brother years ago and he seemed fine to me, so no need to apologize for him being there."

"Richard, Brian's son, has had quite a tough time in the States, so I thought it would be good for them all if I brought him and his kids out. Anyway that's the plan; so we're all set."

✍

"Richard's going to get some money from me and that should help him."

"What about your brother."

He nodded, sipping his wine. "Shit. He is going to be a rand millionaire—I've left him a shithouse full of money."

"Does he know?"

'No, he doesn't even know what's going to happen. He's going to get a nice surprise, isn't he?"

❧

"Looking forward to seeing you again," I said.

"Oh, one more thing," said Irving, "would you and Margie like to come down to Haga Haga with me in November?"

"We would love to, but what do you mean by November? I thought we were going to Zebenine in the last week of January, next year?

"No, we are. But I want to come out before then. I've got a few things to do and people to see and won't get the chance when we go to the bush in January."

"You mean you're going to come in November and stay till February?" He must have picked up the anxiety in my voice as I visualized having Irving as our guest, for two months, including over Christmas.

He laughed. "No, no. I'm coming out for a few weeks in November and then again in January. One of the things that I want to do is to visit the school in Haga Haga which Yvonne and I—and because of our involvement, the Smythes, too—have supported for a few years. I want to see what they've been doing with our money. So if you and Margie want to come along with me, I'll pay of course, we can fly down and stay at the hotel for a few nights. I know you love Haga Haga, so you may as well come down with me?"

"That would be great. Of course it depends on whether I have tours booked. When are you thinking of coming?"

"I think I arrive on the 7th of November. So we could fly down that week and spend say the Thursday and Friday there; visit the school and stay for the weekend."

"I'll check what tours I have booked, but that sounds great. Thanks Irv."

"One more thing. I'll pay all the expenses, as I said, but would it be all right if my cousin's husband, he's a lawyer down in the Cape, transfers some money to your account and you can pay out of that? So you would make the flight and hotel bookings for us, but use that money? Oh, and will it be okay if I stay with you? Not for two months," he laughed again, "only for a few nights before we go to Haga and then again afterwards."

"Sure, no problem. I'll make all the arrangements. Where is the school? It's outside Haga, isn't it?"

"Yes, it's on the Marsh Strand road. It's just a little rural school. I think they were going to build toilets with the last money we sent out. Anyway, I want to see what they're up to."

Sure enough, three days later my bank account was credited with sixty thousand rand.

"Sixty thousand!" I exclaimed, to Margie. "What the hell does he need sixty thousand rand for—I hope he lets us keep the change!"

Margie chuckled. "That's wishful thinking, I very much doubt it."

The next day, listening to Radio 702, I heard a news report that an aircraft belonging to 1Time Airlines had skidded off the runway at Oliver Tambo airport. It was the second incident in as many days. Fortunately nobody was injured in either episode.

That evening the phone rang. It was Irving.

"Robbie, did you get the money?"

"Yes, thanks Irv, I got sixty thousand rand."

"Ja, that's right. Have you made the bookings yet to go to Haga Haga?"

"Well it's not enough to leave the country with, is it?" I joked. "No, not yet. I still have to check on what tours are confirmed with me around that date. Anyway I can assure you the cost of the hotel and airfares for three of us will be a great deal less than sixty thousand."

"Ja, but I'll need some cash while I'm there. Just keep it in your account so that it's handy for me. In fact, if you wouldn't mind going to the bank and drawing ten thousand for me, so that I have some cash while I'm there. And by the way, please, please don't book on any of those mickey mouse airlines. I see in our papers here that one of them—1Time or something— had a crash. Good name for an airline that crashes."

"1Time? They skidded off the runway. I'd hardly call it a crash."

"Never mind what you call it. Book on a reputable airline like South African Airways or, preferably, British Airways. I want to make sure I get there in one piece."

I laughed. "Come on Irv, what difference does it make?"

"They're bloody dangerous—that's what difference it makes. I don't want to crash."

"No, I meant what difference does it make to you? I mean, if you are going to die anyway, if you have a plane crash, it'll save you the bother, won't it? Just kidding. It's obvious that you've changed your mind, otherwise you wouldn't be concerned."

"I haven't changed my mind at all." His tone was serious. "It's just that I will decide when and how I die, and it won't be on some mickey mouse airline. Shit! What if we crashed and I was seriously injured— like paralysed or brain damaged or something? No ways. I want to do the job properly."

I didn't answer because the elephant had returned to sit on my shoulders.

∽

Towards the end of November I made the bookings with South African Airways and at the hotel in Haga Haga for accommodation for the three of us. Because I had tours booked we were going to fly down on the Friday morning, visit the school that day, and stay at the hotel until Sunday. I phoned Phil Conlon in Haga Haga.

"Phil, old Tucker's coming out in a few days' time."

"Really? How's he getting on?"

"He's fine Phil. Says he's going to kill himself, but apart from that he's fine."

"Really? Kill himself? He can't be serious, can he?"

"Well, he's been saying it for almost a year now and hasn't done it, so it's probably a load of bullshit. Anyway he wants to come down to Haga to visit that school that he and some other people have been supporting, so I just called to ask who in Haga knows anything about the school, so I can arrange for us to visit there next week. Margie and I are coming with him."

"That's nice. So we'll see you? Look, the lady you want to speak to is Sylvia Lake. Here's her number," he read out the number, "she deals with the school and will know what's going on."

I thanked Phil and called Sylvia Lake's number. After introducing myself I asked, "Do you know Irving Tucker?" There was a momentary pause while she tried to place him.

"Oh yes. He's one of those people from England who give money to the school, isn't he?"

"Yes he is. He's arriving next week Tuesday in Joburg, from England, and he wants to come down to Haga to visit the school and see what they're doing there."

"Oh, that's good," she paused, "what day does he want to come?"

"We'll fly down early on Friday morning and visit the school on Friday."

"You do know that Eastern Cape schools break up for the Christmas holidays that Friday, don't you?"

I felt an uncomfortable sinking feeling in my stomach.

"Yes, I am aware of that, but we are coming down on Friday specifically to see the school. I'm sure, even though it's the last day of school, the principal will have time to show us around, won't she?"

"No, the school will be closed on Friday. Closing early. Thursday will be the last day. There won't be anybody there on Friday. I think you should come on Thursday?"

"No, that's not possible, I'm afraid. I'm working. Is there nothing we can do? Won't she stay for one day?"

She gave a humourless laugh. "You must be joking. The principal is going on holiday and that's that."

The sinking feeling passed the pit of my stomach and journeyed to my toes.

"Oh hell! I've booked tickets and everything; still, that's my problem."

I thanked Sylvia and hung up.

Chapter Seventeen

A COSTLY JUDGEMENT

I was at home on Tuesday when the buzzer signalled Irving's arrival. I pushed the electronic gate opener and walked outside to welcome him at the same time as he drove his hired Toyota into our townhouse complex.

He clambered out of the car, his face wreathed in a giant smile. Despite his overnight flight he looked rested and well.

"Hello you old bugger," I said, giving him a hug. He smelled of twelve hours of aircraft sweat. "You look bloody well, Irv. You've put on a bit of weight, haven't you? Hell, you don't even look tired after the flight."

"Travelled business class, didn't I? Makes a helluva difference, Robbie." He lifted his right arm and bent his head to sniff his armpit. "Still, could do with a shower. I stink. Then I wouldn't mind a bit of a kip."

He opened the boot of the car. Inside lay three large suitcases.

"Here, let me help you with those, Irv. Shit! How long are you staying for? You've brought a lot of gear haven't you?"

He laughed. I grabbed a suitcase and tried to lift it from the boot. My arm jolted as the full weight dragged me down. The suitcase felt as if it was full of lead.

"Jeez! What the hell?"

Irving bent double laughing, his hands on his knees.

"That's got catalogues and stuff, some wine and other odds and ends that I've brought out to give people here. That's why it's so heavy. Here give it to me."

I carried the two lighter suitcases upstairs to the guest room, while Irving used both hands to haul the heavy suitcase up, walking backwards as he bumped the suitcase up the stairs, one step at a time.

There was a crash as he let the suitcase drop to the floor in the spare room. He was breathing heavily and his face was flushed from exertion.

"You're not very fit are you, Irv? Don't have a bloody heart attack now!"

"No, not really," he said, breathing heavily, "whew! I'll be glad to get rid of all the shit I've brought."

"What the hell have you got in these cases?"

"Oh, all sorts of stuff. Some of Yvonne's clothes to give away, something for you as well, a little surprise. Most of the weight is catalogues."

"What catalogues are you bringing half way round the world? What on earth are you bringing catalogues here for?"

"They're all the catalogues that Yvonne and I collected from the art exhibitions we attended."

"You must be joking!"

"No, of course not. They're beautiful. Some are worth a fortune." He bent over, knelt on the floor and opened the case. It was full of glossy art auction brochures, and bottles of wine, wrapped in flimsy white paper and packed inside cardboard tubes to protect them from breaking. He picked up one of the brochures and, still kneeling, passed it to me. I took it. It was a Sotheby's catalogue. I thumbed the pages, colourful pictures of art blurred past.

"Impressive. Have you got the one for Frank Auerbach's painting? I would like to see what that looked like again."

"Who? Oh, you mean Frankie baby. *Ja*, it's in here. I'll show it to you later."

He reached into the suitcase and rummaged through some clothes tucked into a corner.

"Here this is for you," he passed me a T-shirt with blue writing on it. It looked vaguely familiar.

I held it up and examined it. It was a promotional T-shirt which I had designed for my promotions company, some twenty-five years earlier. The writing on the T-shirt described the events and promotions which we had successfully managed.

"I don't believe it," I said. "I gave the Jolly Green Giant this shirt more than twenty-five years ago. Good grief—and she still had it?"

He chuckled. "*Ja*, she loved it. She used to wear it still."

I held up the shirt. The blue writing and the logo were faded but provided readable descriptions of some of our achievements as a public relations consultancy: 'Saved the South African Grand Prix'; 'Benson & Hedges Night Cricket'; 'Datsun Double Wicket'; 'State President's Air Race'; 'Southern Sun Hot Air Balloon Race'; three Motorcycle Grand Prix races; four World Championship Sports Car races; three Formula One World Championships; 'South African Games' and many more.

I felt a surge of pride at our record of achievements and chuckled as the memories came flooding back.

"Isn't that something? And she was still wearing it? I haven't seen one of these for years."

"Well keep it—it's for you. I'm sure she would have wanted you to have it rather than throw it away."

"Thanks Irv. I will. I love it. Nice reminder of days gone by." I glanced at the wrapped bottles of wine. "Why are you lugging those bottles of wine half way round the world? You can buy good wine here you know," I said with a laugh.

"Those," he said, glancing at the wrapped bottles in his case, "those are gifts I've brought for some people here."

"Well, as I say, that's a bit of a waste of effort, Irv. You could have bought really good wine here. They must be very special if you brought them all the way from England. What are they? French?"

"No, South African."

I shook my head in disbelief. "You bought South African wine in England to give as gifts here? That's a bit like taking coals to Newcastle, Irv."

"No, no, it's South African wine that I took to England when I left."

"What do you mean? Over twenty-five years ago? You must be kidding."

"It's South African wine, but also very special wine. When I worked for PMI we used to do a lot of work with Distillers Corporation. You remember that? Well, before we left, I bought a few cases of their really special reds and took them to England. I laid them down in my wine cellar and now, after all these years, I've brought a few bottles back as gifts for friends."

"That's great Irv. But, after all this time, the wine will either be wonderful or like rotten vinegar. That's quite a gift. Do we get one as well?"

His response slapped me in the face like a dead wet kipper.

"Don't be bloody mad Binckes. I've seen how you keep your wine. You don't give a shit about wine."

"What?" I exclaimed indignantly, "I love wine!"

"No, you don't. If you loved wine you wouldn't keep yours in boiling hot temperatures next to your car in the garage. I felt some of those bottles that you have in there, last time I was out. They are, or should I say were, bloody good wines but you've boiled them. No Robbie. No wine for you. These are for people that really appreciate wine. You'll have to learn to look after wine before I give you my special wine. Anyway, these are the last six bottles, so you've missed the boat, haven't you?"

I pulled a face. "Who are the lucky wine lovers?" I asked, in the most sarcastic tone I could muster.

"Ag, people you don't know. One of them is a mate of Tony's in Cape Town, then there's another for ..." He glanced at my face and saw that I had lost interest. "Well, anyway, it doesn't really matter does it? None for you. Wine has to be treated with tender love and care, not fucking boiled in a garage."

I shrugged. "It's probably crap wine anyway, Tucker. After all these years you'll probably poison the recipients. You wouldn't have done me any favours giving me rubbish like that. I'm glad you haven't included me."

I decided to change the subject. "What do you want to do now?" I looked at my watch. "I've still got a bit of writing to do."

"I'm going to take a shower and then have a bit of a sleep, if that's okay? I'll be a new man after that."

"Right. I'll be writing in my study right next door, so whenever you wake up come in."

"Are you still writing that porn book you sent me part of to read?"

"Yes I am. It's not a porn book, by the way. It's an historical novel with a bit of sex in it," I retorted, "did you ever read it?"

"To be honest, not really. I sort of glanced at it. Yvonne was the reader not me. You and Ray Johnson," he looked at me, smiled and shook his head as if in despair.

I left him to shower and returned to my study to carry on writing *Canvas Under The Sky*.

Two hours later, I heard movement from the guest room, followed by a light tap on my door. I swivelled round as a freshly shaved and refreshed Irving entered.

"Hard at it are you Robbie?"

I smiled and nodded.

"That's one thing about you, isn't it? Never been afraid of hard work. The Jolly Green Giant always admired that about you."

"Thanks Irv, but when you don't have any option, what can you do? Anyway, I love writing as much as I love doing my tours, so it's really not a hardship, rather a hobby that I get paid for."

He sat down in the leather armchair in the study, sinking into the softness.

"Did you get that money, the ten grand, for me? When are we off to Haga?"

I slid open the drawer of my desk where I had tucked one hundred R100 notes behind some papers, took the bundle of money held together by a rubber band and handed it to Irving.

He pushed it into his wallet without counting it.

"Aren't you going to check it Irv?"

"No. I trust you Robbie. Talking about trust, your bloody police can't be trusted hey?"

"Why Irv, what makes you say that?" I was genuinely puzzled by his comment.

"All this bullshit about the British tourist whose wife was murdered on their honeymoon."

"You mean Dewani? The guy who murdered his wife and won't come back to stand trial?"

"Well, would you? Poor guy. His wife gets killed then your chief of police calls him a monkey who murdered his wife. What chance has he got of a fair trial when the police call him a monkey even before he's been tried? No, it's obvious that the whole thing is rigged. It's a conspiracy by this country to try to protect its shitty image."

I looked at him in amazement, trying to see if he was joking. He wasn't. I felt my blood pressure soar like an overheated radiator.

"Come on, Tucker. Get real. The guy killed his wife and now is too scared to come back to stand trial. Look at his pics in the papers. He looks terrified."

"Well, wouldn't you be? Poor guy. He's distraught at the loss of his wife and now, and now," he spluttered, waving his hand in the air dismissively, "and now, going through all that trauma, he gets charged on a trumped up case of murder."

"Irving, Irving, Irving," I said, shaking my head. "I can't believe you think like that—"

He interjected. "What do the papers here say? I suppose they all say he's guilty?" He snorted. "See, I told you it was a conspiracy. Your judicial system is corrupt, everyone knows that."

"That's crap, and you know it—or if you don't you bloody well should. He's as guilty as all hell and there is nothing wrong with our justice system in terms of honesty."

"Ja, well, we'll see, won't we? When are we flying down to Haga?"

"Friday, and staying for the weekend."

"I hope you didn't book on that airline that crashed?" he asked, a concerned look on his face.

I laughed. "Come on Irv. You mean 1Time? No, I booked on SAA."

He nodded his approval. "Good. At least we'll get there."

"But, there's a little problem with the trip to the school."

He furrowed his brow. "What's the problem?"

"I phoned there to make arrangements and spoke to Sylvia. She knows you."

He nodded. "Yes, she's our sort of liaison with the school."

"Well, the thing is, it's the end of the school year on Friday and the school is going to be closed."

"Yes, but we're flying there on Friday. So although they're closing that day, we can still see the school, can't we?"

"No, actually the headmistress is closing a day earlier, on Thursday."

A dark cloud passed over Irving's face.

"Why? She can't do that. Bugger her. If the school term closes on Friday then she has to stay open, doesn't she?"

"In theory, Irv. This is a rural school and the headmistress has decided to close early. We can still go and have a look at the physical state of the school."

Irving exploded—his face as fiery as his voice. "Bullshit! Jeez! Closing early because she wants a bloody holiday? Let me tell you her little move of closing early, not staying open for us to visit has just cost that school and the kids a shithouse full of money."

Tiny fingers squeezed my intestines as I realized what he was thinking. I felt guilty and responsible.

"Well Irv, it's more my fault. Maybe I should have contacted her earlier. I couldn't go down any earlier though, because I have tours booked. She didn't know you were coming; I'm sure if she did she would have made an effort."

"It's not your fault. Bloody hell. She's obviously a crook, she's probably been stealing all our money for herself."

"Aw, come on, Tucker. Forget it. She's a headmistress of a little rural school and she's decided to close on Thursday instead of Friday. It's not a big deal, Irv, and it doesn't make her a crook. Come on."

"She probably is though, just like the rest of them. Shit. I wonder what they did with the money we sent?"

"Well, let's still go down and see. The tickets are booked, accommodation is arranged. We can still take a drive out there. How much money was it and what were they supposed to do with it?"

"Twenty grand or thereabouts. They were supposed to build toilets for the school."

"Maybe they have. We'll at least be able to see that."

He shook his head.

"No, no way. I'm not helping a bloody crook. Cancel the flights. Have you paid already?"

"Yes, I have."

"Well, see if you can get the money back. I'm not going. That's the end of that woman and her school. I was going to leave the school money in my will. That's over now. I'll find somebody else who deserves the money to leave it to. Cancel the trip Robbie, it's not worth going if the school will be closed."

I was disappointed with his response and felt he had over reacted—but it was his money so I had little choice.

"I'll cancel. And if you don't know who to leave your money to you could try Friends of Alexandra, couldn't you?" I suggested, laughing.

Irving looked at me with a strange expression on his face; one that I couldn't really work out. In retrospect though, I realized that according to his personal values, leaving money to Friends of Alexandra ranked lower than crawling through a thorn bush.

He shook his head. "No Robbie. I'm not doing that. I would rather leave it to you personally."

Like a sweet with a sour centre, I felt as though I had sunk a thirty-metre putt on the golf course, but on the other hand felt a surge of acid disappointment that Friends of Alexandra would not benefit instead of the school at Haga.

"No, I'll find something else to benefit. Yvonne was keen on the Haga school, but of course she didn't know that the headmistress is a crook."

I snorted. "Cut it out, Irv. Closing a day early doesn't make him anything other than someone keen on his December holiday."

"Well, whatever, it has cost her a lot of money ... a *lot* of money." He emphasized the second 'lot', making his point.

"Seeing as we aren't going to visit Haga, I think I'll go and stay with Jacques out at Broederstroom for a few days. They asked me to come out and I would like to see them. I can give them these art auction brochures at the same time. That's who I brought them for."

"Do they get any wine?"

"Yes, I've got a bottle for them as well. He looks after his wine."

I didn't respond.

"I'd better give them a call now to see if it's okay."

He took out the cell phone he had hired at the airport and looked at the face.

"Damn. Have to get their number. It's in my book in my room." He passed the cell phone to me. "I'll call out the number Robbie, just dial it for me."

He shouted the number from his room. I wrote the number down and hadn't started dialling when he came back into my study. I held out the phone to him.

"No, Robbie. I asked you to dial."

My arm remained outstretched. "Well, here's the number, you can dial it yourself. You're here now. You're not helpless."

He took the phone and looked at me sheepishly. "I can't, Robbie. I'm dyslexic."

I could feel the surprise on my face as I flushed with embarrassment. I had known him for years and not been aware of his problem.

"Sorry Irv. Shit, I didn't know, sorry about that. Here, give me the phone. I'll do it, I was only kidding. Of course I'll do it for you."

He gave the phone back to me.

"Well, thanks. You see, that's why Yvonne always had to do everything with writing and reading for the two of us. I've always battled, particularly with numbers. I can do it, but things come out wrong," he smiled bitterly, "numbers always come out the wrong way round."

"You certainly hid it well. I've known you for years and had no idea."

I wondered how he managed on the farm with no Yvonne to help him cope with his dyslexia.

The next day Irving drove to Broederstroom to stay with his artist and sculptor friends, the Malans, returning to us on the Friday, in time to go out for dinner at Turn 'n Tender in Parkview. We were joined by my cousin Sharon, a very attractive divorcee, and her recently widowed, equally attractive friend, Carol. My daughter Samantha and her partner, Jacques, completed our party of seven. Sam had always been fond of Irving and he of her.

Irving greeted Sam with a broad smile and a big hug.

"Hello Sammy. It's good to see you again. My, you are looking well. Come and sit next to me here." He patted the chair he meant for Sam and sat alongside her, with Sharon on his other side. There was a great deal of laughter around the table. An attractive waitress placed menus in front of us and took our drinks orders.

"Order the wine Irv, you're the expert," I called out.

He ordered three bottles of very good Merlot and then turned to Margie. "You like white don't you, Margie?"

She nodded.

"We'll have two bottles of Jordan Sauvignon Blanc," he said to the waitress. His eyes scanned her shapely figure and came to rest on her well-shaped breasts, temptingly exposed by her low cut dress. Sam was watching him. Her eyes met with mine and she smiled knowingly, with an expression that said 'all men are the same'.

"Why is it so smoky in here?" Irving asked the table in general and the waitress in particular. I glanced around. It was smoky. Light blue smoke blurred the sharpness of my sight and there was a strong smell of meat being grilled.

"Can we open a window and let out some of the smoke?" Jacques asked.

"No, I'm sorry sir, we can't. It's pouring with rain outside and those people next to the window will get wet. Afraid we can't." She looked embarrassed at her inability to solve the problem and the smoke appeared to be getting thicker.

"No, this is terrible," said Irving in a loud voice. Some of the other diners turned round to see the cause of the disturbance and the background noise of conversation and laughter took a dip. "What's the problem? What's causing all the smoke? I mean, I know they're cooking but this isn't normal, is it?"

"No sir," said the waitress, directing her answer to Irving, "I'm afraid the extractor fans are not working. I'm sorry, sir."

It seemed that, for Irving, the waitress had lost all her appeal.

"Well that's ridiculous. This is a health risk, you know."

I looked at Irving in amazement, trying to see if he was joking. He wasn't.

"You shouldn't be trading. You should be closed if you can't serve meals to your customers in decent conditions. This is terrible … you're not going to charge us normal prices, are you?"

The waitress made the mistake of thinking he was joking. She smiled and said, "No sir, we're not charging extra for the smoke."

"I'm bloody serious! I'm not joking. I expect a discount, at least, on our bill. I would go somewhere else but it's too late for that. Anyway, why must we be inconvenienced? We made a booking—when did this problem start?

"This morning, sir."

"Exactly. Why were we not phoned to tell us that you had a problem? That would have given us the choice as to whether or not we kept our booking. Now we're here. When I go out for a meal, I don't choose the restaurant for the food only. I choose a restaurant for its ambience and atmosphere as well. You have reneged on the deal. You are not providing me with the ambience, plus you are poisoning my lungs, and still you insist on charging us full price? I think it's scandalous, a bloody rip-off."

The waitress stared at Irving. From where I sat I could see her large eyes starting to brim with tears.

"Leave it, Irv."

He looked at me in surprise.

"Leave it," I said, "she only works here, she's not the owner. Anyway, we're here now, so we may as well order and stay. It's not *that* bad. Come on, give her a break."

"Not bad? It's bloody terrible," and he broke into what was obviously a forced bout of coughing to make his point.

The attractive waitress disappeared into the cloud of blue smoke, which was thicker near the cooking area. The buzz of conversation around us increased as the other diners realized that the entertainment was over.

I spent most the evening chatting to Margie and Jacques who sat nearest me, occasionally glancing towards the end of the table where Samantha and Irving were deeply engaged in earnest conversation. From the look on Sam's face I knew, without hearing their words, the topic of their conversation. Towards the end of the evening I saw Sam dabbing her eyes with a tissue and it wasn't the smoke causing the tears. She pushed her chair back, excused herself and disappeared into the still thick blue smoke in the direction of the ladies toilet. I allowed sufficient time to elapse so as not to arouse any suspicions and followed, waiting for her outside the ladies loo. She was a long time coming out. Her face had been freshly made up and there was no trace of tears.

"What upset you my girl?"

"Irving, Dad. Do you know what he's going to do?" she said, her voice tinged with accusation.

"Yes. Well, I don't know that I *know* what he's going to do. I know only what he *says* he is going to do."

"Dad! He's going to kill himself!"

"Is that what he told you? That he's going to kill himself?"

"Well, he started off by saying that he was 'going away'. Then after I questioned him as to where he was going, he admitted that he was going to kill himself."

We paused as a woman brushed past us on the way to the ladies.

"Maybe he's just talking crap. Maybe it's all to get attention."

"No. No, Dad. I'm sure he'll do it. What a waste. One minute he's talking about killing himself, the next, he's ogling the waitress. I saw him looking at her tits. How can he do that?" She sniffed and dabbed at her eyes again.

I tried to make a joke of it. "What? Look at her tits? Don't be upset about it my girl, all men do that."

"Don't be silly Dad. I meant talk about killing himself?"

"Well, I don't know. Did he say when he's going to do it? No? Come on. Let's get back to the table. Don't worry about it. I don't think it's going to happen." I wasn't as confident as I sounded.

"He says he's going to leave you some money so that you 'won't have to work so hard any more'."

I shrugged. "First time I've heard of it. News to me. I'll call you tomorrow and we can chat about this."

We returned to the table and our respective places. Much to my annoyance Irving had already called for and paid the bill.

"That wasn't the deal, Irving. We didn't bring you here for you to pay. Come on."

"It's my pleasure, Robbie. My pleasure. You've all been very kind to me and put me up and all. No, it's a done deal, I've already paid, so let's go. The sooner we leave, the sooner we can get some fresh air into our lungs." He forced another coughing spasm. "Shit, I hope I haven't got lung cancer from all this smoke." He coughed some more.

When we arrived home Margie went straight to bed, leaving us alone in the lounge.

"Feel like a glass of wine as a night cap, Irv?"

"As long as it's not any of that boiled wine in the garage."

He saw the expression on my face and grinned. "Only kidding, Robbie, only kidding."

I poured him a glass of wine, opened a beer for myself and sat down in my favourite chair.

"Cheers, Irv," I said, holding up my can in salute before taking a long pull of the ice cold beer.

"Cheers Robbie. Lovely evening," he laughed, "even if I did get lung cancer from all that bloody smoke."

"Well. I believe you told Sam that you are going to kill yourself anyway, so I don't see what difference a little smoke in your lungs is going to make."

"She told you, did she?"

"You really are going to do this stupid thing are you?"

He nodded. "Mmm. Wine's good. Yes I am. Might be stupid to you but it makes good sense to me."

I shook my head.

"Irving, you've been talking about killing yourself for a year now. I mean, to be honest, I think if you were really intent on doing it you would have done it by now. When do you intend bumping yourself off?"

"What do you think I've been doing this past year?"

I shrugged; I didn't quite know what he meant.

"I've been getting my affairs in order. I'm almost ready now."

I felt a sudden chill.

He continued. "There are a couple of things that I'm busy with and then I'll be ready. You know there are a helluva lot of things you need to do before you die?"

"Like what, for example. Some people die without any preparation, killed in a car crash, or a sudden heart attack."

"Ja, well, I'm not one of those. I know when I'm going to do it and I don't want to leave a mess behind, so I'm tying up all the loose ends."

"When?" I probed, forcing the issue.

"Soon, Robbie."

"So what have you been doing that takes a year to sort out?"

"Lots of things. For example, you know that Yvonne is buried on the farm?"

I nodded and sipped my beer.

"Well, I want to make sure that her brother, even though he's a bit of a prick, has access to her grave, you know, if he wants to visit the grave? And as the farm will be put on the market, to be sold as soon as I die, I've applied for a rezoning that will preclude from the sale one acre surrounding her grave, plus a pathway across the farm to the grave site. That means he will have access in perpetuity. I have also deepened Yvonne's grave to take another coffin because I will be buried there as well."

I stared at him, stunned, as he coolly and without any emotion detailed his plans. Eventually I shook my head, like a boxer who's taken a punch.

"All of these things take time, Robbie. They all take time."

"The farm will be sold, when you die?"

"Ja. Hang on," Irving stood and walked out of the lounge, leaving me alone. I felt as though I was in a bad dream and couldn't escape.

He returned a few minutes later and handed me a brochure. It was a sales brochure from a firm of estate agents; the front cover showed the rolling green hills of the area and the title 'Bryn Uchaf'.

"What's this?"

"It's the sales blurb for the farm. I had the agents come down in summer so I could show them the farm at its best. They took pictures while everything was looking green and lovely. As soon as I do it, the farm will go up for sale. We've agreed the price and everything."

"Do they know what you're planning?"

"No, of course not. I'll send them an email when I'm ready. So you see, these are all the little details I've been sorting out. Takes time. You know that."

He sipped his wine, smacked his lips in appreciation and wiped his mouth with the back of his hand.

"Who knows about this Irv?"

"Oh, very few people. Only you and a couple of others."

"Tony Taylor?" I asked.

"Ja, he knows."

"And what does he say, Irv? Does he try to talk you out of it?"

"Not really. We don't really discuss it."

"What about your friend who owns a school, Murray, back in England?"

"Him? He knows."

"And doesn't he tell you how mad you are to be even thinking things like this? I mean with all your bloody money ..."

"No. He won't discuss it. He avoids the subject." He sounded irritated at the thought.

I made another attempt at dissuading him from this course of action.

"Irv, come on. You have so much to offer. Now, with all your money, you could do so much good. You could do charity work."

"Like what?"

"You were particularly impressed with the hospice and how they treated Yvonne; you could work with them, I'm sure? Or, why not consider teaching young kids how to farm? That's your expertise. There must be thousands of under-privileged kids in London who have never even been on a farm. You could bring them down to your farm, teach them about animals, and farming. I don't know; I'm sure there are thousands of ways that you could do good—now that you have some money and a great deal of time. Don't be so selfish. Do some good with the time you have, now, and your money."

"Well, I am going to do some good with my money. And by the way, you have to be careful nowadays, in England, about doing anything with young kids. You can't just go and bring a crowd of kids to the farm—everyone will think there's something wrong with you."

"Like what?"

"Like you're a paedophile or something. You have to be very careful, you know."

I snorted. "Well that's hardly an excuse Irv. What about hospice, giving some help there? You were impressed with them weren't you?"

"Yes, so much so that after Yvonne's death I made them a substantial donation. I never even got a letter of acknowledgement, let alone a 'thank you'. So I wouldn't be too keen on helping them again."

"You say that you are going to do some good with your money—what are you planning to do?"

"There are a number of people that I know, that Yvonne and I knew, who I am going to leave money, to help them out."

I felt the stirring of anticipation.

"Like who?'

"Like your pal Johnson in France, and others."

"Do they know? I mean, do these people know that you're going to kill yourself?"

"No, nobody who is in my will knows about that."

My heart took a deep dive. That ruled me out of any bequest.

"So Johnson doesn't know?"

He shook his head. "No, only a few people know; and none of those who are going to benefit."

"Why, do you think they might beat you to it and bump you off for the money?"

He laughed. "Something like that. No, they don't know."

"Irv, really, I mean ... are you really going to do this stupid thing? Why? Why are you doing this?"

"Yes, I am. Because it's what I want."

"When?"

"Quite soon, Robbie."

My heart faltered. "Do you mean while you're here?"

"No, no," he laughed, "I'm going back to the UK and then coming out again in December, and we're all going up to the bush in February, remember? I wouldn't have made those plans if I wasn't going to be around, would I? Then I'm going back."

"To kill yourself?"

He looked at me and shrugged.

"Explain to me why. You've got money, you're healthy, you've got everything going for you. I mean, you're not even bad looking. Why?"

"Look Robbie, I've had a brilliant life. I really have. I met and fell in love with Yvonne. We were soul mates; we were one. We had a great life together. Without her there is no point in carrying on. I'm not going out filled with regrets and bitterness; on the contrary, I'm going out deeply satisfied with my life. I don't want to start over."

"Do you think you're going to see Yvonne on the other side?"

"No—there is no 'other side' Robbie. There is nothing when you die. You know how I feel about all that religious crap. No, I've just had enough. We're all going to die, aren't we? I'm just choosing when and how I die. There's nothing wrong with that. I know I'm a little young, but I would rather die when I choose than wait till I'm locked away in some home, dribbling, having someone I don't even know wiping my bum. You should understand that I'm totally comfortable with my decision."

"Well, I must say, you might be comfortable with your decision, but I certainly am not. You say there's nothing wrong with that, but it's illegal—I think?"

He laughed. "So what are you going to do about it? Have me arrested? Ha ha! Don't *worry* about it, Robbie. As I said, I'm quite comfortable with it; looking forward to it actually. Come on, let's go to bed."

I switched off the downstairs lights and we made our way upstairs.

I was climbing into bed in the dark, trying not to disturb Margie, but she stirred and whispered drowsily, "Sam says he's left us some money, so you don't have to work so hard."

"Could have fooled me," I whispered back, "we've just been discussing the whole fucking thing again and he never mentioned money to me."

"Didn't he?"

"No. He said he was leaving money to quite a few people; but all the folk who will inherit are unaware of his decision to kill himself. And we don't fall into that category because we do know."

"That's a shame, isn't it?" she murmured.

"Mmm," I replied, "a big shame."

Margie was already dozing off. I lay in the dark, peering at the ceiling, my hands clasped behind my head, thinking about my discussion with Irving. Why had he ever told us what he was going to do? He might not care but we certainly did. I didn't want him to die, but if he was so intent on carrying out his threat, with all that money around, couldn't he have left us some, not a lot, just some? Shit. We could do with a windfall. Oh well, I guess you don't miss what you never had. Even that jealous bugger Johnson is going to get something. I wonder who else? Wonder why he left us out? All those years he and Yvonne stayed at Haga Haga for nothing. Hell, if we had charged him rent we would have made quite a lot. Say twenty years for a month at R300 per day ... that's too little ... say R500 per day. Twenty times thirty days, that's six hundred days times R500 per day, that's R300,000. Three hundred thousand! That's a shithouse full of money. Shit! Maybe I should tell him? What will I say? Maybe: "Irv, you owe us R300,000 for back rent at Haga Haga, but we've given you a discount—you can pay us R250,000."

I smiled to myself in the dark. Perhaps Tucker will change his mind anyway—that's probably why he hasn't told any of the people who are going to get some money. Yes. That's it. Allowing himself an escape route. No, he won't really kill himself. He's not depressed or anything. If he tells people he has left money to them and then doesn't kill himself, maybe one of them would murder him for the money. This time I chuckled to myself.

With this thought I felt better. I rolled over and, helped by the beer, fell into a deep sleep.

I dreamed of a bloodstained bedroom.

Chapter Eighteen

THE COPPER BANGLE

Irving left us the next day to journey down to the Cape and then on to Tony Taylor's farm. He came into my study where I was writing, to say goodbye.

"Listen Robbie," he said, "when I come back in a few weeks' time, to go to Zebenine, I will be coming a week or so early. I intend going to Cape Town for a few days, to visit my cousin; she's married to the lawyer who transferred that money into your account. By the way, you still have it, don't you? The money, I mean?"

"Of course. So far I've drawn only that ten thousand that I gave you. I still have about fifty thousand rand of yours in my account."

"Good. So, I would like to stay here for a bit when I come back, if that's okay, and then I wondered whether you would be interested in coming to Cape Town for a few days? On me, of course. It would be nice to have you there. I'm going to stay at Tony Taylor's place and of course you can as well."

"Staying here is fine Irv. That'll be before we all go up to Tanda Tula?"

He nodded.

"Of course that's fine. As far as Cape Town is concerned, Margie won't be able to come because of her job, but I was planning a trip down there anyway, to go to the archives to do some research for my book. So *ja*, we can make a plan and I'll come down."

"Good, Robbie. Keep that money for when I come back if you don't mind? I'll have quite a lot of expenses for the trip to the bush; food and booze, and I will probably need your help to buy it all, anyway."

The following day I received a phone call from Sam.

"Hi Dad. Is Irv still there?"

"No, my girl, he's gone down to the Cape and then to Tony Taylor's farm, and then he'll leave for England. But he'll be back in a few weeks when we're going to the bush with him to do an elephant collaring."

"So, he isn't going to kill himself now?"

"Doesn't look like it. In fact, I don't think he is going to, anyway. Do you?"

"Well, Dad, he says he's going to. I don't really know. It's so sad, he's such a lovely man." I could hear the tremor in her voice. "It's such a waste, isn't it? I mean, there was Sharon's friend Carol at dinner with us that night, at Turn 'n Tender, still grieving because her husband died of cancer a few months ago, and here is Irving, perfectly healthy and jolly, telling me that he is 'going away'. And he's got all that money."

I sighed. "I don't really know either, to be honest. Most of the time I think he will do it and then something happens and I change my mind. So, really, I don't know. What did he say to you?"

"He started by saying that he was 'going away'. When I pressed him, asked him where, he just smiled. But later that night he said he was determined to kill himself. Then he said he would be leaving you and Margs some money."

"That's news to me—he hasn't mentioned a word of that to me. You didn't tell him I had already told you he was going to kill himself, did you?"

"No, I didn't. I behaved as though it was the first time I'd heard about it. Anyway he says that you will be looked after and that he wants to give you some money when he dies, so that you don't have to work so hard."

"Pity he doesn't tell me that. I'll believe it when I see it. He told me he had only discussed his suicide with people he was *not* leaving any money. Seeing that he has told us he plans to kill himself, I don't think we've cracked the nod."

"You don't think he would join Sharon and me on a skiing trip to Austria, do you Dad, and pay for all of us?" We both laughed, trying to instil some humour into our bizarre conversation.

In December Margie and I flew to the Victoria Falls for a few days of R&R. Sitting on the gracious rolling green lawns of the Victoria Falls Hotel, which sloped down and slid over the edge to the giant river below, with the spray of 'the water that thunders' ever present, rising in a white cloud above the dark green trees in the distance, the thought of Irving killing himself became as large as the falls themselves in my mind. The quiet and the majesty of the surroundings seemed to make Irving's threat even more inexplicable. The dream of his brains splattered across the bedroom, blood running down the walls, repeated and repeated—like the smell of asparagus in urine.

On our final day there we were doing some last-minute shopping at the local market for small gifts to take back for family. While at a stall selling local curios my eye fell on a copper bracelet, the type that people with arthritis wear as a form of 'healing aid'. I've never been sure if they work or not, but have always felt that they add to a sort of macho image. I had a sudden urge to buy a gift for Irving; something that sort of connected us to him. I don't know why, but the copper bracelet seemed ideal, a band of friendship.

"I'm going to buy one of these copper bracelets for Irv," I said to Margie, "a sort of 'going away present' from us, for when he returns home after his next visit?"

The grateful Zimbabwean wrapped the copper bracelet in soft tissue paper and handed it to me, with the smile of a man who knows he has received a payment double the value of the item sold.

I forgot about my purchase until Margie came into my study a few days after our return, and placed it on my desk while I was writing. I glanced up at the interruption.

"That's yours, you bought it for Irv."

"Oh yes. I'll give it to him when he comes back."

The unobtrusive tissue-wrapped parcel remained on my desk.

⟋

Irving returned on 8 January 2011, and from the very first day he seemed different; slightly uptight and distracted.

The next morning he took Margie and me for breakfast at the new Pick n Pay superstore on William Nichol Drive. We sat outside in the sunshine under an umbrella and waited for our order.

"Quite some store, isn't it?" he remarked. "I'll have a good look around while you do your shopping Margie. What's their meat like? Would you like a braai? Or would you prefer some prawns for a braai this evening? Or should we have both?"

Margie and I laughed, "No, that would be too much."

Over breakfast we agreed on a prawn braai that night and a meat braai the next. While we sat sipping our coffee Irving looked around at the busy restaurant.

"Very impressive, lovely store. They seem to have taken some of your ideas from RB's Theatre of Food, Robbie? That really was a lovely store you had."

"Yes, it was, Irv."

"Bit ahead of its time, if you ask me."

"Okay, you two can buy the meat, or the prawns, whichever you like, while I do the shopping for our weekly groceries," said Margie, as we made our way into the store.

"Let's get these," Irving said, pointing at a box of Tiger Giant prawns, "I'm paying, well you are, but take it out of my money that I left here. You still have it, I hope, Robbie?"

I nodded. "Sure. But let's get smaller ones. I think the large or medium prawns are better than those giant ones."

A flush of annoyance crossed his face. "That's not right, you know." And then he remembered and corrected himself. "Oh, I'd forgotten you were in the fishing business. So, you think those smaller ones are better? Didn't we used to eat the big buggers in the old days at the LM?"

162

"Yes we did, but we didn't know any better then. Anyway, the smaller prawns are a better price."

"That doesn't matter," said Irving, "but okay, let's get three kilos of the smaller ones, if that's what you want. Now let's look at their meat."

We walked across to the display of fresh meat.

"Lovely display. Their meat looks really good quality. Here, look at this."

He stopped, picked up a pre-packed parcel of meat and read the wrapper.

"Grain fed, aged and matured porterhouse steaks. These look good. Take three of these Robbie, one each, and we'll try them tomorrow."

That evening, beer in hand, I lit the fire in the Weber while Irving, holding a glass of cold Jordan Sauvignon Blanc looked on.

"Why are you piling the charcoal on two sides and not across the whole braai?" He asked, a puzzled expression on his face.

"So that I can move the prawns off the direct heat if the fire gets too hot, to stop them from burning."

He watched me and sipped his wine.

"There's another story about Dewani in the paper today," he said.

"Well, if you read our papers, I'm sure you'll see a different side to that presented by the English papers. They're very biased."

"English papers biased? Rubbish Robbie!. They are the best papers in the world. Did I tell you that Newton who invented gravity was British?"

I ignored his comment about Newton. Quite frankly I couldn't have cared less.

"Ja Irv. I suppose the next thing you'll tell me is that your star cricketer, Kevin Pietersen, is British? We saw that with the World Cup, didn't we? We saw how accurate the British media is; they were talking about race riots in the streets, snakes attacking the teams ... we've never heard such rubbish."

"Oh that. Those were the tabloids."

"Well, like Newton, even the tabloids are British."

The two fires in the Weber danced happily, bright orange flames on each side, between them a no-man's-land of open grill under which there was no fire.

"So where do you put the prawns to cook?"

"Above the hot coals, when they are ready. But I can move them to the middle where there are no coals if they start to burn, as I said."

"Don't you have one of those griddle things, that you can put the prawns into? You know, those things that fold in two? Then you hold the prawns over the coals and turn the griddle? That way they don't get burned."

I felt like asking him how often he braaied prawns in England, but held back and changed the subject.

"Won't you do me a favour Irv? While I'm preparing the prawns just nip upstairs for me, won't you? There's a parcel wrapped in tissue paper lying on my desk. It's for you."

"How are you going to prepare the prawns, Robbie?"

"What do you mean? I'm going to brush them all with lemon butter sauce. Is that okay?"

He saw that I was becoming irritated by his questions.

"I'll get that parcel."

While he was gone I dipped the prawns into the mixture of lemon butter sauce and, one at a time, put them on the grill. When he returned with the parcel all the prawns were on the grill. A plume of smoke ascended as the butter dripped onto the coals, causing a momentary flare.

"Shit! Careful Robbie! You're burning them."

I glared at him, hoping he would get the message and leave me to do the prawns.

"Come on Irv, it's just the butter, the prawns aren't burning, man. Oh, you found it?" I said, glancing at the tissue-wrapped parcel. "Open it. It's for you. We bought it in Zim when we were there a few weeks ago."

"For me? That's nice of you. What is it?" He tore the thin tissue paper, took out the copper bangle, and held it between the fingers of one hand, looking at it.

"Oh, very nice. Thanks a lot." He put it on the table.

"Aren't you going to put it on, Irv?"

"Oh, yes, of course." He picked up the bangle and slipped it over his hand onto his right wrist, looking at it admiringly. I thought his admiration a little forced. "Great. Thanks a lot." He held up his arm up to show me.

Another burst of flame seared the prawns as butter dripped onto the red coals.

"Move that one, Robbie. It's burning," he said, pointing at a slightly blackened prawn.

"It's not burning, Irv," I said none too confidently. At that another burst of flame licked the prawns.

"Here," said Irving, "you really should have one of those griddle things, you know. Here let me do it." He picked up a spare braai fork and pushed a prawn to the side, away from the direct heat.

Inside me I felt a wall of anger burst, and the words poured out: "Fuck off Tucker! Fuck off! Don't you fucking well know that in South Africa you *never* interfere with another man's braai. Christ Tucker, I don't know what you do in England but it's bloody bad manners to tell someone else how to braai. Particularly if you're an Englishman. You probably never braai there anyway. What the fuck does an Englishman know about braaiing, prawns or meat? Now fuck off. Leave me to do the braai. I'm sick and tired of your interference. I'll call you when the food is ready. Fuck off."

Irving looked as though I had struck him. He backed away, holding up his hands like a boxer under a flurry of blows, flinching as my words lashed him. Without a word he turned and entered the house.

Margie was busy making a salad in the kitchen. She looked up as Irving entered. "Is the braai ready, Irv?" she asked.

Irving ignored the question and announced, "I've really pissed Robbie off. He's furious with me."

Margie laughed. "Oh, don't worry about it, he'll get over it. He's getting touchy in his old age." She continued cutting avocado for the salad. "What did you do to upset him Irv?"

Irving looked embarrassed, "Interfered with his braai."

Margie laughed. "Now that is a problem. He takes his braaiing very seriously! Can't stand other people interfering with his braai."

"Ja, I can see that—particularly an Englishman."

I entered the kitchen carrying a tray piled high with the still smoking, hot, braaied prawns.

"Sorry about that, Robbie. They look bloody good anyway—even without my help."

I laughed. "I have braaied before Irv. Anyway, no problem. You paid for the prawns so I suppose you have a right to say how they're cooked. Anyway, let's sit and enjoy them."

After the meal Irving smacked his lips and complimented me: "Delicious Robbie. Well cooked."

"Thanks Irv," I looked at him and grinned, "despite you trying to interfere."

He held up his hands like a boxer again, smiled and shrugged.

"So what are your plans this time?" I asked. "I know that we are going to the bush in a few weeks' time to do the elephant collaring, but what are you going to do until then?"

"Well, I thought I would stay a few days here with you. I have some things that I want to attend to and people to say goodb ..." he bit off the word and then continued, "I mean, see again. Then I'm going to Cape Town for a few days to stay with my cousin."

"Presumably you'll see your brother while you are there?"

"No, he's coming to the bush with us. I told you didn't I? Of course I did. Shit. I'm sorry about that. Anyway it'll be for a few days only that you overlap with him and his family."

I laughed. "Irv, I don't know why you go on about Brian. I met him years ago and he was fine, nothing wrong with him."

"Well, you'll like the others when you get up there. Helen and Steve will be there. They are friends from Oswestry. You'll really like them. He's South African and is a bloody good surgeon, specializes in spines. They've lived in the UK for years. Helen is a mad Irish woman. They're a good pair. Then of course the Taylors and the Maythams are coming. You know them anyway, so we'll have a nice crowd." His face clouded over for a second. "Except for Brian; well it's really his wife. She's RC, you know?" as if being Roman Catholic fully explained his dislike of her.

"So what Irv? So is Margie; you don't dislike her because of that, do you?" I asked with a laugh.

"No, well she doesn't ram it down your throat all the time, does she?" he replied. "Anyway, while I'm here I want to see some friends that I haven't seen for ages. In fact I'm meeting a guy that I was at school with, tomorrow, for lunch. By the way, Robbie, I need quite a bit of that money of mine, which you still have, I hope?"

"Sure Irv. How much do you want? I've got a bit here, but if you want a lot we'll have to go to the bank in the morning."

'You may as well draw it all. I want about twenty thousand tomorrow, and then if you wouldn't mind, I'll give you a shopping list to buy stuff to bring up to Tanda Tula when you come?"

"Sure, no problem."

As I was getting into bed that night Margie turned to me and asked: "Do you still think he's going to kill himself? He hasn't referred to it, has he?"

"What do you think he's doing here now? He's come to say goodbye to people he knows, hasn't he?"

"Do you think so?"

I nodded. "Yep, I'm afraid so. He even started to say as much earlier on tonight and then stopped himself. I get the feeling he *is* going to do it."

"Well, I hope he doesn't do it when we're around. Wouldn't that be ghastly? Is there nothing we can do to stop him?"

I shook my head. "No, I don't think so. Look I'll have another go at talking to him but if he's made up his mind to do it ..."

"Funny that he hasn't referred to it this time, don't you think?"

"Yes, but it all adds up. I mean why has he made two trips out here in the last two months? He says he has to take care of a few things and also that he is waiting ..." I made quotation marks in the air with the index finger of each hand, "for 'some things to happen', then he'll do it."

That night the dream came back.

❦

The next day Irving accompanied me to the bank to draw the money from my account.

I had offered to drive him to the Bryanston shopping centre where he had arranged to have lunch with his friend

"Who's the guy that you are meeting for lunch today, Irv?"

"Oh. He's an old school friend and we were friendly for some time after school. I haven't seen much of him lately, but decided to connect with him one last time. He's fallen on hard times, so I'm going to give him a bit of money."

"That's good of you, Irv."

"Well, I told you, didn't I, that I would do something good with the money from uncle Frankie—you know, Frank Auerbach's painting? So I'm going to give him a present; that's why I need you to draw some money."

I glanced at him.

"You still going ahead with this damn crazy thing, Irv?"

He nodded vehemently. "Absolutely. Absolutely. It's not crazy. It's what I want."

"Is there anything I, or anyone else, can do or say to change your mind?"

"No. Absolutely nothing. My mind is made up."

I shook my head. "Christ Irving. Killing yourself? You must be shit scared. I certainly would be—I couldn't do it."

"Not at all. In fact I'm looking forward to it. And you'll see a lot of people will benefit out of my money. So, my money won't be wasted."

I felt my stomach muscles tense, hoping he would say something to indicate that Margie and I were some of those people. I didn't want him to die, but if he had decided, why shouldn't I get some of the money?

"Do the people coming up to Tanda Tula with us all know about it?"

"Yes they do—except my brother and his family, I haven't told them."

"Well presumably you are going to tell him, aren't you?"

"No, I don't know, I haven't decided yet."

"Gee Irv. You can't not tell him, can you? I think that would be very unfair. Will it offend you if we talk about it at Tanda Tula?"

"Not at all. Certainly doesn't offend me, but trying to talk me out of it does."

"Okay Irv. I get the message."

It was early evening when he returned from the lunch with his friend.

I looked at my watch. 'Hiya Irv. Must have been a good lunch?"

"Ja, well, sort of."

"Sort of? How can you sort of have a good lunch. It's either good or bad isn't it? How was your friend? Must have been good to see him again?"

"*Ja*, it was. He's having a tough time though."

"Well, he must have been pleased with the money you gave him?"

"Twenty grand I gave him Robbie. He didn't even say thank you."

"What do you mean? Didn't say thank you.? Surely not!"

"Well I put the money in an envelope and at the end of the lunch I gave it to him."

"Did he know what was in the envelope?" I asked.

"I don't know. I handed him the envelope, he put it into his pocket without opening it, and that was it. He did say thank you when I gave him the envelope, but that was it."

'When he gets home and opens it I'm sure he'll phone to thank you. I'm sure he will."

"You just don't know with people, Robbie," he said shaking his head. "Do you remember last time I was here I brought wine for some people; lugged it all the way from England after keeping it for over thirty years, and gave it to people I thought would appreciate it?"

My stomach tightened like a thumb screw at the reminder. I had been hurt at the time because he hadn't given me any of that wine, because he felt I didn't know how to look after good wine. I hid my disappointment at the memory.

"Yes, I remember. Very well. You didn't give me any wine."

He ignored the comment.

"So I gave a bottle to Tony Taylor's mate—Tony had introduced me to him in Cape Town. The bastard never even acknowledged getting it, let alone thanked me for it. No, people, shit, difficult to fathom sometimes. Much prefer working with animals on the farm. Far less complicated than humans." He paused, then almost under his breath he muttered, "Ungrateful bastards, that's what they are."

I felt a surge of pleasure that at least one of the people who had been given some wine had now fallen to the bottom of the popularity stakes. I turned the knife slightly to inflict another stab of pain.

"Pity you didn't give me any of that wine. I would have shown true appreciation at your gift. That is, if the wine was palatable after all this time. Probably wasn't Irv, that's why he never thanked you."

That night we again visited the Grill House, this time with our friends Doug and Mar Sutherland. We had already warned them in advance of Irving's intentions. Throughout the evening Irving kept us entertained with jokes and stories, at times laughing so much at the memories that tears ran down his cheeks. I looked carefully to see whether they were tears of laughter or sadness being camouflaged by humour. I couldn't tell. He was the life and soul of the party and again he picked up the tab.

We strolled to our cars in the car park, Mar walking next to me. In a tone that wouldn't carry to Irving walking behind us with Doug and Margie, she said, "That was a lovely evening, thanks so much. Your friend is a scream, isn't he? *Skattie* (sweetheart), there is no way he is going to kill himself. Seriously *skattie*, I'm quite sure that he's been having you on. No way at all. You'll see, *skattie*. He won't kill himself."

"I hope you're right Mar, I really hope you are right."

When we arrived home Margie went straight to bed as usual, while Irving and I settled down in the lounge for our customary last drink.

I opened a Castle and poured Irving a glass of Jordan Sauvignon Blanc.

"Thanks Robbie," he said as I passed him the glass, "are you working tomorrow?"

I shook my head.

"No Irv. Day off. Why?"

"It's just that I'm going to Cape Town, the day after tomorrow, to my cousin, and then we are going to meet up there next Tuesday, aren't we? You are coming down aren't you?"

"Yes I am."

"Well what about you and me going to the Johannesburg Art Gallery tomorrow? Have you ever been?"

"No, I'm ashamed to say I haven't."

He sipped his wine. "*Ja*, I used to go there a lot with Ray Johnson. That's when I developed a love for art, as a kid, all those years ago. I would like to see the place again before I ..."

"Before you what, Irv?" I asked, raising an eyebrow quizzically.

He laughed. "Before I go home."

"So let's do it. I would like to go. I'll share a bit of culture with you."

⊷

The next morning Irving and I set off for the Johannesburg Art Gallery, with me driving. Irving scanned the morning newspaper while I navigated through the traffic. As usual, there were several intersections at which traffic lights were out of action. The car on my right broke the unwritten law of 'one-one-one' allowing each car at the faulty lights to go through in turn. I hooted angrily and Irving glanced up from the paper.

"Bastard!" I whispered to myself, pressing the hooter.

"What's wrong with your robots here, Robbie? Why are so many not working? Shit. It causes chaos with the traffic, doesn't it?"

I nodded. "Yes it does. It's one of the great mysteries of the universe. The authorities just can't get it right: stolen cables, stolen micro-chips, rain, accidents; they give us every reason under the sun—but the bottom line is that the lights still don't work. You should see how many are out of order after our Highveld storms."

Irving snorted and went back to his reading while I concentrated on weaving my way through the morning traffic.

"Jeez! I don't believe it," he said, forcing a hollow laugh, "they're going on about Dewani again. Of course he isn't going to come back here. They must be mad."

I took my eyes off the road for a second and glanced at him.

"Who? Dewani? Why not? Of course he must come back and stand trial here."

"Come off it, Robbie. Everyone knows your judicial system is corrupt. Christ, the chief of police has called him a monkey. It's all a conspiracy, man, a bloody conspiracy. He could never get a fair trial here."

I felt my blood pressure starting to rise like an Apollo spacecraft and my face flushed. I looked at him.

"What do you mean? A conspiracy? What on earth do you mean?" My voice was a few decibels higher than normal conversation as I glared at him.

An orchestra of hooting and squeal of tyres accompanied his accusing shout: "Look out! Look at the road! Fuck it Robbie, you nearly caused an accident."

Alerted by the hooting I had looked back in time to swerve and avoid hitting the car I was careening towards. I heaved a sigh of relief. Oddly, the brief danger had calmed me a little, forcing me to focus and taking my mind off Irving's comments.

'Whew! That was close. Sorry about that Irv, but it wasn't me who nearly caused the accident—it was you."

"Me? Me? You're the one driving. How could I have caused an accident?"

"By making me irritated, talking so much shit about Dewani and a conspiracy. How can it be a conspiracy? Who on earth do you think is conspiring against him?"

"Everyone; it's all to protect the tourism business here. Your judges are corrupt, the newspapers and the police are in cahoots."

I looked at him, scowling angrily."Come *on* Irv! That's enough. Shit man, you're an intelligent person. How can you let yourself down by talking such crap? First, our judges in this country are rated among the finest in the world and our judiciary system one of the best. Where do you get such bullshit from? Secondly, because the chief of police stupidly referred to him as a monkey doesn't mean he won't get a fair trial. The police don't try him, the courts do. And finally, use your head. Can you see the police, the judiciary and the media sitting down and saying 'we have to protect tourism in this country, let's make out that he murdered his wife'? Grow up Tucker. You are being fuckin' stupid and I have had enough of your pro-British crap. Everything British is wonderful and everything to do with South Africa is bad. What the fuck do you keep coming back for if you hate it all so much? Enough! I've had enough of your arrogance. Enough!"

In the silence that followed I concentrated on driving but I could see Irving out of the corner of my eye. He was staring straight ahead. I saw the glint of a tear in his eye. He swallowed hard and turned his head towards me. I looked at the car in front of us.

"Sorry Rob. I am really sorry. I was winding you up. Yes, I do keep coming back to SA. I come back because of people like you and Margie, and the Taylors and Maythams, my friends. That's why I keep coming back. Apart from my friends there isn't much else ..." his voice trailed away and we continued the drive in silence.

I felt like someone who had robbed a blind beggar of all his daily takings.

At the Johannesburg Art Gallery, with our verbal altercation behind us, Irving took me on a tour of the gallery, the likes of which would have been difficult, if not impossible, to better. His deep knowledge and love for art was evident, his enthusiasm bubbling over as he described painters, their different styles and periods. His eyes glowed and he moved from painting to painting like a child in a toy shop.

"Look at this Irma Stern, look at this Anton Van Wouw statue, look at the lines, Robbie. Look at this Tretchikoff, mind you, I'm not that keen on his stuff. Here, look at these Pierneefs, lovely aren't they?"

In each case he stopped in front of the painting and described it in detail, giving the provenance and value. I was very impressed. He certainly knew what he was talking about.

The next day, after handing me the shopping list as promised, Irving left for Cape Town. We had arranged that I would fly down a week later to do my research at the archives and stay one night at Tony Taylor's home.

"You will get all this stuff and bring it up to Tanda Tula? No problem?"

"No problem, Irv," I glanced at the list.

"Shit! How many cases of Chocolate Block? Eight cases? How long you going for?"

"Well, that's only forty-eight bottles, Robbie."

"*Ja*, but you've also got a dozen Pongracz and four cases of Jordan Sauvignon Blanc plus Johnnie Walker, and gin. And we'll be there for only six days?"

"Seven, Robbie." he corrected me with a knowing smile. "Well, we're going to have a party, aren't we ?" he challenged me, with a grin.

Turning to Margie he said, "Please don't forget to buy some of that lovely grain fed and aged sirloin steak for us to have up there as well. I want to give you all a treat, get it at that Pick n Pay, you know the one I mean, don't you?"

Margie nodded.

"Use the money I left for you and if anything is over bring it up to me in cash, if you will? See you next week in Cape Town Robbie, let me know what flight you're on and I'll pick you up at the airport—I'll have Tony's car. See, still wearing our bonding bracelet." He smiled broadly, holding up his right arm, waving it for me to see. With that and a wave of his hand he was gone.

Chapter Nineteen

DRINKS ON THE ROCKS

The following Tuesday I caught the red eye special to Cape Town so that I would have as much time as possible at the archives for my research. I had arranged to meet Irving in front of the magnificent new airport building. I gazed around me in the new arrivals hall, astonished at how much had been done in the two years since I was last in Cape Town. Again I reflected on how great the World Cup had been for us. I wonder what Tucker thinks of all this, I thought to myself, smiling a self-satisfied smile. I stopped at an ATM to draw some cash for the day, putting my small bag and lap-top on the floor, my feet straddling them as I dug in my pocket for my wallet and credit card. I pushed the card into the slot and began entering my pin number when, out of the corner of my eye I saw a stealthy movement, a white hand crept around my leg like a slithering snake—in a blink my bag and laptop had been snatched. My stomach lurched with shock, I was instantly appalled at the thought of losing all the work on my laptop.

"Hey!" I shouted as I spun round, arm outstretched to grab the culprit. It was Tucker.

"Ha ha! Howzit Robbie? You must be more careful. You know how dangerous this place is, don't you?" he roared with laughter as he handed the bag back to me. "Come on, car's out here. Ha ha! Had you, didn't I?"

I smiled sheepishly, knowing I had been careless and could easily have lost months of hard work on my laptop. Once again, I reminded myself to backup all my writing.

We arrived at Tony's car and Irving opened the boot to store my bags. There was already a suitcase in the boot.

"Who's case is that?" I asked.

"Mine. I've been staying with my cousin for a few days, but from tonight and for the next few nights I'll be staying at Tony's place."

"Oh. You haven't been there yet?"

He shook his head. As we climbed into the car he said, "No, came straight from my cousin's place this morning to pick you up. I'll drop you off at the archives, then I've got a few things to do in Cape Town, and then I'm having lunch with Bev and Mike at the Radison Blue at Seapoint. Know it?"

"No. Never been there, Irv. I remember Mike and Bev though, so you're going to see them?"

"Yes, they're down from Joburg, they spend quite a lot of time here. What time are you going to finish this afternoon? I thought maybe I could pick you up and we could go for a drink and then a bite?"

"That'll be great," I answered, "I'll certainly feel like a beer or two after a day of digging through musty old papers."

We arranged that Irving would collect me outside the archives at five that afternoon.

"That'll give me a full eight hours for my research," I said looking at my watch.

I waved as he gunned the engine and left me standing outside the old Roeland Street jail, which in 1989 had been transformed into the Western Cape Archives.

The next eight hours passed quickly as I surrounded myself with the ghosts of the past. I poured through old papers and parchments of letters and memoranda between people like Sir Harry Smith, Piet Retief, governors Somerset and Stockenstrom, Sarel Cilliers, Reverend Smit and more. These great men surrounded me, came alive among the musty old papers and peered out at me from yellowed pages and faded handwriting, which at times I could decipher only with the help of a magnifying glass. For eight hours I was transported through time into another world by these spirits from days gone by.

I glanced at my watch: ten to five. I rubbed my eyes, stood up and stretched. Time to meet the ghost of the future—Irving Tucker—I thought wryly.

He was waiting for me as I emerged from the archives, blinking as the bright sunshine hit me.

"How was it?" he asked as I climbed into the car.

"Fantastic," I replied, "I'm weary though. Bloody tiring going through all those papers. Could do with a Castle."

"I had such a nice lunch at the Radison Blue. Thought we could go back there for a drink, watch the sunset and then have a meal. What do you say?"

"Sure Irv, sounds good to me."

We threaded our way through the evening Cape Town traffic.

"You love that stuff, don't you Robbie?"

I was lost in my own thoughts, still saying goodbye to the ghosts of the past.

"What's that? Oh! You mean the history? Oh yes, I do. You have no idea how much hell those people went through."

"Who do you mean?"

"Those early settlers, and the Voortrekkers. What they all had to put up with against the British government, you have no idea." Then I realized that I had probably touched a nerve and changed the subject. I had forgotten that he thought of himself as English.

"So you had a good lunch?"

He glanced at me and smiled, indicating that he hadn't missed my comment.

"Very pleasant. Always good to see Beverley and Mike. We go back a long way as well." He glanced at me again. "I'm glad you are so happy doing what you do, Robbie. You love the history of this place don't you?"

I nodded.

"Now this book that you're writing—this bloody sex book on the Great Trek ..."

"Aw, come on, Tucker," I said with a laugh. "it's not a sex book at all. There's a bit of sex in it but the history is one-hundred-percent accurate."

"Well whatever. Do you think you're going to make money out of it?"

I shrugged. "Not really Irv. Maybe if it sells really well. But you have to sell a helluva lot of books to make money."

"What's a lot of books?"

"About fifty thousand copies."

"How many copies of your book do you think you'll sell? Enough to give you and Margie a pension?" he sounded concerned.

I shook my head. "No, no way. Maybe enough to have a trip overseas or something. Maybe, if I'm lucky, I'll sell five or six thousand. That would make it a bestseller here ... but certainly not a pension fund. Mind you, my next book, for which I already have a contract, will be a non-fiction account of the Great Trek and the history of the country. It's called *Great Trek Uncut*. Now that one might, just might give us an annual income. The publisher is expecting very big things with that one."

"Well, they say sex sells, so maybe you'll do better than you expect with this book, Robbie. You *have* to make provision for your old age." Stressing the word 'have'.

I felt a weight push on my heart. The subject that I always avoided, retirement and pensions, had raised its head again; Irving's comment was another indication that he would not be including Margie and me in his distribution of wealth. I wondered why.

"We're here," he said, as he manoeuvred the car into the narrow concrete entrance of the underground car park at the Radison Blue Hotel.

"Come on, Robbie. Our cases will be fine in the car I'm sure, they have security here. Let's get that drink."

We walked through the hotel onto the busy terrace, weaving our way through the occupied tables. We found a vacant table at the end of the terrace overlooking the sea, sat down and ordered a Castle and a glass of cold Jordan Sauvignon Blanc.

As we sipped our drinks I gazed at the view and smacked my lips, half in delight at the sensation and taste of the cold frothy beer on my lips, and half in awe at the sight before us.

A few clouds were scattered over the clear blue sky and the late afternoon sunlight danced and sparkled on an azure-coloured sea, which heaved and pushed gently against the rocks in front of us. As the small undulating waves were parted by the black rocks in their path, they foamed and turned to egg-froth white. Seagulls swooped and screeched as they dived for small fish in the gullies, and behind us the hum of conversation and clink of glasses provided the backdrop to a perfect evening. A cloud passed in front of the sun. I glanced up. A dark patch indicated the sun's position behind the cloud and the edges of the cloud shone silver.

"Beautiful, hey Robbie?"

"It really is, isn't it? Where else in the world do you get a view like this?" I asked.

He didn't answer. I saw him surveying the people around us and followed the direction of his gaze. He was looking at a table where two beautiful women, probably in their forties, sat drinking tall, brightly-coloured drinks through straws. The evening breeze carried their voices across to us. They were obviously American.

"Tourists I would think," I said, "sounds like a Texas drawl to me."

"Whatever it is, they're bloody nice, aren't they Robbie. Shit what stunning women. They must be models, don't you think?" He had not taken his eyes off the woman sitting directly opposite him. She was startlingly beautiful and I could see that the two of them had made eye contact; she was keeping her eyes on Irving while her honey-blonde companion chatted away, quite oblivious to the fact that her companion's attention was somewhere else entirely. She had rich black hair cascading to her shoulders and framing an olive skin, an open face with brown eyes and a strong nose. Full lips sucked at the straw as she watched Irving, a little smile tugging at the corners of her mouth. Bright red nails at the end of slender fingers contrasted with the bright yellow of her drink.

"Shit. Not bad hey, Robbie? Not bad at all."

"No. Actually very beautiful. And she's giving you the eye, Irv."

'Well, that's a waste of time isn't it?" he said.

"Come on, Irv. Go over and chat to her. She's made it clear that she's interested in you."

The beauty looked straight at Irving, having realized that we were discussing her.

"Forget it, Robbie. I'm not interested." He looked around for the waiter to order another drink, caught his eye, gestured towards our glasses and looked at me again.

"Not interested, Robbie. Not interested."

I felt a surge of anger at his selfishness.

"How can you talk about killing yourself, Irv? You know, I think it's all a game you're playing. Look at the sight in front of you," I waved towards the sea, "look at that, and look at that woman over there. Are you going to tell me that you are not impressed by the beauty in this world, and the beauty of that woman? Are you going to tell me that you want to end it all? I say bullshit Tucker. You love beauty as much as anyone. You love life and yet you want to end it all? I think, maybe, just maybe, you are jerking us around; that this is a Tucker game. I mean, with all the money that you have, you could have all of this and more—including that woman who has just undressed you with her eyes. I mean Irv, if you told her, or any of the other women around here, just how wealthy you are, they would all come running. Don't you feel like taking one of them to bed? Come to think about it, what about both of them? You could have any one of them. Don't you know that money is the greatest aphrodisiac in the world? Anyway, I think if you were really going to do it you would have done so by now. It's more than a year since you first told me."

"I told you, I've had things to do. Also, I've been waiting for some things to happen and they are almost in place now." He paused, "I'm getting quite a lot more money."

"What do you mean? More than you got for the Auerbach painting?"

He nodded and sipped his wine. He glanced at the table with the black-haired lovely, smiled at her dismissively, turned his attention back to me and nodded.

"Yes," he answered.

I pushed back in my chair and shook my head as I looked at him in astonishment.

He lifted up his right hand and the copper bracelet glinted in the last rays of the sun. He looked at it.

"Still wearing it, Robbie," he said with a smile, "it sort of bonds us together doesn't it? Like tied to each other. That's our symbolic bond, hey? Thank you for thinking of me and thank you for giving it to me. It means a lot."

I was slightly embarrassed at his unusual expression of emotion.

"Tell me about the money," I said.

"It's quite a story." He began to explain: "You know that Yvonne's father had to flee Germany during World War Two?"

I nodded, sipped my beer, hardly tasting it this time so engrossed was I.

"Well, some time ago I received a telephone call from a lawyer in the USA who specializes in tracing and recovering the stolen property of refugees from Germany. As you know, Yvonne's father had a great art collection. Of course, he had to leave most of it behind in Germany when he fled. Well, the lawyer told me that he had traced a painting that had belonged to Yvonne's father and that he could claim it back from the current owner. The law states that if a painting was stolen in the first place, the current owner has to hand it over and that's that; he loses out, no matter what he has paid for the painting."

"Shit Irv. Not another Auerbach?" I let out a roar of laughter at his good—and wasted—fortune. The black-haired lady looked at us and smiled at my obvious mirth. Irving shook his head.

"No it wasn't. Incidentally, the lawyer wanted one third of the value if he recovered it. He would get one third, I would get one third and Yvonne's brother would get the remaining third. But I had to tell him I knew that Yvonne's father had sold the painting that the lawyer thought had been stolen, so we couldn't go along with his little plan. I was tempted, I can assure you. Michael wanted us to proceed but I said no. Anyway that was that. However, after Yvonne died, I came across an old ammunition box on the farm filled with papers belonging to Yvonne's father. They were all in German. I sent them to the lawyer in the states and asked him to go through them to see if there was anything of value among them."

He paused, sipped his wine, smiled again at the beauty (we had overheard her companion address her as Lynn) then continued.

"About three months later he came back to me."

"Had he found anything of value?"

"Yvonne's father had owned a piece of property in the centre of Berlin."

I couldn't believe his news.

"How much Irv? What's it worth? Are you getting that as well? Jeez, Irv. Keep your voice down," I said lowering my voice to a whisper, "that Lynn will be over here like a shot if she hears this conversation."

He laughed. "It's gone through the courts there, so we are getting about a million between us. One third, one third, one third.

"Shit Irv, that's another three hundred and thirty thousand rand. That's not bad."

"No, not rands—dollars. So we will each get about two to three million rand."

I exhaled hard in a long slow breath. "Whew! Even more bucks. What on earth are you going to do with all this money?" I shook my head in amazement.

"Oh, I am seeing that it goes to the right people. People who need it."

I shook my head, downed the rest of my beer and called the waiter over.

"So that's what you've been waiting for, before you ... do it?"

"Exactly. I wanted that money to come through."

"And has it?"

"In the next few weeks. By the time I get back home after Tanda Tula it should be done."

"So that's when you are going to ... kill yourself?"

There was a sudden chill in the evening breeze and the sun had disappeared. The sea which had appeared so bright and sparkly was now a dark, dark blue as night charged in. I had been so engrossed by Irving's story I had not noticed the two women get up from their table and leave.

"Ja. The time is getting near now. I have to wait for the auction of another painting on the ninth of February, and then it will all be finished, and I will be ready."

"What do you mean, another painting?"

"This one is being auctioned on a collection of Irish art. It's by Yeats, the brother of the Irish poet, you know? Also worth a few bob and I want to see what it realizes on the auction before ..."

"What do you think? Another million quid?"

He laughed again and finished his wine before answering.

"No, this should go for about fifty to sixty thousand pounds. The market is a bit depressed, with the recession and suchlike, particularly in Ireland."

I shook my head. "Shit Irv. You are a rich man. I mean not just well off, rich. What do you think you are worth?"

"I've worked it out, Robbie. Had to see who gets what. I'm worth about forty million rand."

I expelled my breath in a whistle. "So you've left it all to charities?"

"No, to friends, Robbie. Let's go and have something to eat."

Chatting over supper, in the intimate atmosphere of a small Italian restaurant overlooking the now darkened bay, I felt very close to Irving. After supper I leaned back in my chair, raised my wine glass to him in salute and said, "We will miss you Irv. Please don't do it. Your friends don't want you to go, despite you being a difficult bugger we do care about you, you know?"

He raised his glass in return.

"Thanks Robbie," he said softly, looking at me. He smiled, almost sadly, almost apologetically. I felt my eyes begin to water. I felt stupid. He noticed.

"Don't be sad, Robbie. I'm not sad at all. I'm looking forward to it. I've had a great life. I know that I am young, but I want to decide when I go; and as I've told you, I have no interest in starting over. My money will benefit people who could do with it, so there's nothing wasted, is there?"

"Except for the rest of your life. What about your friends? What about us? Don't you realize what this is doing to all of us?"

"Ja, well."

"How are you going to do it?"

He shook his head and smiled.

"Are you going to one of those places in Switzerland? One of those clinics with Dr Death where they euthanize you? Shit! Surely not? Shit Tucker, I'll bump you off for half the price!"

He laughed. "No, Robbie. Nothing like that. I'm not prepared to tell you how. Rest assured that it will be well planned and executed."

"Christ Tucker, that's a poor choice of words, isn't it?"

He laughed. "You know what I mean. No, I will be in charge."

"What if you fuck it up? What if you turn yourself into the vegetable you dread becoming?"

"No, that won't happen. I've been into the whole subject very carefully. I can assure you I won't make a mistake."

He tilted his head back, drained his glass, dabbed his lips with a table napkin and said, "Let's go home."

We drove down the long darkened drive to Tony Taylor's home where we were to spend the night.

"Here we are, Robbie".

I looked at the big house in the dark shadows.

"Tony does all right for himself, doesn't he? Still, very nice that he lets you use the place even when he isn't here. You must remember to thank him from me."

We climbed out the car, slammed the doors and walked around to the boot in the dark to collect our suitcases. Irving clicked the latch. He lifted the boot lid open and a blaze of light, contrasting with the blackness surrounding us, lit up the interior of the boot. There was nothing in the boot. It was empty. Our suitcases were not there.

We both stared into the well-lit interior of the car boot as if the harder we looked the more chance there would be of the suitcases suddenly appearing.

"Fuck! What the hell?" said Irving, "they've gone—the suitcases have gone."

"What do you mean, Irv? Gone? Gone where? Where are our cases?"

My heart plummeted as I thought of my laptop with my book saved in 'documents'. Not much good now. It certainly wasn't saved or safe. My entire manuscript—gone! Surely this could not have happened?

"They've been pinched. Shit! They must have been pinched at the hotel when we were having a drink. I thought they had security there?" The light from the boot accented Irving's worried expression.

I felt nauseous, thinking of the two years of writing that had disappeared with my suitcase, together with all my research notes. My stomach had dropped through my shoes. I couldn't think of what to say. We both stood staring into the empty boot.

"You didn't move the cases into the car, Robbie?" Irving asked, hopefully.

I grimaced and shook my head.

"No. How did they get in? There's no damage is there?" I looked at the bottom of the lock to see whether it had been forced. It hadn't.

"Oh well, Robbie. You didn't have much in there did you? Just your overnight things and shaving stuff I suppose?"

"No. Shit Irv. My laptop."

He put a hand to his mouth in dismay.

"My laptop, but that's not all. My book. My entire book is in my laptop. Jeez, this is a disaster."

"Surely you had backed-up your book? I mean, you have got a back-up haven't you?"

My mind raced as I thought about when last I had backed-up the book. It had been some weeks earlier and I had done a great deal of writing since then.

"Some of it, not all. Fuck!"

I kicked the tyre of the back wheel in anger. Added to the loss of my book the thought of not being able to shave in the morning (I never missed shaving) and not being able to clean my teeth added to my anger. I kicked the tyre again.

"Come on … let's go inside anyway. Standing here isn't going to find them."

Irving unlocked the front door and we walked into the dark house. He fumbled on the wall for the light switch before clicking it on and bathing the room in light. I blinked as my eyes adjusted. I looked around. It was a very comfortable house. Big old leather chairs and sofas, books lining the walls. I flopped into an armchair, shaking my head.

"I can't believe this has happened, Irv. Shit a brick. What a blow."

"Tell you what, Robbie," he said, with what I took for forced enthusiasm, "why don't I phone the hotel and ask if the cases are there? Maybe someone took them inside."

"Don't be stupid Irv. How can they be there? They must have been taken from the boot of the car. They've been stolen, man. They are *not* at the hotel."

"I'm going to phone anyway. Do you have the number? No, of course not." He took his mobile phone out his pocket and I heard him ask directory enquiries for the number. I shook my head and thought what a stupid thing to do, phone the hotel. They wouldn't know a thing. I was looking at the titles of Tony's books on the bookshelf and half-listening as Irving made contact with the hotel. I heard him ask for reception. I could hear only his side of the conversation.

"Hello? Reception? Ah, good evening."

Pause.

"Look I wonder if you can help me?"

Pause.

"My name is Tucker," he glanced across at me and shrugged helplessly.

"No, that's Tucker with a 'T'. T – u - c – k – e – r. T for Tommy ..."

I smiled to myself. Welcome to Africa, I thought.

"Look we were there earlier and parked the car in the car park ..."

Pause.

"Yes, the hotel car park, the one underground."

Pause.

'Yes, well, when we got back to the car our suitcases were gone."

Pause.

"I was wondering if you have our suitcases there?"

Pause.

He took the mobile away from his ear, covered it and whispered loudly to me, "She's going to have a look."

I wrinkled my forehead in puzzlement but before I could say anything he resumed his conversation.

"Yes I'm here ... yes ... yes. Oh!" He sounded disappointed. "They're not there?"

Pause.

"Taken to our rooms? No, you don't understand, we are not staying there."

Pause.

"Look in our rooms? Yes I will, but we are not staying in the hotel. Okay."

I was becoming irritated by Irving's pointless conversation and wasted effort.

"Leave it, Irv. You're wasting your time. The suitcases are gone."

He ignored me and continued talking on the mobile.

"Okay, hang on. I'll go and look in the bedroom as you say ..."

I sat watching Irving as he walked out of the lounge still with his mobile to his ear.

"Yes, I'm going to check in the bedroom …"

I shouted after him as he disappeared out of the lounge.

"Don't be bloody mad Tucker—how can they possibly be in the bedroom?" At the thought of my missing work on my stolen laptop, my stomach again did a minor flick flack.

"Here they are! Robbie! She's right! They *are* here!"

Then he spoke again into the mobile.

"Thank you very much. You've been most helpful."

I shouted after Irving: "What crap are you talking, Tucker? They can't be here!"

"But here they are, Robbie. Come and look."

I thought he was being ridiculous and I was in no mood for more of his silly behaviour. Impatiently I walked into the bedroom where Irving was standing—right next to our unopened suitcases.

A grin lit up his face and stretched from ear to ear. I looked from Irving to the cases and back to Irving, in amazement.

"But how … how could … how did they get here?"

He burst into peals of laughter and doubled over, wiping tears of laughter from his eyes.

"Your face Robbie! What a picture!"

"Well, I still don't know how the fucking cases got here, unless …" as the penny dropped "… Tucker you bastard! You came back here during the day and dropped them off, didn't you? You sod! You planned this whole thing the whole day? How could you do that? You know how valuable that laptop and its contents are to me. Shit you bugger, that's cruel, really cruel."

I charged at him, laughing, realising that he had made me the butt of the joke, and delivered a hard punch to his arm. He held up his hands in defence, roaring with laughter and then rubbed the spot ruefully where my punch had landed.

"Mark my words, Tucker. You'd better be on your guard. I'm going to get you back. You had better look out. I owe you a big one for what you've just done to me. You'd better watch your back. Given what you've done I might just hasten your departure from this world."

He let out another roar of laughter.

"I really had you going, didn't I Robbie? I really had you."

He doubled over, holding his stomach, wheezing with laughter.

Chapter Twenty

BLACK HUMOUR

The following Friday, 28 January, Margie and I set off for the Timbavati in our heavily loaded car. The cooler boxes were filled with fresh meat, and several cases of wine and beer were piled high in the back, leaving little space for our suitcases. I glanced over my shoulder at the assortment of boxes.

"Gee, it looks like we're going to feed an army for a month with this lot, doesn't it? Hope we got everything. Did you get that special meat for Irv from Pick n Pay? He wanted the grain fed and aged sirloin, didn't he?"

"Well, I did get the meat there, but I'm not sure if I got the right meat."

"Oh well, I'm sure whatever we have will be fine."

Seven hours later. It was already dark as we bumped and bounced over the dirt road leading to the camp. The headlights of the Jeep at times pointed into the dark heavens above and then plunged downwards, like a trawler in a storm, as we jolted over the rough terrain. I slowed as we entered the perimeter of the camp. The bright beam swept over two figures: a man and a woman were caught in the probing head lights like startled buck.

It was Irving, barefoot, check shirt hanging out of khaki shorts which reached to his knees, carrying the ever-present glass of red wine. Next to him stood a black-haired lady, a full head shorter than Irving, also holding a glass of red wine. Her hair was shoulder length and her spectacles flashed as the headlights shone on her. She wore three-quarter khaki bush pants, ankle socks and tackies (tennis shoes).

"That must be Irv's friend, Helen," said Margie as I pulled up in front of the two figures. Irving waved his hand in greeting, a wide welcoming smile on his flushed face. I could see that he had been drinking heavily.

"Come on you guys," said Irving as he held open Margie's door, "did you get all the stuff?" He cupped his hands against the window and peered into the dark interior of the Jeep.

"Christ. You've got a lot of stuff here, haven't you?" he laughed. "Looks like it's enough to feed an army. Did you get that lovely meat? Anyway, come on, we're going to have a braai. You guys must be starving. At least now I have some decent company. I was getting tired of talking shit to this bloody Irish woman."

Helen looked at us behind Irving's back and smiled ruefully.

We helped carry the boxes of wine and cooler boxes into the kitchen and then dropped off our suitcases in the bungalow at the back. Irving indicated the bungalow would be ours for the duration of our five-night stay. When we returned to the wooden deck, Irving was already braaiing the meat while Helen sat at the table. Both had replenished their wine.

"So Helen, where is your husband while you are up here in the bush?"

"Her husband, Steve, is a bloody good spine surgeon, Robbie," Irving shouted from the fire. His voice floated to us out of a cloud of blue smoke rising from the fat dripping from the lamb chops and *boerewors* (South African traditional sausage) onto the fire.

"Where?" I asked.

"In Oswestry."

"Oh, is there a hospital there?"

"A bloody big hospital and very, very good," Irving said earnestly, "you'd be amazed at what we have in Oswestry. Amazed."

"Oh, really?" I raised an eyebrow.

"Abso-bloody-lutely. Shit. We have Mount House on the High Street—a school that was started in the 1400s; the largest organic fruit and vegetable market in the whole of England; BAE has a factory there that makes the wings for the 747s ... and ... and—"

"Comeon, Irv, Stop bullshitting."

"No, no, I'm not kidding you. All that is true, plus there's a twenty-five pounder cannon from the war ... and talking about the war, one of the famous war poets, Wilfred Owen, you've heard of him of course?"

I nodded.

"Well, he was from Oswestry, as was Darwin."

He looked smug. I covered my mouth to hide my amusement.

"And the orthopaedic hospital of course, where Professor Steve Eisenstein carries out his work. And Laura Ashley—you've heard of her haven't you? Laura Ashley's factory. We even have a bloody hot air balloon factory on the High Street. What's it again, Irish git, what's it called? Oh yes, Lindstrand Balloons. Quite a street we have, quite a High Street."

"He's South African, isn't he, your husband, I mean?" I asked Helen.

She nodded.

"Yes. We've just been on the most fantastic trip for ten days in Namibia; then I came up here and joined Irving while Steve stayed in Fochville to visit his brother. He's dying of cancer."

"I'm sorry to hear that. When will Steve get here?"

"Sunday evening, at least I think it's Sunday evening. What day is it today? I've lost track here in the bush."

Irving shouted from the fire where the meat was sizzling.

"Don't talk crap, you Irish git. You never know what day of the week it is. Don't blame the bush. You Irish only know about growing potatoes!"

Helen laughed. "Yes, and rugby, don't we? Better than the poms."

She had a lilting Irish accent and took his jibe without offence. I thought that she must know Irving very well not to be offended by him.

"That's true," said Irving with a good natured smile, "very true."

Irving arrived at the table carrying a tray of chops and *boerewors*. The delightful rich smell of braaied meat rose from the platter. Around us were the night sounds of the bush. As Irving sat down next to Helen the night air carried the sound of a lion cough.

We piled our plates with salad and freshly cooked meat. Margie and I were both hungry from the long drive from Johannesburg and were quite content to enjoy Irving's cooking and listen to the good-natured banter between the two of them.

"Helen is the one who has been helping me in Oswestry."

"Oh, are you the counsellor?" Margie asked.

Helen nodded. "Yes I am, but I've been seeing him more as a friend than a client."

"So you know all about it, do you?" I asked.

"Uh huh, I do. Terrible isn't it?"

Irving got up from the table and returned with a new bottle of Chocolate Block. He replenished the glasses and sat down.

"So how many people know about this thing Irv?" I asked, and we all looked at him for the answer.

"Oh a few friends. Not many. Really, just a handful."

"How many is a handful exactly? I mean, do your other friends here and in England know and talk about it.? Like Tony Taylor and your friend who we met last year, the guy who owns a school or something. Do they know?"

"You mean Murray Smythe?" he snorted. "Well, I've told him but he just ignores the subject. Doesn't talk about it. Tony knows as well, and the Maythams. Actually Murray pisses me off. He avoids the subject like the plague. Irritating, really."

"Can't say I blame him. So you've known each other a long time?" I addressed my question to Irving, but looked first at Helen

'Yes, Yvonne and I were friendly with Steve and Helen, despite Helen being Irish. Steve's a good guy and he married her because he felt sorry for the Irish ..."

"What do you mean?" Helen asked with a laugh. "He's Jewish—I felt sorry for him!"

"What a combination," said Irving. "A Jew with a holy Roman Catholic!

What a combination. The man deserves a medal."

The bottles of wine that Irving had drunk that day began to surface. "Mind you I would have thought that Steve had more sense than to marry an Irish peasant like you."

Helen smiled and said, with her Irish lilt, "He's a very 'looky' man, and he knows it."

"Bloody holy Romans," Irving slurred, "can't stand the bastards. Bloody hypocrites."

"Hold on Irv. Margie's also a Roman Catholic," I pointed out.

"That's fine. Then she knows about how all those bastard priests behave. Buggering little boys and then praying for their souls. You know all about that, don't you Margie?"

"Not really. I did go to a convent though."

"Well, you're lucky if those nuns didn't try to get into your pants, aren't you? The nuns are just as bad as the priests."

"Well, can't say that I ever had an experience like that," said Margie.

"Bastards. Real bastards. I hate them all for their hypocrisy."

"But didn't you tell me that your brother's wife, who is coming up here, is Roman Catholic? You have Catholics in your family." Helen said in a shocked tone.

Margie and I laughed.

"Exactly. That's why my brother and I don't get on. Those filthy Catholic priests, up to all sorts of tricks and then praying to the Lord for forgiveness. Makes me furious at the thought. Fucking little boys at every opportunity they get—and each other."

"Come on Irv," I said, "you can't lump all Roman Catholic priests together."

"Why not? Why not?" His face was red with anger and wine, "they're all bad, anyway. Yvonne hated them as well; you should have heard what she had to say about them. Anyway, I'm going to bed. See you in the morning. No game drive for me in the morning. G' night."

He lurched into the shadows then reappeared on the edge of the light from the fire, half in the light and half in the dark. I looked up and at him. He stood swaying slightly. His face was in the dark but I saw the flash of his white teeth as he smiled and pointed to the copper bracelet on his right wrist, "Still wearing it Robbie ... still wearing it ... symbol of our friendship," he called in an almost incoherent mumble, then turned again and disappeared into the shadows, walking a crooked line to his chalet, leaving Helen with Margie and me.

I threw another log onto the fire. A shower of sparks like fireflies darted, swirled as if looking for direction, then scattered and climbed into the black sky above, which danced and glittered with the matching millions of stars like diamonds on a black cloak.

We were silent as Irving's footsteps receded into the night.

I looked up at the sky. "Lovely here isn't it? Hear that?" as a wild dog, slightly closer now, cried for the second time. "That's a wild dog," I said.

Helen nodded.

I sipped my wine.

"Difficult old bugger isn't he Helen? A bit like that wild dog howling."

"Well, to be honest, I'm seeing him in a totally new light. I've known him for a long time but have never seen him behave like this—this isn't the Irving I know."

'What do you mean, you've never seen him behave like this? How does he behave in England, in Oswestry?"

"Totally different. He and Yvonne used to come for dinner. Maybe have a couple of glasses of wine ..."

I snorted. "A couple of bottles you mean, surely?"

"No, not bottles. He was always very quiet. This is a totally different character. I have never heard him swearing and being rude to anyone like this, let alone all this drinking. They would have dinner, always very sober evenings. Then Yvonne would give the sign and they would go home. She wore the trousers I can assure you."

I nodded thoughtfully. "Well, I suppose if you are planning to kill yourself, you would change personality, wouldn't you?"

"Do you think he'll do it?" she asked.

Margie and I exchanged glances. I nodded and tightened my lips.

'Yes, I think he might well kill himself. I don't know when or how, but he's pretty determined. Do you know about his paintings?"

She nodded. "Yes, and all that money. I wonder what he's going to do with it all?"

"He says he's leaving it to friends who 'could do with it'—maybe you are included?" I asked, casting a line into the water, to see if she had any idea of who was going to benefit.

"No, we aren't included. Maybe you are? He's very fond of you, you know. Always talking about you. Robbie this, Robbie that. He's told us a lot about how you have recovered from your financial disaster, as he says, 'by working your arse off!'"

I shook my head. "That may be so, but no, he's made it clear that none of the people he has left money to are aware of his intention, so that rules us out. We are very much aware of his plan."

"Us too. We're getting some of his firewood though, so he tells me."

I laughed. "What do you mean? Firewood? Firewood? I've never heard of that in a will?"

"Don't you know about his firewood?"

"No, afraid I don't; first time I've ever heard of it."

"He's been collecting and storing firewood for years. He keeps it stacked in piles by the year. You know, like someone who collects and stores wine? A small sign stating the 'vintage year' identifies each pile of wood. He's got piles of 'bluddy' firewood around his farm, all neatly stacked and labelled."

"You are kidding me?" I said.

"No, not at all. Each pile is a dedicated year and we are getting one of the 'good vintages' of wood, so he tells me. Quite frankly we would rather have a couple of his pictures. They're worth a few bob. But no, we are getting firewood; and some of his other friends in the UK are getting the same; not sure what year we are getting, though," she added ruefully.

I shook my head in amazement.

"This is like something out of a movie, isn't it? So, so, sad. I mean, Helen, he doesn't even appear depressed. He's invited us all here," I waved my arm expansively, another log shifted and a shower of sparks danced heavenwards, "he's partying, having fun, and yet he says he's going to kill himself. I mean in England, where you live, is he lonely? Does he walk around looking miserable?"

"Not at all. Not at all. For a while, after Yvonne's death, he was very down. Then, I think he saw a doctor and was on medication for depression. Not sure if he's still on the medication though."

I shook my head in disbelief at the absurdity of the situation.

"I sometimes feel I'm letting him down by not trying harder to talk him out of this madness. But, quite honestly, I don't believe any amount of talking is going to make an iota of difference. He's made up his mind and that's that."

"I agree. Irving has made up his mind. You won't change it."

"Well, then we can only give him support and try to help him, somehow."

We finished our wine and stumbled through the dark along the path to our respective bedrooms.

That night the dream of Irving's blood and brains on the walls came back.

✍

The next morning I volunteered to make breakfast.

"A big greasy fry-up Irv, that's what you need," as I sliced tomatoes and cut bananas lengthways.

"That'll be good," Irving's voice floated into the kitchen from the wooden deck. I glanced out. He was leaning back in his chair, binoculars glued to his eyes.

"What you watching, Irv?" I put oil in the pan and began to fry the tomatoes and mushrooms. I planned to do the bananas last, just before frying the eggs.

"Unbelievable. Fish Eagle down here at the river and over there, some ellies. Hell, I love it here. Look at that for a sight."

I glanced out the door and across the river to where a herd of about five elephants were tugging at some mimosa branches. The yet-to-be-scorching morning sun bathed the scene in a soft glow.

"Absolutely beautiful, isn't it Robbie?" he said without taking the glasses from his eyes.

Soon the kitchen filled with the morning smells of bacon frying and hot fat as the tomatoes and mushrooms cooked.

Irving carefully put his binoculars away in their case and left them on the table. He stood behind me as I cooked.

"Have you got a good pair of binocs, Robbie?"

I shook my head. "Not really. I have a pair but I wouldn't call them particularly good."

"Mine are brilliant. You must use them on the game drive this evening. You can spot a pimple on an ellie's knacker at a distance of three hundred metres with these. Great magnification. You see all sorts of things with the animals that you miss with the naked eye. Try them this evening. You'll see what I mean."

'Thanks Irv, I will."

The tomatoes, mushrooms and fried banana were ready. I removed them from the stove and put them in the oven.

"How many eggs do you want?"

"Two please. Sunnyside up if possible, not too soft."

I cracked the eggs and managed to spill them into the frying pan without breaking them. I selected an egg-lifter from a forest of assorted utensils and began to paddle hot oil over the sizzling eggs.

"Are those mine?" Irving asked his voice slightly raised in alarm, looking at the eggs.

Surprised, I looked at him and nodded.

"Then don't use that bloody plastic fryer to do my eggs; plastic is carcinogenic. In fact, don't use it on anyone's eggs. Christ Robbie, we'll all get cancer. Here," he said as he grabbed a metal egg lifter from the collection of utensils, and passed it to me, "use this. Much safer."

I looked at him in astonishment. How could he be so worried about getting cancer if he planned to kill himself?

"You are joking aren't you, Irv?" I asked, not sure myself if he was.

"Not at all. Don't you know that a plastic egg lifter could cause cancer?"

"Well, what the fuck do you care, Irv? Shit man. You talk of killing yourself in the next few months and now you're worried about getting cancer? I can guarantee you that if I had carried on using that egg lifter there is no way you would have got cancer before you died. Or, maybe, Irv," I said, looking at him accusingly, "maybe this whole thing about killing yourself is bullshit? If you worry about getting cancer that must mean that you enjoy life and don't want to lose it, don't you think?"

Irving shook his head gently from side to side, looking slightly sheepish. "The eggs are getting hard," he said.

I took his eggs out of the frying pan and began frying the other eggs while he wrapped his hand in a tea towel for protection, opened the oven door and removed the hot platter with the fried tomatoes, mushrooms, and bananas. I brought out the platter of eggs.

"Here's what we need," said Irving, as he opened a bottle of Amarula liqueur and poured it over the fried bananas, "that'll set us up for the day."

He was right. The bananas were delicious

Later that day Steve, Helen's husband, arrived. Steve was a tall gaunt-looking man, built like a long distance runner. His greying beard and moustache made him look like an Arctic explorer, but without the ice on his whiskers. Large spectacles gave him a severe look, his hair was receding at the temples and he was as reserved as Helen was outgoing. Steve remained at the camp that evening while Helen, Irving, Margie and I set set out on our game drive, in the company of Martin, who turned out to be an outstanding bush guide.

Irving passed me his Kamakura binoculars. "Here Robbie. Try these. You'll see a helluva difference with them."

He was right. You could see the hair on a gnat's ball.

"They really are great Irv." I handed the glasses back to Irving and wondered what he was going to do with them when he killed himself.

As dusk was falling Martin pulled the Land Cruiser to a halt in a clearing in the bush. We all clambered off the vehicle and marvelled at the sky which was streaked with broad brush strokes of brilliant pink as the sun, now only a flaming quarter orb, slipped down over the horizon. In the distance a lion coughed. We were surrounded by a thick silence that cloaked us like treacle. The engine of the Land Cruiser ticked quietly as it cooled, almost as regularly as a clock ticking.

"Beautiful, isn't it Margie?" Irving asked as he opened a bottle of Sauvignon Blanc and poured three glasses. I opened an ice cold Castle with the familiar *shook*, took a long drink and felt the cold liquid refresh my throat with that special, slightly bitter flavour.

"Ah, lovely. Beer, the bush and friends. What more can anyone want, hey Irv? Pity this is one of the last you'll be seeing, isn't it?"

"Aren't you coming out again?" Martin shot a glance at Irving.

"Something like that," Irving chuckled and looked embarrassed, "you could say that. Not for a long, long time."

I looked at him. His eyes were brimming with tears. I looked away.

"Pity," said Martin, "anyone want some biltong (salted, dried meat)?" He offered us a plate of the sliced dried meat.

When I saw that Irving was engaged in conversation with Margie and Helen, I took Martin aside.

"Martin, I need your help."

"Sure thing. What can I do for you?"

I quietly outlined my plan for exacting my revenge on Irving, for the practical joke he had played on me in Cape Town a few weeks earlier. Martin listened attentively, nodding agreement as I quickly went through my scheme. He agreed to assist and we arranged to execute our prank on the Tuesday, when Irving went to fetch his brother and family from the airport at Hoedspruit.

That night, after supper, sitting around the roaring log fire drinking wine, Irving reminded us that his friends the Taylors and the Maythams were arriving the next day.

"What's her name again?" I asked. "I always remember Alistair but—"

"Who? Oh, you mean Gale? Think of a big wind."

"I'll call her Storm; for some reason Gale doesn't stick with me. I remember them. Nice people. Do they know what you intend doing?"

"Yes, they all know, except for my brother."

"I bet Tony Taylor isn't too impressed, is he?"

Irving shrugged dismissively. "I don't know. He doesn't say anything. Actually, except for you Robbie, I talk more to the wives than the men. They seem to understand the whole thing more. Gale, Helen, Anne—even in France I didn't say much to your pal, Ray Johnson, but I chatted to Lynne. The men don't seem to believe me. Alistair's okay though."

More likely they don't want to be sucked into the play, I thought. Strange, Irving considered that anyone who listened and talked about his intended suicide 'okay' and those that avoided the subject irritated him.

"How many people actually know?"

"Not many. Just the people here."

"Well, that can't be," I challenged, "you chatted to Lynne Johnson."

"Oh yes. Just them."

"What about your friend Murray? You told him didn't you?"

"Oh, yes. Yes, I did. That's all though. Very few people know."

"Bullshit Irv. Lots of people know. What about Michael, Yvonne's brother? Doesn't he know as well?"

"Yes. Well," he added lamely, "I had to tell him. He's the executor of my will. I had to tell him."

"And what did he have to say?"

"Not much. He's a bit of a prick anyway," Irving stood up, stretched and yawned, his head tilted back, looking up at the sky, making it clear that the discussion was over.

"I'm off to bed. See you in the morning."

Gale and Alistair Maytham arrived the next day and soon after that the Taylors. Auburn-haired Gale, whom I called Storm, was a lively, bubbly person whose personality matched her name. Her husband, Alistair, was balding with grey hair and appeared more serious, but turned out to have a wicked sense of humour.

Irving's behaviour changed when the Taylors arrived. In front of Tony he became far more serious and seemed to look to Tony for approval and recognition. That evening, after the game drive followed by supper under the stars on the veranda, sitting around the fire, the conversation and humour was particularly dark. Talk turned to the Rugby World Cup which was to be held later in the year in New Zealand.

"What do you think of the Boks' [nickname for the South African rugby team] chances? Mind you," Irving added, "they start at a disadvantage under that loose cannon of a coach. What's his name?" he asked, looking at Alistair.

"You mean Pieter de Villiers?" Al answered, "ja, he is a bit of a liability, but we have a strong team. Feeling is that they could take it, even with de Villiers as the coach."

"Forget it," said Irving, "us poms will thrash you. Don't we play you in a pool game? Shit! It's going to be a bloody good tournament, isn't it? The All Blacks are starting to peak, so it could be between us—England—and the All Blacks."

We all stared at Irving in amazement, taken aback by his enthusiasm for an event for which he was not going to be alive.

Alistair said what we were all thinking: "I don't know why you are getting so excited Irving."

"Why not? We've got a bloody good team."

"That may be," said Alistair, "but you aren't going to be around to see it are you?"

Irving laughed. "*Ja*, but that doesn't mean that I can't get excited about it, does it?"

Tony Taylor stood up.

"We're going to bed. Come on Anne, let's go. Don't forget, Tucker, I'm doing breakfast tomorrow."

To a chorus of 'goodnights' from the rest of us they disappeared into the dark shadows.

There was silence for a few moments as we watched them go. The fire crackled and spat.

"Come on Irving. This whole thing is bullshit, isn't it? Admit it. You got excited about the Rugby World Cup. Why not put your plan on hold until after the World Cup? In fact why don't you cancel it altogether?" I said.

"Absolutely, Irving," said Alistair.

Steven nodded his head in agreement. His glasses glinted in the firelight with the movement.

"Forget the whole thing, Irving. Get on with your life. Stop this rubbish about killing yourself. You've been talking about it now for a year ... let's just forget the whole thing," I said.

We were all gazing at Irving. He looked back at us, a small smile tugging the corners of his mouth, and shook his head gently. "No, I'm not forgetting about it. I've planned the whole thing and I'm going ahead. That's definite."

"What do you mean you've planned the whole thing. I bet you haven't thought of all the details?" I challenged.

"I think I have. I've spent the last year planning."

"Do you think you've covered everything?" I asked.

"Well, I think so. I've tried to."

"Who's going to find you when you kill yourself, then?"

There was a stunned silence around the fire at my question.

Irving looked embarrassed then laughed. "Well, it doesn't matter does it? I won't be around." He sipped his red wine.

"Of course it matters. That's very inconsiderate. What if it's one of your friends who finds you dead? Jeez, it would be a helluva shock to find you as a corpse. Even you."

"Mmm. I suppose you're right. I'll have to give it some thought. Anyway at least I won't stink." Someone dropped their wine glass. It smashed into little diamonds that sparkled in the light of the fire. "I'm doing it in February. It's still cold in the UK then, so I'll be sort of refrigerated."

"February? That's next month Irv."

He looked at me, his eyes glistening in the firelight. I wasn't sure if it was the reflection of the flames or tears. I shook my head. The others were watching me. Their eyes switched between us, following the conversation like spectators at Wimbledon.

I swallowed hard. "Next month Irv. You are going to do it next month? When?"

"Not sure yet of the exact date. I'm still waiting on a couple of things. I discussed them with you Robbie."

"Irv, I think you're actually enjoying this. It's all a bit of a game to you, isn't it? I actually think this is a giant bullshit on your part. In fact now that I think about it, here is a good plot for a book. It goes like this: first, you tell us that you are going to kill yourself and tell me that you have left me quite a lot of money, say a million pounds. Then after getting me all excited you later tell me that you have changed your mind. I am devastated, because I had counted on the money and now you aren't going to die, so I am not going to inherit the shit load of money. So I decide to fly to Oswestry, the capital city of England—"

There were chuckles around the fire. "Not England, the 'bluddy' world," Helen asserted quietly. More chuckles from the others.

"—and I murder you. Seeing as you had told so many people that you were going to kill yourself, I bump you off, make it look like suicide, and head back home. It'd make a great story," I said as I leaned back and sipped my beer.

"But here's the sting in the tail, Robbie," said Alistair, "after you've murdered him you discover that he had changed his will and you weren't getting anything anyway."

Irving led the roars of laughter from the others that followed.

"Seriously though Irv," I said, "I do have a good idea as to how I could make some money if you do it—I'm going to write a book."

"About me?"

He looked pleased.

I nodded. "Ja. A book about this bizarre event. It'll be a bestseller."

He laughed. "I hope so Robbie. Shit. About me … that's nice."

We all laughed.

I looked at Irving. He looked happy. I think he was enjoying being the centre of attention. I smiled and directed my next question to Helen.

"Oswestry is the centre of the world is it, Helen?"

"It is, you know. Michael Palin comes from there, as well as Michael Hesseltine; and RAF Shawbury is there. We even have a walkway under which lie the bodies of 500 people who died in the Great Plague of 1347, as well as a plaque in memory of one of the sons of Oswestry who died in the Frontier Wars in South Africa."

"Must be helluva congested, that street," someone muttered, and again there was laughter.

Helen took a sip of wine and continued, warming to the subject.

"And outside the town there is even an ancient fort that goes back to the Iron Age, over two thousand years ago ... lovely place, Oswestry."

There was silence for a few seconds, finally broken by Irving.

"Amazing place," he said, taking another sip of Chocolate Block, "actually, you're wrong Robbie. Not the centre of the world."

"Not?" I asked, with a glance at Helen.

"Centre of the bloody universe," said Irving. He drained his glass and refilled it immediately, splashing some of the Chocolate Block on the hard earth underfoot. In the half-light the stain looked like a dark patch of blood.

"I suppose there's even an undertaker on that High Street, Irv? I asked.

Everyone laughed.

"Yes. David Davies, the best undertaker in the world is there ... right on the High Street, along with all the other famous people and buildings."

"Well, he's going to be handy isn't he?" said Alistair. "That's who you should get to find your body Irv. Send him an email just before you do it. Tell him to come around and collect you."

"I can't bear to think of you lying there on your own, Irv," said Helen with a shudder. She tipped her head back and drained her glass of Chocolate Block.

"Hey? I won't know, will I? I'll be dead. So don't worry about that Helen."

My eyes were glued to Irving's face. This time I was sure that tears caused the glistening in his eyes in the dancing light.

"Do you really think you are going to a better place? Do you think you are going to join Yvonne?"

"Absolutely not," said Irving forcefully, "of course there is no 'better place'."
He made the sign of the apostrophes in the air with his forefingers. "In fact there is no place at all. There is death and nothing. I've said so to Robbie, haven't I, Robbie?" he said looking at me.

I nodded.

He continued: "I've told Robbie, that I don't expect to see Yvonne. I don't expect to see my father. I don't expect to see anyone, because there is nothing. Nix. Nil. Zero. A great big fucking nothing."

"Jesus Christ," I said softly to myself, and shook my head in disbelief.

Irving heard and fired a glare at me. "Not even him, Robbie. Definitely not him. He is just a popular fable, an urban legend and, of course, the fictitious hero of the biggest selling book in the world—the bible. A book of fables. You'll do well if your book sells one per cent of what the bible has sold."

"Well, you'll never know, will you Irv? You've decided not to be around."

He shrugged.

Silence met this last statement. Broken by a log tumbling off the fire, sending a shower of sparks dancing into the air. As the glowing log rolled across the hard baked earth it left a spoor of dancing fireflies.

Like a ten-ton truck descending a steep incline, rapidly changing gears down, the mood around the fire had skidded from the heights of humour and companionship, to settle in a low, rumbling dark reality.

That night the dream came back. This time it started with the stain of the Chocolate Block that had spilled earlier onto the hard earth floor. The stain spread and crept up the walls of the bedroom, finally to trickle and drip down the walls.

Chapter Twenty-one

REVENGE

The next morning I walked into the kitchen to see Tony Taylor at the sink cutting onions. I felt a pang of irritation. Breakfasts had been my territory.

"Hi Tony," I said with a lightness I didn't feel.

He glanced over his shoulder and continued cutting.

"Hi Robbie. Doing you a Polish breakfast I learned from my grandmother."

"Oh yes? What's that?"

"You'll see. Better still, you'll taste it."

Won't be as good as my fried eggs and bacon, I thought.

Tony continued slicing and dicing the onions.

"You guys have a late night last night? We were tired so left you quite early."

"Not really late," I replied, "we were discussing Irving's death."

He glanced up from his cutting. "Oh?" he said, in an offhand manner.

I left it.

"What on earth are you making us for breakfast, Tony? Looks like a shithouse of onions?"

"Ja. Well wait till you taste it. You'll see."

He poured the chopped onions into a frying pan and began to stir.

"The trick is to have them almost burned. Not quite burned but browned and very soft."

I watched him as he sliced up the tomatoes.

"The tomatoes have to be very ripe; as ripe as you can get them Robbie".

When the onions had fried for ages, it seemed to me, he poured the finely chopped mushy tomatoes into the onions and stirred. Then he added pepper and salt.

"Lots of salt and pepper, Robbie, lots."

He used a spoon and sampled the mixture.

"Right. We're ready. Call the others."

"Is that what we're eating for breakfast? Did I give up my fried eggs and bacon for this?"

"Not quite Robbie. Watch this."

Tony smoothed the mixture in the pan and then cracked an egg over it. He broke the yolk with a fork and whipped the mixture so that the white and the yolk seeped down filling the holes in the mixture as it cooked. He stirred and cracked eight more eggs into the mixture of onion and tomato.

"*That* is what you gave up your eggs and bacon for. Come and eat." I piled my plate high. The others sat down at the breakfast table. It was delicious. I decided that losing my role as breakfast chef wasn't so bad after all.

The Taylors and the Maythams departed for home after breakfast. We returned to admiring the view from the veranda.

Irving turned to me and said. "I'm going into Hoedspruit to fetch my brother and his family later. They arrive here at midday. Hope you and Margie will be able to stand it?"

"Come on Irv. I am sure he's not as bad as you make out. Anyway we are here just till the collaring and then we're off to Sabie Bungalows. I'm sure that we can stand being with your family for that short period of time, even if they are as bad as you make out. Does your brother know yet?"

"No. I've decided I'm not going to tell him. I think I'll tell his son, Richard. He can tell Brian."

"Why don't you tell Brian, Irv? I mean we all know, why not him? He is your brother, after all."

"*Ag*! Can't be bothered really. I'll tell Richard and he can tell his father. You'll see what I mean when they arrive."

"I can't wait," I said sarcastically, "actually Irv, I think you are a shit judge of character. I bet your brother is a bloody decent guy. In fact, I think you are scared to tell your brother what you intend doing, and so you are taking the chicken run and telling his son. Secretly I actually think you are frightened of upsetting your brother."

Irving snorted and raised his binoculars to watch a herd of elephants across the river. I saw movement out of the corner of my eye and turned my head. It was Martin, our ranger.

I waved a hand in greeting. "Hi Martin. How you doing?"

Martin was carrying a piece of paper in his hand and wore a worried expression on his face. He glanced at me and then turned to Irving who had put the binoculars down and was watching Martin approach.

"Hi Irving."

Irving smiled and held up a hand in greeting.

"What brings you here Martin? You're too early for the game drive. Anyway we're about to depart for Hoedspruit."

"I've just received this email; you had better have a look at it."

"Why? Is it about the collaring tomorrow?"

"No, not quite. Here—have a look." Martin passed the email to Irving. Irving read the email. He furrowed his brow and looked irritated. He passed the mail to me. I read it out aloud. By this time Margie, Steve and Helen had joined us.

Dear Martin

We have a report that members of the Rhino Poaching syndicate that has been so active are in our area. We have names and are checking with all akomodation places in the area of their guests. Please submit by return the names of people staying at present at Fig Bush Lodge.

Thank you.

Inspectr Sizwe Velapansi.

Endangered Wildlife Division. South African Police Services

"Are they active in this area?" asked Irving, looking at Martin.

"Who? The Endangered Wildlife people? Oh, you mean the rhino poachers. Well, they're all over. We haven't had too much trouble here up to now, though."

"They are obviously taking precautions, aren't they? Bastards. Killing the rhino. Shit. They use the horns as aphrodisiacs don't they? Give me the email, Robbie."

Irving scanned the page. "Shit man, is this from the police? They can't even spell. Look at it. No wonder you have a high crime rate with a police force like this. Look how he spells accommodation." He chuckled to himself.

"So, can you write down the names of yourself and all your guests?" asked Martin, slightly sheepishly. "Including those that you are fetching from Hoedspruit today."

"My brother and his family?"

Martin nodded.

Irving spotted a folio pad lying in the kitchen, tore a page out and wrote down the names of each of us staying there.

"What about the Taylors and the Maythams? They've been here but have already left."

"You had better include them," Martin answered.

I smiled to myself; the revenge I had planned to wreak on Irving seemed to be working—and he was unsuspecting. Martin could have been nominated for an Oscar for his performance so far. I wondered if we'd be able to take my joke to its end.

Irving scribbled away, then triumphantly passed the list to Martin.

"There. Total bullshit really, isn't it? I mean, do my friends and me look like rhino poachers?"

"You'd be very surprised," answered Martin, "some very respectable people have been caught as part of the syndicates currently operating in this area."

"Ja. But what good is getting our names going to do?"

Martin shrugged. "Well, maybe they have names of suspects, I don't know. Anyway, we have the names now and that should keep the cops happy. Thank you." Then, changing the subject, he said, "So are you off just now to fetch your new guests?"

His gaze was drawn, as though by a magnet, to a bin piled high with empty bottles of Chocolate Block. I saw his eyes widen in surprise and he commented, "You guys have had quite a party here, haven't you?"

"Quite a party," said Irving, grinning, "and it's still going on."

Martin smiled. "Thanks for this Irving. I'll see you all later for the game drive?"

He left us and Irving studied the email that he had delivered. I was worried in case he smelt a rat, but needn't have bothered.

Irving snorted and tossed the email onto the table.

"Have you seen how they spell, Robbie? Can't even spell correctly—how are they going to catch any poachers?"

"Come on Irv, everyone spells badly on emails, don't they?"

"Not like this," he said waving a hand in the direction of the message lying on the table.

"Anyway, I'm going to my room for a bit. Have to leave for Hoedspruit in an hour to fetch the family."

He walked off to his room. I sat and watched the elephants over the river through his wonderful binoculars. They really were impressive. An hour later Irving returned to the deck where I was sitting, still watching the elephants who had now been joined by a herd of impala.

I looked up and noticed his eyes were red.

"You off then Irv?" I asked.

He nodded. "Listen Robbie, if you see me crying at any point, don't think it's about my own death. It's about Yvonne, how she suffered and how I miss her. That's all it's about."

"Okay Irv, I'll remember that."

"See you in a few hours—enjoy my glasses."

A few moments later I heard the noise of his vehicle fading into the distance as he disappeared into the bush.

I switched my attention to studying the birdlife across the river. Through Irving's binoculars even the smallest detail was visible. So engrossed was I that I didn't hear Steve and Helen approach. It was only when they sat down at the table that I noticed them. I put down the binoculars. Steve blew his nose loudly on a handkerchief and Helen was clutching some tissues. I noticed that Helen's eyes were red, as if she had been crying, so were Steve's.

"You guys okay?" I asked, "what's happened? Your brother hasn't ...?" I looked at Steve.

"No, no, he's okay, as far as I know," said Steve.

Helen explained, "No. It's Irving, Rob."

"Yes. It's bloody pathetic, isn't it?"

"We've just been to talk to him in his room."

I must have looked surprised.

Helen added, "Before he left, while you were sitting here. We went to his room to talk to him."

"I don't suppose you had any joy? I've tried as well, but I don't think any of us will change his mind."

"No, it wasn't that; well, we tried as well. We went to see him now to offer to find his body after he kills himself. Remember, we were talking the other night as to who was going to find him?"

I nodded.

"I couldn't bear to think of him lying there, dead, all alone. So Steve and I discussed it and decided we would volunteer."

"Well, that's really good of the two of you. Don't think I could volunteer for a job like that, even if I lived in England. I admire your guts."

"It isn't something that we want to do. We just felt that we should offer." Helen's eyes brimmed with tears and her nose was shiny red. She sniffed and wiped her nose with a tissue.

Silence descended as each of us thought of finding Irving's lifeless body. A pigeon cooed from the bushes alongside the river. I broke the heavy silence.

"How will you know when he has done it?"

"That's what we have been discussing; we've worked out a code. He will send us an email asking us to come to tea at eleven o clock the day after; and that will be it."

The silence descended again.

"So you think he is going to do it?" I asked.

Helen nodded vehemently. "Oh yes. I am pretty sure."

"When?"

"I don't know," she replied.

Steve shrugged then added, "Pretty sure it will be quite soon after he goes back. He says he has a few things still to sort out. I know he's going to stay with the Maythams and the Taylors when he leaves here, and he thinks he'll go back home about the middle of February."

"Yes, he told me that a painting of his is going on auction—an Irish auction of art. I think he said it was taking place on 9 February. I know he's waiting to see what he gets for it."

"It's not another Frank Auerbach, is it?"

I laughed. "No, this time it's a Yeats—brother of the poet. It's called 'The Cat Among the Stars'. Not in the same league as the Frank Auerbach, although I'm sure it's worth a few bob. I wonder what difference it makes to him what it goes for?"

"It'll make a difference to those in his will, not to him. Do you know who is getting his money, Robbie?"

I shrugged and shook my head. "No, not really, although he has mentioned a couple of people, like his friend, Ray, in France."

"What about you?" asked Helen leaning forward. She had stopped crying, but still sniffed and dabbed at her nose with a screwed up tissue.

"No, afraid not. Well, if I am he hasn't mentioned it. At least you are getting some of his vintage firewood, aren't you?"

"So he says. My God, he's a strange bloke isn't he? Now he's gone off to meet his brother that he doesn't like. You know he's paid all the costs of his brother's son and kids to fly out from the USA, plus of course he's paying for all of us to stay here. That's quite a tidy sum, I'm sure. Yvonne would never have done that I can assure you."

"Not?" I asked.

"Never in a thousand years," said Helen. "And he goes on about his brother, and how he feels bad about imposing him on us. Bit of a joke really. I bet his brother and his wife are really nice people."

"Well, you know Irving, don't you? I met his brother years ago. Good guy. Why don't we make a big performance of welcoming them when they arrive? Make them feel glad to be here."

"Great idea," said Margie, who had joined us. I saw that Margie had noticed the red-rimmed eyes of Steve and Helen. She looked at me and raised an eyebrow quizzically. Just then we heard the sound of a car engine approaching. So the four of us, glasses of Chocolate Block in hand, went and stood next to the parking area, as a welcoming party for Irving and his family. As they climbed out of the vehicle all four of us prostrated ourselves on the ground, arms outstretched in salute. The two children, climbing off the vehicle, looked at us in amazement, as did the adults.

Irving let out a roar of laughter: "What on earth are you buggers doing?"

"We are greeting your family, Irving. If they are your family they have to be very important people."

I shook Brian's hand. He was a good-looking man with open features. Despite being five years older, he looked like a younger version of Irving, without the beard. His sparkling blue eyes looked earnestly into mine as he shook my hand warmly.

"Hi Brian. We met some years ago."

"Of course we did. I remember you well, and Irv has often talked about you."

He turned and introduced the lady next to him, who looked slightly dazed by the welcome they had received.

"This is Brenda, my wife, my son Richard, and his two children, my grandchildren, Blake and Annika, all the way from Las Vegas."

I looked at Brenda and was impressed by her calm and grace, evident from the way she carried herself, with a dignified air. She was a pleasant looking woman and despite searching I could see no evidence of the dreaded RC factor that Irving was so uptight about. The two children looked around with wide eyes.

I directed my comment to the children.

"Las Vegas, hey? Wow! Now here you are in Africa. Come and have some tea and then we'll be off for a game drive."

We helped carry their luggage onto the veranda where tea had been set out. Martin was already there, holding a saucer in his left hand and sipping from a cup of tea. He winked at me as I approached.

"Hello Irving," said Martin. "Could I have a word with you before the drive? Won't take a minute." Martin put his cup down, wiped the palms of his hands on his thighs, and took a folded letter from his top pocket. He unfolded the letter.

Irving looked slightly irritated. "What's this about Martin?"

"Well, it's just that I've had a reply from the Endangered Species people about the email that I sent this morning; you know, my response to the one I showed you?"

Irving nodded.

"Well, I've had their reply—this is it."

Martin held out the letter to Irving, who had a suitcase in each hand. Brian and his family were listening to the conversation.

"What's this Irving?" asked Brian, "the Endangered Species division? They're quite on the ball you know?"

"Ja, ja," said Irving, then he asked Martin: "What do they say? Read it out." Martin read the email, stumbling over the spelling errors.

Thank you for informaton. Do thes people have wepons with them or helicopter? Plees let us know if any attempt to hire helikopter. we have name of I. tucker, british citizen as one of thos possibly involved in plans to poach rino. We are not sure if he is same one. Can you send description of I Tucker?

Sorry for causing you work.

regards

Inspektor Sizwe Velapanzi. Endangred Wild Life Division.

South African Polce Services

There was a stunned silence. Then Irving let out a shout: "What! What's that? I. Tucker—that's my fucking name! Here, let me see that."

He dropped the suitcases he was carrying, grabbed the email from Martin's hand and scanned the page swiftly.

"Come on, this is bullshit! I mean, how do they have my name? Send a description?" he muttered, reading the message. "Shit. They think I'm a rhino poacher ... hire a helicopter ... of course there's a helicopter chartered for tomorrow's collaring. Bullshit man, how can they possibly think I would be involved in rhino poaching? Tell them to fuck off Martin."

Irving's face was flushed with indignation. I looked away, hiding the smile tugging at the corners of my lips.

"I can't do that," said Martin, his face straight and sombre. "You don't mess with these people. I need to send your description, seeing as they have asked me, and also inform them that we have chartered a helicopter."

"Well, we haven't. It's Michelle and her elephant people. I mean we aren't involved, it's just that I am paying for it."

I could see that Martin was struggling not to laugh.

"Yes, Irving, you *are* paying for it, aren't you? That means that you are responsible for what the helicopter does, doesn't it?"

"Well, not really Martin. I mean, I'm paying an overall price for the collaring, something like forty thousand rand. I don't know how that's broken up. You'll have to talk to Michelle, the elephant lady, she'll be here tonight. She's the one responsible for the helicopter charter."

Martin put his hand into the top pocket of his bush jacket and pulled out an iPhone.

"Just stand there, please Irving," he said, indicating a place in the sunlight on the veranda.

Irving looked incredulous. "What on earth for Martin?"

"I'm going to take your photo and send it to the Endangered Species people by email. Wonderful thing technology.? Easier than trying to provide a description of you. Just mail a photo." He looked pleased with himself.

Martin held up the phone in front of his face to take the picture. Irving looked as though he was going to explode—and didn't move.

"You can't be serious Martin? Shit man, you aren't going through with this are you?"

"Have to Irving, these people are serious, even if they can't spell. I also need you to sign an affidavit as to what you are doing here. I'll have to go and fetch it. It came as an attachment but I left it at the office. Unfortunately it has to be witnessed by a Justice of the Peace and I need to send it back today, tomorrow at the latest, so unfortunately you will have to go back to Hoedspruit, to a police station or magistrate; that's the nearest JP to here."

"What?! Do we *all* have to do that?"

'No, just you. They're only interested in you, it would appear. Come on, come and stand here where I can get a pic."

Irving let out a groan, and moved a few paces to the spot that Martin had indicated.

While they were talking I had snatched a sheet of paper from the table in the kitchen and scribbled on it with a black koki pen lying nearby. Irving was so wound up that he didn't notice what I was doing.

"I can't believe this is happening," he said, looking at the ground and shaking his head, "I really can't believe this is happening. Hoedspruit is forty kilometres away; I'll have to go back today. We've got the collaring tomorrow."

"I thought you said we were going to be briefed by Michelle and the elephant people this evening? Will you be back in time?" Helen asked.

"Oh shit! What a bugger up. I don't know that I *will* get back in time."

Irving was now in position for the photo. Martin held the iPhone in front of him and looked at the screen. Irving posed. Quietly, I moved behind Irving and stood there, holding my piece of paper above Irving's head. Above the paper I held my two fingers in a 'V'. Smiles tickled the faces of all those watching, including the two children. Irving had no idea what was going on behind his back. Everyone watching started to giggle, hiding their faces behind their hands. Irving stood still, glaring straight at the iPhone in Martin's hand, still unaware of what was happening

Martin took the picture.

"Hang on, Irving. Don't move. Let's make sure you're happy with it." He glanced down at the picture in the iPhone and smiled broadly. "Very good. Do you want to see it, Irving?" Without waiting for an answer he walked over to Irving, who was still spluttering and cursing at having to go into Hoedspruit, and held out the iPhone for Irving to approve the photo.

"That's fine." And then he registered what he was looking at. "Wait! What the shit is that?" He was looking at a picture of himself, but above his head was the paper with the words 'JOKE'S ON YOU!' and above the sign were my two fingers held in a V—the internationally recognized symbol for 'FUCK YOU'.

A look of realisation and relief spread over Irving's face. His face broke into a broad grin and he let out a roar.

"Robbie you bastard! It was you the whole time? It's your doing. I should have guessed. You sent those bloody emails. You've been taking the piss out of me. You little sod! I'll get you for this! Anyway, well done. You had me going for a while." He charged at me and punched my arm. "You shit! How could you do that to me?"

There were howls of laughter from Brian and his family, the children laughed louder than anyone else. Helen laughed so hard that tears ran down her cheeks. Even Steve, who rarely displayed emotion, was chuckling so much that his body shook like a man on a giant vibrator.

"I'll get you back, you bugger!" Irving promised, earnestly.

"No Irv, I got *you* back. That's for what you did to me in Cape Town."

I watched Brian and his family as they disappeared up the path, waiting until they were out of earshot.

"Actually Irv, to tell you the truth, I was quite reluctant to pull this trick on you, in the light of what you could do back to me. In fact you could play the perfect joke on me in view of what you are planning."

He looked puzzled. "What do you mean?"

"Well, here you are, about to kill yourself. Let's say you do it with a gun." Again I pictured the walls, blood dripping down. "You shoot yourself but manage to get my fingerprints or DNA onto the handle of the gun you use, and you frame me with your murder. I mean, I wouldn't stand a chance would I?"

He laughed. "Very good Robbie, very good. Wish I had thought of it. I could really have had you." He stopped laughing and said, seriously, "I wouldn't do that to you Robbie. You are my friend. Look, I'm wearing this copper bracelet you gave me to prove it." He held his arm up for me to see. "My jokes are fun. That one would be too dangerous to play. Besides I won't be using a gun."

"Why? How are you going to do it?"

"I'm not saying Robbie, but it's all worked out. Don't worry. It won't be messy."

"I hope you haven't involved anyone else, have you?"

He shook his head. "No. I've worked it all out myself, from my own experience and, of course, the internet is a wonderful thing you know?"

I saw Brian and his family approaching for the game drive and whispered my response so that they could not overhear: "If you're determined to do it, just don't fuck it up Irv, just don't fuck it up."

We returned earlier than usual from the game drive that evening, to attend the briefing about the next day's elephant collaring. When we arrived at Rock Fig Lodge a small crowd of additional guests had gathered and were standing around in twos and threes, awaiting the arrival of Michelle and other Save The Elephants personnel. The extra people were guests from the main Tanda Tula Lodge who would be joining us for the collaring. More chairs were brought out and about thirty people waited expectantly.

Michelle and three others arrived in a flurry, carrying rolled-up maps and documents and Michelle outlined the procedure for the morning.

"Those of you who were here last year will remember that we collared an elephant and named it 'Yvonne'. Unfortunately, the elephant chosen didn't suit the name, as it was a bull. A male. It was a bit like that song 'A Boy called Sue'. In this case it was a boy called Yvonne." There was a ripple of laughter from the audience. Damn! I thought, she's pinched *my* line. Michelle continued: "This year, we are again going to collar and rename an elephant. But, to make life less confusing, we are going to rename Yvonne, giving 'her', the bull elephant, the more appropriate name of 'Irving'. And then tomorrow's elephant, who is a female, will be named 'Yvonne'."

I glanced at Irving sitting next to me, his eyes glistening with emotion.

Michelle went on to show us the movements of the collared elephants in the park over the past few months, some having travelled thousands of kilometres over the year. She explained about the intelligence of elephants and how in Zambia the elephants knew the reserve areas where they were safe from local villagers. So much so that if they wished to travel to another reserve and had to pass through territory which was not a reserve, they would travel at night to escape detection by the locals.

After supper that night Irving and I found ourselves the last two sitting next to the fire. Everyone else had retired early in preparation for the collaring the next morning. Irving threw a log onto the fire.

"Chocolate Block, Robbie?" As he held up the bottle, head cocked enquiringly.

I held out my glass. The ruby red liquid gurgled as he filled the glass.

"So, are you and Margie off after the collaring tomorrow?"

I nodded and sipped the wine.

Irving looked pensive as he stared into the fire.

"When do you go home Irv?"

"Well, I'm going from here to the Maythams place, near Louis Trichardt. I'll be there for a few days and then I'll go to the Taylors; then back to the UK on the twelfth of the month. I have to stay at the Maythams because communication is better there and I want to see what that painting goes for at the auction on the ninth."

"You mean the Yeats?"

He nodded.

"So will you be coming back to us? We'll go from here to our time share at Sabie Bungalows and then back home, so we'll be in Joburg when you come down to catch your plane," I reminded him. "Presumably you'll come and stay the night on your way back, before you fly out, won't you?"

"No, I don't think so Robbie. I'll drive down from the Taylors and go straight to the airport."

"So ..." I said slowly, "... are you saying that we won't see you again, after we leave here tomorrow?"

"Looks like it, Robbie."

"That's a bit of a bummer, Irv."

He smiled ruefully. We both watched the flames hungrily licking the logs on the fire.

"So ... in effect tomorrow will be goodbye?"

"Afraid so," he said still looking into the fire.

"You definitely going to do this?"

"*Ja.*"

"Are you dreading it?"

He laughed and shook his head.

"No, actually, I'm looking forward to it."

"I don't believe that."

We were both quiet. When I could no longer bear my feeling of helplessness I broke the silence.

"How will I know when you have done it?"

"I will be seeing Michael Hess, Yvonne's brother, when I get back. Before the time. He will be one of the executors of my will and I will give him a list of people to contact. So you'll receive a phone call from him."

"Well, anyway, we will talk again before that happens and you can tell me when you are going to do it. You don't have to tell me how, but I would like to know when."

"Maybe Robbie, maybe."

We were both quiet for a few more minutes, sipping our wine. I still found it hard to believe that this man who was so full of life and fun was going to end it all. When I had emptied my glass I looked at him.

"Is there anything I can say or do that might change your mind, Irving?"

"Absolutely nothing."

He was quiet for a few moments, then continued: "Don't see it as something sad. Think about it as something that I want to do. As I told you, I've had a great life. I know that I'm still relatively young. I miss Yvonne every minute of the day and night, Robbie. I am lonely, but I don't want to start all over. Nobody can ever replace Yvonne, so I'm just marking time by being here. I've had a fantastic time but when Yvonne went, it ended. It's just that I am choosing when and how."

I grimaced and stood up. "I'm going to bed. Of course it's sad. Don't you have any consideration for your friends? We love you Irv, I've known you for years and years; think what effect this is having on us."

"I'm aware of that Robbie, and I'm sorry. But it's what I want. I can't say that I'm not aware of your feelings, and I am sorry to be the cause of your sadness."

"Well. That's quite easy to stop isn't it? Just don't do it."

"Afraid that's not going to happen, Robbie." He swallowed hard. I saw his Adam's apple do a jig. His eyes filled with tears and he looked away. I blinked hard, trying to control my own tears.

"Christ! You are a difficult bugger, Tucker. The problem is though, that we all still care about you. In a way I wish we didn't. Would be a lot easier. Oh well," I sighed, "I better go to bed before I lose it with you, you silly old bugger."

He put his hand on my shoulder, squeezed it.

"Don't worry about it, Robbie. Good night my old friend."

He turned and walked away. I watched as the black night swallowed him.

Chapter Twenty-two

A BOY CALLED SUE

Despite the excitement of the elephant collaring I woke up feeling flat. I realized why as I was trying to shake off the thin veneer of sleep that had come and gone throughout a disturbed night. A light sleep, combined with the now chronic dream of bloody walls, made for scratchy eyes.

It was still dark when we arrived at the airfield, our rendezvous point, where we were to wait for the arrival of the helicopter. Steaming cups of coffee burned the lips while we stood around in the dark. Brian and Brenda's two grandchildren, Blake and Annika, were beside themselves with excitement..

"Where's the elephant, Irving?" asked Annika.

Irving was holding her hand in his. "We will see the ellie only when they dart her. She's somewhere in those trees at the moment, they spotted her yesterday evening," he said, gesturing in the direction of dark shadows marking a cluster of mimosa trees which sheltered the herd of elephants.

As the sun peeped over the horizon, almost as if it had signalled to the helicopter, a tiny spot like a gnat appeared in the lightening sky. Its buzz became audible as it approached, growing larger in size. The chopper landed twenty metres from us and was idling, its rotor blades swishing the air when Irving asked, "Do you want to come up Robbie? You'll get a good view of the darting from up there."

"I'd love to Irv."

But Michelle, who was walking towards the machine, overheard us, turned and said, "Afraid that's not possible, Irving. There is room for only one other," as she climbed into the helicopter.

Irving took the last seat and, engines growling, the chopper lifted off, swung its nose into the wind and then, nose tilted earthwards, roared over our heads with inches to spare, to seek out the future 'Yvonne'.

The helicopter disappeared over the trees now standing out sharply against the early morning sky. We clambered onto the Land Cruisers and in a convoy of five vehicles set off in the direction of the herd. I noticed that one of the vehicles carried a group of about ten rangers from the Parks Board, all armed with rifles. We stopped on the side of the track and waited. The helicopter buzzed over the trees, diving and swooping and then climbing higher, to swoop down again and repeat the procedure.

"They've spotted her," shouted one of the rangers, from a vehicle where he was listening to radio communications from the chopper. He started the engine of the Land Cruiser and beckoned over his shoulder for us to follow. The five vehicles bucked and bounced through the scrub while we hung on grimly. The lead vehicle stopped in a clearing and the rest of us pulled up behind. A dust cloud passed over our heads and dissipated. Ahead of us the helicopter danced and dived, disappearing behind the mimosa trees.

"They've darted her. Careful! Here she comes."

The elephant burst out of the scrub some fifty metres from the vehicles, ears flapping slowly, trunk swaying. She saw our vehicles in her path and changed direction. The chopper buzzed overhead trying to shepherd her onto the road. She stumbled, as if she had tripped, and then slowly her legs bent as if she was about to kneel, she gently and silently fell over onto her side. The drug in the dart sticking into her rump had done its work.

We leapt from the vehicles and one of the vets immediately pulled an ear over the elephant's eyes to protect it from the direct sunlight. A bevy of vets and scientists then went to work taking blood samples, dabbing ointment and antiseptic on cuts and wounds, taking samples of hair.

The ten armed rangers had taken up positions in a semi-circle, weapons held ready to fire, each facing outwards about twenty metres from where the elephant lay. We heard the sounds of branches crackling and the earth shook as the rest of the female herd, with a young calf, burst into sight.

"Look out!" shouted the head ranger. "That's her calf! The baby wants to get to the mother!"

The calf charged towards the rangers standing between it and the sleeping mother on the ground. Two of the rangers took flight, a third lifted his rifle to his shoulder and took aim. Ears flapping and trumpeting in frustration, the calf changed direction at the last moment, slowed and then stood looking at the rangers, trunk swaying from side to side

The armed wardens shouted and waved their arms to distract the elephants. The calf looked at the elephant lying on the ground, looked at the game rangers shouting and waving their arms in the air, shook its trunk and reluctantly wandered away to join the rest of the herd in the trees, where they stopped and watched the collaring from a safe distance.

When the samples and tests had been completed and photos had been taken, Michelle delivered the antidote while we all watched from the vehicles. A minute passed. Then the elephant stirred, shook her head and clambered to her feet. She stood swaying slightly, ears flapping slowly, trunk swinging. Then, seeing her calf and the other elephants waiting for her, she trumpeted happily and lumbered off to join her family. Spontaneous applause broke out from the enraptured audience in the vehicles.

"That was wonderful," said Irving, "absolutely, bloody marvellous." He beamed with delight and hugged his great-nephew, Blake. "Wasn't that great, kids?"

The two looked as though they had been given the keys to a sweet shop. Their faces shone with delight at the extraordinary experience, prompting me to think how different their lives must be, living in Las Vegas.

As we approached Rock Fig Lodge for the last time I felt the same sinking feeling in the pit of my stomach that I had last experienced when returning to boarding school, some sixty years ago. I looked at Irving. If he was feeling the same he certainly wasn't showing it as he laughed and joked with Blake and Annika.

Everyone gathered on the veranda to say goodbye while Margie and I collected our suitcases, loaded them into the car and returned to the group. Irving looked up as he heard us approaching, smiled and stood up.

"You guys ready?"

I nodded.

"Yep. Ready to go."

Helen was watching me carefully. My throat felt tight. My emotions were under control but only just, bubbling beneath the surface.

We said our farewells to Brian and his family. I shook Steve's hand and hugged Helen.

"Stay in touch," she said, "give us a call when we get back to the UK."

"You mean Oswestry, the capital city of Europe?"

She smiled shakily, "Yes. Stay in touch." Her eyes were brimming.

I swallowed hard and looked at Irving. He looked pale and tense. Margie stood next to me surreptitiously wiping her eyes.

"Well Irv. This is goodbye," I choked.

His eyes filled with tears and he blinked to hide the fact, his face flushing.

"Cheers Robbie, see you," he said lamely.

"Don't think so, Irv."

I hugged him and felt the wet where his tears had escaped and trickled down his cheek. He sniffed hard and blew his nose loudly.

Brian and his family stood watching. I saw Brian frown in confusion at the emotion on display and remembered that he had not been told of Irving's plan.

"This is difficult isn't it Robbie? Shit! I hadn't thought about this."

"Not too late to change your plan, is it, Irv?"

Brian looked at us quizzically but was too perplexed, or sensitive, to interrupt.

Irving shook his head. "I'm not doing that." He sniffed. "Look, Robbie," he took the copper bangle we had given him and held it out to me, "you had better keep this Robbie, you wear it."

I looked at him. The tears were trickling down his cheeks, and his voice caught as he stifled a sob.

Brian looked from me to Irving and back again, bewildered and concerned.

"Why are you giving that bracelet back to Robbie, Irving? Robbie gave it to you and I heard you say it was a symbol of your friendship. You shouldn't—"

"*Ag!* Robbie knows … it makes my arm go black from the copper. I can't wear those things."

"I don't see any black mark," said Brian.

"Don't worry Brian. It's okay. I'll wear it as a token of our friendship. I understand … copper does give lots of people a black mark on the arm."

I slipped the copper bangle onto my right arm, having great difficulty controlling my emotions. It felt as though a battle was taking place inside me. I turned abruptly, shouted, "Cheers everyone!" and turned my back to hide the tears I was unable to contain. I grabbed Margie by the arm and led her hastily to the car, with tears running down my cheeks.

As soon as the doors closed I turned the ignition and before anyone could walk up to the car for another round of farewells I slammed the car into reverse. The wheels skidded backwards and we roared out of the parking area without looking back. Margie and I were unable to speak for some time; our silence broken only by the occasional sniff and blowing of noses. After about five kilometres I looked at her; her nose shone like Rudolph's and her mascara had run.

"Fuck!" I said weakly. "I hope I never have to say goodbye to anyone like that again in my life."

Margie nodded sadly. "Me too. Me too."

∽

The peace and sanity of Sabie, after the frenzy of Rock Fig Lodge and the week of black humour which had eventually worn us down, was a welcome relief. But of course Irving was very much on our minds.

We received an email from Helen and Steve who had returned to Oswestry. Helen told us how upset Irving had been the day we left Rock Fig Lodge.

"Irv was in a very bad place when you left; I know that he cried a lot but hid his feelings by wanting to be on his own." She added that Irving had told Richard, his nephew, about his plan, but not his brother, Brian.

After a few days I phoned Irving. He was still with the Maythams, at their guest lodge near Louis Trichardt.

He sounded cheerful when he answered the phone.

"Just wanted to thank you for the week we had with you, Irv. Also for the newspaper cuttings you sent to Sam." (He had sent my daughter some newspaper articles about the violence in the townships, in 1993.) "She would have called you herself only I know what she would have said to you, so told her I would call on her behalf."

"My pleasure, Robbie. It was a fun week wasn't it? Lots of laughs. I hope Sam liked the pictures?"

"Oh yes, she's going to frame them and hang them in her lounge. Tell me, what happened to the auction of 'Cat among the Stars'—have they had it yet?"

"Yes they have had it, but no the Yeats didn't sell. They think because of the politics in Ireland at the moment. Unfortunately I would have taken a lower price but the auction house couldn't get hold of me and didn't know, so I've still got it."

"Does that mean that all plans are cancelled? At least until the Yeats is sold? Say 'yes' Irv?"

"Afraid not Robbie. Just have to work out what to do with it."

I was tempted to say that I would take good care of it as I really liked it, but I didn't offer.

"I'll call you from the airport on the way through in a few days' time," he said.

A few days later, in the evening, I was sitting in my study writing when the phone rang.

"Hello" I said.

"Hello Robbie".

"Hi Irv. Good to hear from you. How are you doing?"

"No, Robbie. It's Brian. Irving's brother."

"Sorry Brian, you sounded just like Irv. So sorry. How are you and the family?"

"Thanks Robbie, we are all fine. We had a great time up in Tanda Tula with you chaps. It was good spending time with you and Irving. We had a lot of laughs."

"Yes we did, didn't we?"

"Robbie, I hope you don't mind me calling you but ..."

"I think I know what you are going to ask me, Brian."

"Well, Robbie, after you left, Irving told Richard, he didn't tell me or Brenda, that he is going to ... to ... to kill himself. I mean, is that right? Has he said anything to you?"

"Yes Brian. He has. That is what he says he is going to do."

"I don't believe it—do you know why? I mean, what reason has he got to kill himself?"

"Well, Brian, he says he doesn't want to live anymore, after losing Yvonne."

"Really?"

"Yes, but it's a bit more than that. He also says he doesn't want to have anyone that he doesn't know wiping his bum for him, in his senior years. Well, that's how he put it."

"Did he say that?" There was silence while Brian digested this piece of information. "I don't think he'll do it, do you Robbie?"

"I'm not so sure, Brian. I wish I could agree with you but I can't. I am pretty sure now the odds are that he will."

"Really? I think my mom must have affected him. She was bedridden for the last nine years of her life. Then my father went on to live until age one hundred and one. But surely he isn't serious? You don't think he will really do it, do you?"

"I'm afraid I think it's very probable, Brian."

"I wonder why he didn't tell me. He told Richard, my son. You know that we haven't always got on, don't you?"

"Yes, he told us."

"We were very close growing up. He was always one step ahead of me, you know, even though I was a few years older. Later on he became very difficult. I think it was really after he married Yvonne. Don't know what to do about it. I suppose it's my fault that I have allowed our relationship to drift for so long. Too late now, I suppose."

"Why don't you phone him and bury the hatchet? It's really never too late to do that, is it?"

"You think?"

"Definitely. Particularly now. You don't want him not to have closure, sort of unfinished business? And you don't want that for yourself, either."

"I might just do that," said Brian.

On Tuesday, 15 February, ironically the day of my daughter Sam's birthday, Irving called me from Oliver Tambo airport.

'Hi Robbie. Just wanted to say thanks for everything."

"Well, I hope you had a good time?"

"Absolutely. Had a great time with you guys and then with the Maythams and Taylors this last week. Gale took me to a school that a friend of hers runs for underprivileged children. Most impressive. The woman is doing a great job. So, I'm going to ensure that she gets something."

"What do you mean? In your will?"

I felt an unwelcome pang of anger and jealousy.

A Boy Called Sue

"*Ja*, instead of that Haga school where they were robbing me."

"Come on Irv, Just because the headmistress went on leave ..." I didn't finish the sentence.

"Anyway. Just wanted to say how much your and Margie's friendship has meant to me. It meant a lot to Yvonne as well. Thank you both."

"Are we going to talk to one another again Irv? Or is this it? Are you going back now to .... to kill yourself?"

"No, we'll talk some more Robbie. Not doing it straight away. Some loose ends still to be tied. No. We'll have plenty of chance to talk. Michael, Yvonne's brother, is coming down at the end of the month to spend a day with me, to sort out a few last details."

"I thought you didn't like him?"

"Not much, but I've made him one of the executors of the estate. He'll be coming down to go through things with me and I'm not going to put up with any of his crap."

"What do you mean? Does he try to talk you out of your plan?"

"No, not at all. Quite the opposite—just doesn't discuss it. Strange chap. Anyway I'll spell it out to him. He'll just have to face up to it now. Okay Robbie, I better go. We'll talk again soon. I'll give you a call when I get home. Bye for now."

"Cheers Irv. Safe flight," I responded, lamely.

Over the next few days there was a flurry of emails and telephone calls between Helen and myself, both of us expressing our sadness and frustration at Irving's determination to kill himself.

There was no news from Irving.

Margie and I discussed the matter continually. As the days passed the tension increased; our edges began to fray and I found myself becoming irritated at the smallest thing. My tours also became harder to do; my mind kept wandering off history and settling on Irving and what could be done to stop him. I also wondered what he was going to do with all his money. He hadn't mentioned his will again. I was sure that if we were included he would have said something, or at least hinted at it.

I sent him an email and copied Helen and Storm, suggesting that maybe if they all wrote a similar mail we could succeed in changing his mind.

From: Robin Binckes <robin@spearofthenation.co.za>
Subject: YOU
Date: 18 February 2011 10:22:14 AM SAST
To: Tucker Irving IYTucker@aol.com
Hi Irv,

I haven't heard from you since you arrived back? How was the flight? How are you doing? The emails between your friends and I have been buzzing. Much as you might be unaware, your decision has caused us much grief and distress.

At this late stage I am begging you to change your mind. I surely don't need to tell you that we love you greatly and don't want you to GO!?!!! You are a difficult old bugger, but a very loveable one! We love you dearly and yes you have lost Yvonne and life will never be the same. However, you have a circle of friends in the UK and South Africa who don't just like you, they adore you. Think of us. Think of African sunsets to come, think of Chocolate Block and all the unopened bottles of wine still to be enjoyed?!! Think of laughter and camp fires under that wonderful star-filled African sky that you love so much, despite your complaints about the country! Most of all, think of your friends and what your going is going to do to them. Think of your art and what more you could see. Think of Yvonne and the fact that she told you to get on with your life. Think of us.

We love you Irv. Don't do this silly thing. You have so much to offer us all. DO NOT DO THIS.

OUR LOVE.

THE BINCKES FAMILY!!!!!!

I was filled with hope that he might, just might be reconsidering, when I received his reply the same day.

On 18 Feb 2011, at 8:00 PM, IYTUCKER@aol.com wrote:
Rob thank you so much for this, you had me in tears. You are a good man!!

I was encouraged by his response and felt that maybe his friends and I were making progress; perhaps some of our arguments were having an effect on his decision. I was pleased that I had encouraged Helen and Steve and the Maythams to write to him, to explain how strongly they felt about his course of action. Maybe, just maybe, our combined pressure against his plan might dissuade him from going ahead.

That same day I received a full and descriptive email from the Maythams in which Storm told us how Irving had been during his stay with them. He had obviously enjoyed himself immensely. He, Storm and Al had been on a Boer war tour of the area known as the Skirmishes Route and he had loved every minute of it. The following day they had taken Irving to meet a friend of theirs who farmed in the area. Irving had given the farmer friend advice on the rearing and slaughtering of chickens and ducks. Storm commented that, "Irv is really a fountain of knowledge; an amazing practical and capable man."

Then she described how she had taken him to see the outreach project run by Leigh, a friend of hers, which Irving had told me about when he called me from the airport. Even though I knew about it, my stomach lurched with disappointment. Irving had been so impressed with Leigh's work that he had described his disappointment with the school at Haga Haga and had told Leigh that he would support her project instead.

Storm described how they had enjoyed (hardly the correct word) a 'last supper' with Irving and their mutual friends, the Taylors, who had come down from their farm for the occasion. During the dinner and fuelled by many glasses of wine they had all frankly discussed the impending event. After the Taylors left, with the words "see you again next year", Storm and Al sat and talked with Irving until the early hours. The discussion had become very emotional for the Maythams but Irving had been adamant that he was going ahead with his plan.

Storm ended with:

> He is simply and utterly resolved and at peace with this and eagerly awaits it, and that is what we have to accept. Anyhow Robbie, I have written to Irv from the two of us and underscored and underlined all you said in your mail to him. I'm afraid I hold no such hope for a change of mind—we talked and talked about it all with him, pushed the pros of being alive and revelling in the best of both his worlds: the beautiful farm and Africa and he was not moved in the slightest. BUT you never know—maybe his longest standing pal might have the final push!

That night there was a glimmer of hope when Helen skyped me from Oswestry:

> I had a long chat to Irving today. We discussed the whole thing at length. I think, although I can't be sure, that maybe he is having second thoughts. I explained to him what he has put us and all his friends through, you included. He really listened and seemed concerned about it. Maybe we are getting through to him.

The next day she sent me an email.

From: Helen Rooney <hel.rooney@tiscali.co.uk>
Subject: Re: YOU
Date: 20 February 2011 10:52:13 AM SAST
To: Robin Binckes <robin@spearofthenation.co.za>
Reply-To: Helen Rooney hel.rooney@tiscali.co.uk

Hi Rob
Had a fun-filled evening with the Smythes and Irv. No mention of anything else. Please do not disclose our conversation about Irv to Irv when you chat today. I am really not at all convinced that Irv has changed his plans. Time will tell. We can do our best but it is all in Irv's hands.
It is a desperate situation we are all in because we care for Irv so very much.
Love to Margie
Xx
Sent using BlackBerry® from Orange.

That Sunday morning I phoned Irving. "Hello. Tucker speaking."
"Is that Tucker with a 'T'?" I asked.
He laughed. "Hi Robbie. Good to hear your cheerful chappie voice."
"Thanks Irv. How's it going?"
"Not bad, not bad, Robbie. Just sorting out a few things. Had a nice dinner with my friends the Smythes last night. Helen and Steve were there. Good to see them again."
I didn't say I knew he had been to dinner with the Smythes, or that I had spoken to Helen.
"So presumably your plan was discussed in detail."
He laughed humourlessly.
"Not at all. Whenever Helen tried to steer the conversation in that direction, Murray avoided talking about it like the plague. Pissed me off actually. He just will *not* talk about it."
"Well, maybe he doesn't know, or else he doesn't believe you."
"Of course he knows. I have given them pictures, wood, all sorts of things; they know what's happening but they won't talk about it. Pisses me off," he repeated, sounding irritated.
My heart sank. He sounded so definite that I knew he hadn't changed his mind.

"So I gather you are still intent on going down this road?"

"Yes I am, Robbie." This time he sounded tired.

"Don't you want to talk about it?"

'No, I mean yes. I don't mind talking about it, rather than avoid the subject like Murray and others. I can't believe that despite me telling them, they avoid the subject. They obviously don't believe me, which irritates me like hell, or they just don't want to."

"Maybe they can't handle it, Irv? You know, it's not every day that a friend says he is going to kill himself. I know I've asked before, but is there nothing that I or anyone else can do to change your mind?"

"No. Definitely not. Don't try anymore. It just irritates me."

"Okay Irv." I was quiet for a few moments. "So is the time getting close now?"

"Yes. I have a couple of things to do this week and then it's all over. I've asked Michael and his wife, rather strange that she is also called Yvonne, to come down next weekend to go through everything with me. He's another one that won't face up to it. Anyway I'm not going to take his crap. He will have to face up to it next weekend when we go through what I want him to do. He's a joint executor of the will."

He sounded so exasperated that I decided to change the subject.

"What have you done about your binoculars, by the way? You aren't going to need them are you?" I wanted to ask him about his money as well but avoided the temptation.

"Well, you never know whether I will need them. Why do you ask? I left them with Alistair Maytham. Did you want them?"

"Ja. Me and everyone else. They were terrific. Helen and I were going to arm wrestle for them."

"That would have been a very interesting spectacle. Sorry, Robbie. I remember now that you liked them."

"What arrangements have you made about a funeral?"

"No, I don't want anything like that."

Silence.

"Do you want me or anyone else to come over? Will that help?"

"You mean now? No, there is nothing anyone can say, or do, to change my mind. No Robbie, after ... after ... well, there's little point, is there. I won't be here. Maybe you guys could have a couple of beers if you feel like it, but no big deal. Waste of time and money. They must just bury me in Yvonne's grave. Anyway it's up to Michael. I won't be around to interfere."

After that conversation I think I finally knew, for absolute certain, that he was going to kill himself. I had always been fairly sure, but had hoped I was wrong. That hope had now disappeared. I sent Helen an email and told her the sad news that nothing had changed, that in my opinion Irving was definitely going ahead with his plan, and it would probably be some time over the coming weekend.

I was fortunate that I did not have many tours that week. My head was in a whirl and I found it impossible to focus on anything. My mind kept returning to Irving. What does a man do in the last week of his life? Does he read the newspapers, listen to the news? Watch television? What's the point of knowing what's happening? Was he frightened and having second thoughts? Was he hoping that we would persuade him to give up the idea? How was he going to do it and when? Can you still laugh at jokes when you are going to die? Irving proved that he could.

On Monday 21 February I sent Irving an extract from an article written by Professor Jansen of the University of the Free State titled 'My South Africa' which set out many of the reasons why so many of us love this country. He didn't respond for two days and when he did there was no mention of the article. Instead he sent me a joke.

> A policeman spots a huge black guy dancing on the roof of a Ford car so he radios for backup.
> "What's the situation?" asks the operator.
> "A big, fat, black dude is dancing on a car roof."
> "You can't say that over the radio," replies the operator. "You have to use the politically correct terminology."
> "Okay," says the cop, "Zulu, Foxtrot, Sierra."

Tucker humour, I thought, even at this late stage he wants to share a joke.

Meanwhile the telephone lines and cyber space were filled with emails and phone calls between his family and friends. Irving's brother, Brian, called me that evening.

"Do you still think he will do it Robbie?"

"Yes, Brian. I am pretty sure that he will."

There was silence for a few seconds.

"When?"

"I think it's going to be this weekend. Apparently Michael and his wife are coming down on Saturday to sort out things and last minute details. Have you called him?"

"Yes, Robbie, I have. I have made my peace with him and feel a great deal better about our relationship. It would have been terrible if he killed himself before we had sorted out our issues. I am, of course, still devastated that he wants to do this thing, but at least I feel that we have buried the hatchet and put the past behind us."

"That's good to know. I'm going to speak to him later tonight. Anyway Brian, I will keep you posted."

That same day, Wednesday, I received an email from Storm in which she said that Irving had called and asked them to give his binoculars to me, together with a book that he had left at the Maythams for me, *The Rise of the South African Reich*. He told the Maythams that he thought that I would be very interested in the book because of my interest in history.

Chapter Twenty-three

DESPERATE EFFORTS

On Wednesday 23 February, Helen sent a mail informing me that she had seen Irving for the last time. Irving had called in for a bowl of soup at lunchtime. He had been to town, had a haircut and filled his car with petrol instead of diesel. He was in a pre-occupied state. He was going to soccer that night with a friend from the village, a self-made millionaire, and he and Irving were going to watch Stoke City play Arsenal.

I found it hard to think of someone who was going to end his life in a few days' time doing everyday things such as having a haircut, filling up his car and going to watch a soccer game. Again I wondered how much of the game he would actually see and absorb. Surely his mind would be elsewhere, as it had been when he filled his car with petrol instead of diesel? Helen mentioned also that Irving and Michael were going to watch the rugby— England against France—at Murray's home on the Saturday.

She sent another mail referring me to an article she had researched on the internet regarding suicide. Helen gave me the link and suggested that Margie and I read the article as it had certainly helped her to understand better what Irving planned to do.

> Hi Rob and Margie
> Fascinating stuff about Suicides
> Please read Rational Suicide and Suicide pacts in Couples
> Very interesting reading and think of Irv and Yvonne. Helped me to make sense of the whole thing.
> Helen xx
>
> http://www.deathreference.com/Sh-Sy/Suicide-Types.html

I followed the link and found the well-researched article interesting. But of course it changed nothing. This is what I read:

Rational Suicide
The question of whether or not suicide can sometimes be rational is a controversial topic that has been the subject of considerable debate among mental health practitioners, scholars, and laypeople alike. Some suicides are obviously irrational, for example, when

a schizophrenic man kills himself because he hears voices commanding him to do so. However, the possibility that some suicides may be rational can be debated on both philosophical and scientific grounds.

In 1964 the philosopher Jacques Choron defined rational suicide as being when there is no psychiatric disorder, there is no impairment of the reasoning of the suicidal person, and the person's motives appear to be justifiable or at least understandable by the majority of contemporaries in the same culture or social group.

Choron's first requirement that there is no psychiatric disorder eliminates the majority of suicides, since most persons who die by suicide suffer from a mental disorder, such as clinical depression, alcoholism, or drug abuse. Given these data, rational suicide, if it exists, is a phenomenon that can characterize only a small minority of suicides. Even the most vocal proponents of rational suicide exclude persons suffering from mental disorders. In his defense of the Hemlock Society's support of rational suicide, the society director Derek Humphry stated in 1986 that there is another form of suicide called 'emotional suicide or irrational self-murder'. The Hemlock Society view on emotional suicide is to prevent it when you can. The Hemlock Society, which supports rational suicide, specifically does not encourage any form of suicide 'for mental health or unhappy reasons'. (1986, pp. 172–176).

Even when the suicide victim does not suffer from a serious mental disorder, some suicides may still be irrational by any standard; for example, when the suicide victim is in a temporary state of extreme agitation or depression or his or her views of reality are grossly distorted by drugs or alcohol, or a man whose wife has just left him, has a loaded gun in his house, and then consumes great quantities of alcohol that distorts his judgement, may become highly suicidal even though he was not suffering from a previous mental disorder. There still remains the question of whether or not some suicides can be considered rational.

The psychiatrist Ronald Maris has argued that suicide derives from one's inability or refusal to accept the terms of the human condition. He argues that suicide may effectively solve people's problems when non-suicidal alternatives may not do so. Although no suicide is ever the best alternative to the common human condition, for some individuals suicide constitutes an individual's logical response to a common existential human condition.

The researcher and ethicist Margaret Battin, while admitting that no human acts are ever wholly rational, defines rational suicide in terms of the criteria of being able to reason, having a realistic worldview, possessing adequate information, and acting in accordance with a person's fundamental interests. Battin indicates that meeting the criterion of 'ability to reason' may be very difficult to establish because of research and anecdotal information indicating that persons who commit suicide often leave messages that are illogical and tend to refer to themselves as being able to experience the effects of their suicide after their death as if they were to continue to be alive.

One of the basic criteria for being able to act rationally is the ability to use logical processes and to see the causal consequences of one's actions. It can be argued that many suicides do not accurately foresee the consequences of their actions. Furthermore, one can ask the philosophical question of whether or not it is possible to foresee the final consequence of suicide, which is to know what it is like to be dead. Battin suggests that when one imagines oneself dead, one generally imagines a view of one's own dead body surrounded by grieving relatives or located in the grave, which presupposes a subject being around to have those experiences. This may be an indication that one does not accurately imagine death. However, Battin points out that two classes of suicides are not necessarily irrational: first, those with religious or metaphysical beliefs that include the possibility that one goes on to have humanlike experiences after death; and second, persons whose reputation and honour are of primary importance, such as the case of the Japanese suicide of honour by a samurai who had been disgraced.

There is also the question of what is considered rational decision making. According to *Webster's New World Dictionary of American Language*, rationality is 'exercising one's reason in a proper manner, having sound judgement, sensible, sane; not foolish, absurd or extravagant; implying the ability to reason logically, as by drawing conclusions from inferences, and often connoting the absence of emotion'. This definition implies a degree of autonomy in the decision-making process, the presence of abilities to engage in logical and reasoned thought processes, and the absence of undue influence on the decision-making process by external factors. In a 1983 review of contemporary philosophical writings on suicide, the scholar David J. Mayo presented the definition that a rational suicide must realistically consider alternatives concerning the likelihood of realising goals of fundamental interest to the person and then choose an alternative which will maximize the realisation of those goals. More than a decade later Brian L. Mishara argued that the most important human decision making is more emotional than rational, including the most significant choices in life, such as whom a person marries and what career a person chooses. If important decisions have a predominantly emotional basis, what would lead one to expect that the paramount decision of ending one's life could then be different and more rational? Those who argue for rational suicide generally insist that the act must occur when a person is experiencing interminable suffering. Mishara argued that in the presence of severe suffering true rational decision making is even less likely to occur; the emotions associated with the suffering compromise one's ability to reason rationally.

Battin's second criterion for rational decision making is that the decision is based upon a realistic view of the world. She points out that there are multiple worldviews that vary depending upon cultural and religious beliefs; what appears to be irrational for some is considered quite rational in other cultural contexts. Her third criterion, adequacy of information, may be questioned because of the effect of one's emotional state on the ability to look for and see the full picture. Still the suicidal person's actions cannot be seen to be more inadequately informed or less rational than in any other important moral choices.

Battin's criterion of avoidance of harm is essentially the justification that organisations such as the Hemlock Society propose as their fundamental justification of rational suicide. They cite the cessation of the harm of unbearable suffering as the most common reason for suicide. The organisation lists grave physical handicap that is so constricting that the individual cannot tolerate such a limited existence as a second reason. This justification goes against the Christian religious tradition that purports that pain and suffering may serve some constructive purpose of spiritual growth, has some meaning, or is part of God's plan.

The decision to end one's life when terminally ill is frequently construed as rational. The acceptance of ending life when extreme pain or handicap is experienced assumes that no relief for the pain is available and that the severe handicap may not be better tolerated. Derek Humphry defends people's 'right' to refuse to experience even a 'beneficent lingering' and to simply choose to not continue to live any longer when they are terminally ill.

Battin's final criterion of being in accordance with a person's fundamental interest raises the question of whether one can actually satisfy any kind of personal interest by being dead (and not around to be satisfied). Nevertheless, some individuals have long-standing moral beliefs in which the decision to foreshorten life under certain difficult circumstances is clearly condoned as in their interest.

The concept of rational suicide may sometimes be confused with the concept of 'understandable' suicide. David Clarke's work suggests that the concepts of rationality and autonomy are less useful than the concepts of 'understandability' and 'respect' when considering the expressed wish to die. However, what an outsider considers to be understandable or respectful of a person's wishes is not necessarily congruent with the suicidal person's experience. In some situations, when outsiders often feel that a person would be 'better off dead', persons who actually experience those circumstances feel differently. For example, despite popular beliefs, very few persons who are suffering from terminal and severely disabling chronic illnesses actually consider or engage in behaviour to end life prematurely.

Debates concerning rational suicide usually centre around society's obligations to provide easier access to suicide under certain circumstances. If one accepts the possibility of rational suicide, there is also an implicit moral acceptance of suicide under the circumstances in which rational suicides may occur. However, developing criteria for when a suicide can be considered rational is not an easy task. What constitutes unbearable suffering for one person may be an acceptable level of discomfort for another. Furthermore, individuals differ to the extent that rationality is an important component of their decision-making process. On what basis may one say that rational decision making is more justifiable than emotional decisions? Most suicidologists choose to try to prevent suicides that come to their attention, assuming that rational suicides, if they exist, are rare, difficult to identify, and merit interventions to challenge their reasoning.

See also: Philosophy, Western; Suicide; Suicide Influences and Factors: Mental Illness

Bibliography

Battin, Margaret P. 'The Concept of Rational Suicide'. In Edwin S. Shneidman ed., *Death: Current Perspectives*. Palo Alto, CA: Mayfield Publishing Company, 1984.

Choron, Jacques. *Modern Man and Mortality*. New York: Macmillan, 1964.

Clarke, David M. 'Autonomy, Rationality and the Wish to Die'. *Journal of Medical Ethics* 25, no. 6 (1999): 457–462.

Humphry, Derek. 'The Case for Rational Suicide'. *Euthanasia Review* 1, no. 3 (1986):172–176.

Maris, Ronald. 'Rational Suicide: An Impoverished Self-Transformation'. *Suicide and Life-Threatening Behavior* 12, no. 1 (1982):4–16.

Mayo, David J. 'Contemporary Philosophical Literature on Suicide: A Review'. *Suicide and Life-Threatening Behavior* 13, no. 4 (1983):313 345.

Mishara, Brian L. 'Synthesis of Research and Evidence on Factors Affecting the Desire of Terminally Ill or Seriously Chronically Ill Persons to Hasten Death'. *Omega: The Journal of Death and Dying*, 39, no. 1 (1999):1–70.

Mishara, Brian L. 'The Right to Die and the Right to Live: Perspectives on Euthanasia and Assisted Suicide'. In A. Leenaars, M. Kral, R. Dyck, and S. Wenckstern eds., *Suicide in Canada*. Toronto: University of Toronto Press, 1998.

Brian L. Mishara

Suicide Pacts

A suicide pact is a mutual agreement between two or more people to die at the same time and usually at the same place. This is a rare phenomenon that occurs in less than 1 per cent of suicides in the Western world. However, suicide pacts are a little more prevalent in the Eastern world where they represent approximately 2 to 3 per cent of deaths committed by suicide.

Nazi mayor Alfred Freyberg, his wife, and eighteen-year-old daughter (wearing Nazi armband) died by poison in a suicide pact before the Allies captured Leipzig, Germany, in 1945.
Bettman/Corbis

Because suicide pacts are rare, they are difficult to study. Despite their rarity and the fact that suicide pact victims generally choose nonviolent suicide methods, suicide pacts are generally lethal and the chances of survival are low.

Suicide Pact Commonalities

Suicide pacts have some common characteristics. The suicidal persons have a close and exclusive relationship, often free of significant bonds to family or friends. The isolation can be caused or exacerbated by a recent retirement, loss of work, disease, or social rejection—for example, two lovers or two friends who are not permitted to be together. The suicide pact is often triggered by a threat of separation of the dyad [something that consists of two elements or parts], death of one of them, or social and familial restrictions on seeing each other. The fear of losing the relationship with the other person motivates the majority of suicide pacts.

The dyad is generally composed of a dominant person who initiates the suicide pact and convinces a more submissive person to agree to this plan. The dominant member is usually the most suicidal member and the dependent person is the most ambivalent. In most cases, the male plays the dominating role. However, there are no indications that someone can become suicidal only due to the suggestion of another person.

Most suicide pacts use poisoning. This nonviolent method allows the synchronisation of the deaths and, at the same time, allows the pact members to change their minds. It appears that when the pact is aborted it is frequently because the passive member changes his or her mind and saves the instigator, sometimes against his or her will. However, some researchers claim that the dependent member may ask the dominant one to kill him or her in order to not survive and be left alone.

The prevalence of mental disorders is lower in suicide pacts than in individual suicides. However, researchers have found that at least one member of the dyad usually suffers from depression, borderline or antisocial personality traits, or substance abuse. Physical diseases are frequently observed, particularly in older suicide pact victims. Often, at least one pact member has attempted previously or has been exposed to the suicide of a close relative. This has led some researchers to suggest that suicide pacts are related to suicide clusters (a series of suicides in the same community) because there is a contagion effect. Besides these commonalities, some important differences exist. Three types of suicide pacts can be identified: the love pact, the spouse pact, and the friendship pact.

The love pact. Generally the love pact occurs between two young lovers who are faced with the threat of separation as imposed by their parents or society. There are some cases of love pacts in the Western world, but this type of pact is particularly frequent in the Eastern world where there are strict rules concerning dowry and marriage. For example, in India and Japan many young people are forced to break off a love relationship to marry the person that their parents have chosen for them. Some of these young lovers view suicide as the only way that they can stay together. Lover suicide pacts are often also seen as rebellion against parental authority and linked to the intense guilt of giving priority to one's own desires instead of respecting social conventions.

The spouse pact. Typically occidental, the spouse pact is the most prevalent. Generally it occurs between a husband and a wife, aged fifty or older, who are childless or not living with their children. At least one of them is likely to be physically ill. In most cases, there is interdependence and devotion to one another and the couple engages in a suicide pact because neither member wants to be separated by the other's death. However, the members are sometimes motivated by the fear of chronic pain or fear of losing their physical and mental integrity because of old age. Usually, a dominant/dependent relationship is present.

The friendship pact. The friendship pact has a lower prevalence. Usually it takes place between two or three adolescents of the same sex. This type of pact appears to be less planned and results in less lethality than adult suicide pacts. Attempters tend to share similar life stories; for example, they have been separated from their parents since childhood because of parental divorce or the death of a parent. As a result, adolescents see each other as a narcissistic double and this dynamic seems to be a mutual facilitator. In the days before the suicide members of the pact stay together almost all of the time, in isolation from the rest of society. This social withdrawal prevents them from seeking help. The dominant/dependent relationship seems to be less prevalent in the friendship pact.

Prevention of Suicide Pacts

Numerous risk factors associated with individual suicides are linked to suicide pacts. For this reason, it is important for health practitioners and loved ones to pay attention to general signs of suicide risk, such as major behavioural or emotional changes, sleeping or eating disorders, disposal of important possessions, loss of interest and energy, substance abuse, and hopelessness. One should also be watchful for signs of suicide pacts, such as the isolation of an older couple with a physical illness or emotionally unhealthy exclusive relationships in young friends. Moreover, the people who engage in suicide pacts often talk about their plans to family and friends.

Mental health practitioners suggest that one asks direct questions to verify suicide intentions and plans, such as, 'Are you thinking of suicide?' 'Did you plan your suicide (i.e. decide when, where, or how to do it)?' The more the suicide is planned, the more important it is to be direct and act quickly. One should be empathic and warm with a suicidal person, and try to find new solutions or alternatives to the person's problems, and encourage him or her to seek professional help if needed. Finally, despite the fact that suicide pacts share a lot of characteristics with individual suicides and are a rare phenomenon, health practitioners believe that education programmes on suicide prevention should incorporate information on suicide pacts and guidelines for preventing suicide pact behaviour.

See also: Suicide Influences and Factors: Physical Illness; Suicide over the Life Span: Adolescents and Youths; Suicide Types: Theories of Suicide

Bibliography
Brown, Martin, and Brian Barraclough. 'Partners in Life and in Death: The Suicide Pact in England and Wales 1988–1992'. *Psychological Medicine* 29 (1999): 1299–1306.
Cohen, John. 'A Study of Suicide Pacts'. *Medico-Legal Journal* 29 (1961):144–151.
Fishbain, David A., and Tim E. Aldrich. 'Suicide Pacts: International Comparisons'. *Journal of Clinical Psychiatry* 46, no. 1 (1985):11–15.
Fishbain, David A., Linda D'Achille, Steve Barsky, and Tim E. Aldrich. 'A Controlled Study of Suicide Pacts'. *Journal of Clinical Psychiatry* 45, no. 4 (1984):154–157.
Granboulan, Virginie, Alain Zivi, and Michel Basquin. 'Double Suicide Attempt among Adolescents'. *Journal of Adolescent Health* 21 (1997):128–130.

Noyes, Russel, Susan J. Frye, and Charles E. Hartford. 'Conjugal Suicide Pact'. *Journal of Nervous and Mental Disease* 165, no. 1 (1977):72–75.

Vijayakumar, Lakshmi, and Natararajan Thilothammal. 'Suicide Pacts'. *Crisis* 14, no. 1 (1993):43–46.

Read more: http://www.deathreference.com/Sh-Sy/Suicide-Types. html#ixzz2MDi061Va

I wondered whether there was any point in forwarding it to Irving, and decided that little purpose would be served.

That same Wednesday, I had arranged to have lunch with an old friend, ex-Springbok cricketer, Lee Irvine. He had a friend who he said wished to talk to me about charities in Alexandra. We met at the restaurant at his work premises and were joined by his wife Helen and their friend, Helen Johnson. My mind was on other things while we talked about Friends of Alexandra. Eventually Lee commented: "You seem distracted Rob? Anything the matter?"

I winced. There was silence as I told them about Irving.

"No!" exclaimed Helen Irvine, while Helen Johnson, wide eyed, shook her head.

"How terrible. Surely he won't do it, will he?" Helen Irvine asked.

"Afraid so."

Helen Johnson finally broke her silence. "I think it's a cry for help; I really do."

"Afraid not. It's this weekend. I'm pretty sure about it. I've tried—we've all tried. He's not going to change his mind."

After we had finished lunch I apologized for being preoccupied and we went our separate ways.

"Talk to your friend, you must change his mind," Helen Johnson said, as we walked out of the restaurant.

I shrugged and gritted my teeth. "I'll try. Don't hold out much hope though."

As I drove home I realized finally that it was going to happen. I had always felt deep down that it was definite, but had held on to the slight feeling that Irving wouldn't do it. I knew now that the ifs and buts were over; it was now only a case of when.

On Thursday morning I did not have a tour and I phoned Irving.

"How are things going?" I asked.

"Good, thanks Robbie. Went to watch the soccer last night."

"I believe so."

"Bloody good game. Arsenal pipped Stoke City one nil."

"So you enjoyed the game?"

"*Ja*. Very good. We had a good night."

"How about your plans?"

"All on track. Went and had a haircut yesterday and then—don't know what I was thinking—put bloody petrol into my diesel car. Must have been thinking about something else."

"You had a haircut? Whatever for?"

"Well, don't want to look bad, you know. Must look my best when they find me."

"I'm sure you will be the best looking corpse around, Irv."

"*Ja*. And then I put bloody petrol in the diesel car. Bloody stupid."

"Well, I do think that under the circumstances you have an excuse, and I don't think that it really matters, does it?"

"Well, I'm just worried that I've fucked up the engine."

There was silence.

"What do you care? It doesn't really matter to you whether you have or have not, does it?"

"I suppose not Robbie. Still ..."

"I spoke to Brian, your *boet*, last night. I believe you spoke to him?"

"Yes, Robbie. I did. We spoke at some length and cleared up a lot of issues. We had a good chat. Glad that that baggage has gone. Anyway he is going to be well looked after by the will ... as you ..."

I waited. He seemed on the point of saying something else concerning his will but he let the words die. We were silent for a few seconds.

"Well, I'm glad that you chatted to Brian and from his account things are better?"

"Yes they are. We had a lot of issues. I suppose I realize now in the current circumstances that I have been rather cruel and unkind to Brian and his wife. To be honest it was certainly more me than him. Anyway, I'm glad we had that time together in Timbavati at the elephant collaring, and the chat."

"I hope you apologized to Brian?"

There was a pause.

"Well, not exactly apologized ... you know me, Robbie, I'm not one to acknowledge when I am wrong. Still I think he got the message that I thought that the fault was mainly mine."

"Good. I'm glad. He's a good guy and we all felt that you were being very unfair to him and Brenda."

There was another silence.

Then: "Where are you with all this? Are you okay?" he asked me.

I sighed. "Me? Yes, I'm okay. But you should know that this hasn't been easy for Margie or me or any of your friends. In fact it's been bloody rough. Now is the worst. Just waiting. We all feel helpless, and of course very sad. We shall miss you Irv."

"I know Robbie. I'm sorry to be the cause of your distress. You've been a good friend. Both you and Margs. The Jolly Green Giant was always very fond of the two of you. Anyway, Robbie, you have that copper bangle, our bond, to wear as a reminder of me and our good times together. Have you still got it?"

I glanced down at the copper bracelet on my right wrist.

"Yes, Irv, I'm wearing it right now."

"Really?" He sounded surprised. "That's good. That'll always remind you then, won't it?"

We were both silent. Then I asked: "Have you decided exactly when yet? Look Irv, is there anything, anything at all that any of us can say or do, even at this stage, to stop this madness?"

"No. Not at all. Nothing. I have decided. It'll be this weekend, Robbie. I always told you by the end of February ... so it's this weekend. I've finished everything, just have to sort out the details with Michael on Saturday, then we are going to watch England give France carrots on Saturday afternoon, and then ..."

"So. Looks like Sunday. When do Michael and his wife go back?"

"I'm taking them to catch the train on Saturday evening."

"How will I know when it is done?"

"I'm giving Michael a list of names to notify. Yours is there of course."

My throat tightened and I swallowed hard. Before he could pick up the signals I said, "Okay Irv. Chat over the weekend. Enjoy the game and good luck to England."

"Cheers Robbie!" came the cheerful answer.

I held out my hands in front of me. They were trembling and I felt nauseous. There was a black hole in my stomach. I sat and looked out my study window. The sun was shining brightly; a hadeda was pecking at some insects on the lawn; our two Scottie dogs lay looking out of the window in anticipation of seeing the enemy they loved to hate, the neighbour's cat. Life looked normal. I shook my head, thinking: six thousand kilometres away my friend is going through the last stages of preparation to end his life. I wanted to give him something ... some words ... something. I wasn't sure what—not to change his mind, but maybe to make him feel better about going. Then I remembered. For some years a copy of a letter from a Rabbi who had cancer, written to his friend, a,Roman Catholic priest who also had cancer, in which he explained his philosophy of life, had been lying on my desk. I dug it out from under a pile of papers and re-read it. It might not have been perfect but it expressed life far better than I could have done. I used the Rabbi's words as the basis for the mail that I sent Irving.

From: Robin Binckes <robin@spearofthenation.co.za>
Subject: Irv
Date: 24 February 2011 3:14:57 PM SAST
To: Tucker Irving IYTucker@aol.com

Dear Irv,

Thought you might like this so decided to share! You possibly wonder where I am in all of this journey of yours? Well, this pretty much sums it up. The Talmud says: "Every person should walk through life with two notes, one in each pocket. On one note are the words 'Anti afar ve'efer'—I am nothing but dust and ashes. On the other 'Bishvili nivra ha'olam'—For my sake was this world created."

These are in contradiction to each other yet the Talmud says they are both true. When I sit on the bench facing the sea at Haga Haga and watch the waves roll in, one after the other, one after the other, never ceasing, never tiring, and look at the endless blue of the sea and sky, I am aware of how insignificant I am. All this was here millions of years before and will go on millions of years after. I am not even a radar blip. I am not even a point on a line. I am totally insignificant. My death, like my life, means nothing in the long run. Even the pain my family and friends feel will be lost in the full scheme of things. 'Ani afar ve'efer'—I am nothing but dust and ashes.

On the other hand 'Bishvili nivra ha'olam'—For my sake the world was created—I am so significant. I am so important, so critical. That all this is worth being just so that I can experience it!

The mathematical probability, said Einstein, of my being born who I am is not 000000001; it is zero!!!! Yet I am here and you are there. And every moment of life is a moment beyond comprehension. That I can see those waves. That I can walk on the shore. That I can feel the sand under my feet. That I can love and be loved. That I can hear the call of the hyenas. That I can smell the bush. That I can gaze on the African sunset. That I can laugh and cry with friends like you. These are experiences that quadrillions of souls have never had and never will. I am in awe of this universe and *my* presence in it. Every moment of my life is a miracle.

Lots of love and thoughts with you.

Go in Peace and with great memories and love, my friend.
Rob & Margs

On Friday he called me: "Thanks for that piece you sent me, Robbie. It doesn't change anything, but I liked it."

"No Irv. Didn't think it would; just wanted to share some words with you. Are you okay?"

"Yes. I'm fine. Pretty much all done here; just waiting for Michael to come down from London in the morning."

I was quiet. "Robbie?"

"Yes? I'm here. I was just thinking. Sorry."

"Thought you had hung up. I was saying, once Michael has been here then everything will be done."

"Yes, that's what I was thinking about. So it could be tomorrow night?"

"No. Won't be tomorrow."

"Well, let's speak before you do it, okay?"

"Okay Robbie, in the meantime, we have the rugby to watch on Saturday afternoon. Hopefully we can teach those frogs how to play our game."

"Where are you watching?"

"We're all going to Murray's and then after the game I'll take Michael and Yvonne to the station and they'll go back to London."

"Well Irv, enjoy the game. I'll give you a call afterwards to congratulate you on your victory or commiserate on your loss."

"Thanks Robbie—you still wearing that copper bracelet?"

I glanced down to check. "I am Irv, of course."

"Good. Chat after the game. Cheers."

That evening I kept my appointment with my friend, Doug, for a beer at the Wanderers Club, as I had done every Friday for the past three years.

Doug, a man who always lives life to the full, looked at my face.

"You look a bit less happy than normal. Are you okay?" he asked.

"You remember my friend Irving?"

"Yes, yes. Fun guy. We all had dinner together. Remember him well."

"Do you remember I told you he was going to kill himself?"

Doug laughed.

"Yes. I remember that. He hasn't done it has he? I mean, that was like a year ago?"

"No, he hasn't, but I think it's this weekend."

"Really? I wouldn't worry too much about that. Any man who tells you a year ago that he is going to kill himself is just looking for attention. Drink your beer. I really don't think you have any cause for concern."

I shrugged and drank my beer. I didn't think he was correct.

Margie was cooking sausages for supper when I returned home. I opened the fridge and took out a beer. A picture, stuck to the fridge door with a magnet, caught my eye. It was of a smiling Irving, taken on the day we had done our tour in Soweto at the Hector Pieterson memorial. I blinked rapidly as my eyes began to water.

"Here, let me do that," I said to Margie.

The oil in the pan splattered and spurted as I turned the sausages over, trying to brown them evenly.

"Spoke to Irv today."

"Oh, did you?"

I nodded.

"How did he sound?"

"Same as always. He seems fine, it's the rest of us who aren't."

Assisted by the alcohol in the four beers I had drunk, my eyes welled up with tears. I blinked to clear them before Margie could see.

"I think it'll be on Sunday," and wiped my eyes with the back of my hand.

Margie continued chopping tomatoes for the salad. I glanced at her.

"I hope you aren't cutting the tomatoes into wedges are you?"

She laughed. "Of course not. He would give me hell. Do you? Sunday?"

I didn't answer. The sausages in the hot oil in the frying pan spluttered and crackled in the silence.

"I wonder what he's going to do with all his money?" I muttered.

"Well, maybe he'll leave some to Friends of Alexandra?"

"No, he ruled that out. You know what he's like. I think that day I took him into the township and he saw Ernest ask me for money for cell phone time and I gave it to him, Irving thought that I just handed out money to anyone who asked for it. He didn't realize that Ernest is my contact at the hostel and that it's essential that he can communicate with me at all times. Irving's pretty unforgiving that way. Unfortunately he jumps to conclusions and even when he's wrong, he won't change his mind."

"Pity. Maybe he'll leave some to us. He told Sam that he was going to and he's always saying that he is going to leave it to people who could do with it."

"Well, we certainly qualify in that department. He has never said anything to me, so I very much doubt it. But he has left us his binoculars—they're with the Maythams. I guess that's our lot."

"They are lovely binoculars. Better than a pile of wood that some people are going to get. They'll be very handy at Haga Haga and in the bush."

That night the dream returned.

Chapter Twenty-four

OU DAE (OLD DAYS)

I had no tour on the Saturday. Margie was out doing the weekly shopping. I sat at my desk in the study, writing. I found it difficult to concentrate. I checked my emails. There was a mail from Helen Johnson, the friend of Lee and Helen Irvine who had joined us for lunch a couple of days earlier. That's funny, I thought. Wonder why she is writing to me?

From: Helen Johnson<rg.johnson@intekom.co.za>
Subject: A letter to a whole soul.doc
Date: 26 February 2011 1:39:30 PM SAST
To: Robin Binckes <robin@spearofthenation.co.za>

Hello Rob
I have been so distressed at your story of the imminent waste of a life. I have written your friend a letter. You have given all these arguments already. I needed to get this written down as another take on why *not*.
Regards
Helen

I opened the attachment and read:

What purpose does this monstrously self-indulgent plan serve?
How does this honour the memory of someone you have loved?
Would you take a ram into a field and shoot it because it was grazing?
Would you cut down a mature Yew tree because it blocked your view?
Would you cast your rod into a river knowing that you had no fly attached?
Would you burn your fields the day before the harvest?
Would you contaminate your water troughs?
Why cancel out all the good you have done in your life in one pointless moment?
People in communities all over the world make conscious decisions to sacrifice their own lives to save the lives of others.
Think of the young teenager in the floods in Australia who sent his

239

little brother off on the lifeline before he was swept away.

Remember the little girl who ran back again to pull other kids out of a burning hostel then succumbed to smoke inhalation.

How self-serving have you been in your planning? Where is the sacrifice? What is the payback for the rest of your team?

Have you donated your last pint of blood?

Have you offered your kidneys, your corneas, your liver or in due time, your heart for transplant? What about harvesting your bone marrow?

Have you donated your body to research?

Come back to South Africa! We need you!

You don't like us enough to get close to the dirty, everyday stuff of life?

There are wonderfully proactive initiatives you could to be part of:

The Smile Foundation for Cleft Palate Repair

The Keiskamma Valley Renewal Project

Habitat for Humanity

Courage in the battle of life is surely more honourable than ignominious desertion.

I was debating whether to forward Helen's message to Irving, and had just decided not to, when the landline rang. The ringing jangled my nerves further. I answered and was startled to hear Irving's voice.

"Hi Robbie."

"Hi Irv. How's it going? Wasn't expecting to hear from you. Thought you would be tied up with Michael?"

"Yes. Well, I am. That's why I'm calling."

"Oh?" then quietly, in case Michael was nearby, "how's it going with him?"

Irving's response sounded forced and I gathered that Michael was nearby and listening.

"All fine here, Robbie," he said, slightly too loudly, "listen, there's something I want to discuss with you."

"Go ahead Irv. I'm listening."

"Well, going through all of my papers and affairs I've come across a bank account that Yvonne and I had with some money in that I hadn't sort of taken into consideration."

I listened and felt a slight rush of anticipation.

"I would like you and Margie to have it."

I could hear someone speaking in the background.

"What's that?" The question was obviously directed to someone else in the room, presumably Michael. Then to me: "I need your bank details to transfer the money."

I gave him my bank details and added, "I receive quite a few transfers from overseas clients, so I know that you also need the swift number of my bank to transfer any money." I gave him the swift number.

"Thanks Robbie. I'll contact the bank and see that it is transferred."

I wanted to ask him how much was being transferred but felt that it didn't really matter. Whatever it was would come in handy.

"Thanks a helluva lot, Irv. It's really appreciated—whatever it is."

"There is a condition attached though."

"What's that Irv?"

"It is not to be used for paying those old business partners of yours. Not one cent. This is for you and Margie. It's for your *ou dae* (senior years). You lost your money. This will help give both of you something for when you have to stop working. Invest it, earn some income from it."

I didn't know what to say.

"Thank you. Thank you. I'll do that Irv. Enjoy the rugby. I'll call you and we can chat tomorrow."

I hung up. My mind whirled like a wind devil. I wondered how much he was talking about. So he hadn't forgotten us. What a lovely surprise. Whatever the amount, large or small, it would be useful. Maybe it was a large amount? If he and Yvonne had an account that he was clearing it might be worth millions. No, this was probably just a small account for a rainy day. We would have to see. He was going to transfer the money today.

I tried to continue writing but could not concentrate. I heard the 'ping' from my laptop indicating that I had mail. I opened my inbox. The mail was from Western Union. I opened the attachment and my eye was immediately drawn to the paragraph below and the amount shown stood out like a dog's balls.

> To celebrate our 150th Anniversary United Kingdom, we're rewarding our customer with prizes of USD 1,000,000.00 from Western Union Online Sweepstake Promotion held on January 3rd 2011.

One million US Dollars! Wow! About seven million rand. For a second or two it felt like I was flying through the air with delight. I forced myself to look away from the amount shown and read the rest of the mail—and very quickly realized that it was another one of the hundreds of scam mails that I, and everyone else, received, every day. But I had enjoyed the brief moment of extreme wealth before it had burst like a bubble. As the truth dawned on me and I smiled to myself, I heard the front door open. It was Margie. I shouted down the stairs.

"Hi. Guess what? Irving's sending us some money."

"That's nice," she replied, "what do you mean, sending some money? Do you mean he's left us some in his will?"

I walked down the stairs and joined her in the lounge, flopping into an armchair.

"No, he phoned. He was obviously busy with Michael and told me that he had discovered some money that he wanted you and I to have. Nice hey? Don't know what it is, but anything will be good."

"Absolutely. I don't suppose it's very much. What do you think? Maybe a thousand pounds or something like that? It was probably a bit that he and Yvonne put aside for a rainy day. Anyway, whatever it is, it's very nice of him. How did he sound?"

"He sounded fine."

I then told her of my excitement at seeing the Western Union email.

She laughed. "Teach you to get too carried away." Then she asked, "So you think he's going ahead with it?"

"Afraid so. I don't think there is any doubt."

Her smile disappeared; she shook her head sadly.

That afternoon England beat France 17-9.

I called Irving but there was no reply. I panicked, and then I remembered that he was taking Michael and Yvonne to the station after the game.

❦

I called again on Sunday morning.

"Just phoned to thank you for the money, Irv. Don't know how much it is but thank you anyway."

"Well, it's a bit of a bugger, Robbie. Have to go into the bank tomorrow morning, Monday, to sign certain forms to arrange the transfer. We couldn't get it done yesterday so it will have to wait until tomorrow."

"That's fine Irv. At least it means you are here today. So it will be tomorrow?"

"Yes. I'll go and sign the forms."

"I wasn't talking about signing forms," I said.

There was a pause.

"Yes, Robbie, tomorrow night, after I've been to the bank and done a few things. Then I'll do it."

I was silent. My heart felt like it was being dragged down into the pit of my stomach.

"So tomorrow night? Definite?" It was the first time that he had stated a date. "When, exactly?"

"Between ten o' clock and midnight my time. Anyway I'll be in touch when I've been to the bank."

The next day, the last day of February I received a mail from Irving.

From: Tucker Irving & Yvonne < IYTUCKER@aol.com>
Subject: OU DAG MONEY
Date: 28 February 2011 12:58:24 PM SAST
To: Robin Binckes robin@spearofthenation.co.za

Hi Mr and Mrs Binckes,
I shot into the Nationwide this morning and transferred this money to you. It could take 3 to 5 days before it's in your account and the exchange rate will be determined then, should have done it when I got back as it was over 11.50 to the £.
The reason I am sending you this now and not as part of the will is this was in a tax free ISA so did not have to show as part of the assets for tax purposes.
Put some of it aside for *'ou dae'*.
Love
Irv

Attached to the mail was a swift transfer form from the bank. I opened it and stared. The amount transferred was fifty-eight thousand pounds.

"Oh my God," I whispered to myself. I read the mail again, to make sure that I hadn't made another mistake. There it was, in black and white. No mistake. I wondered why he had addressed his mail to 'Mr and Mrs'. Odd, I thought, and ever since have not been able to understand why he suddenly began to call us Mr and Mrs Binckes.

I replied to Irving immediately

From: Robin Binckes <robin@spearofthenation.co.za>
Subject: Re: OU DAG MONEY
Date: 28 February 2011 1:18:24 PM SAST
To: Tucker Irving & Yvonne IYTUCKER@aol.com

Hi Mr Tucker!
Wow! It is ALL going to go for *ou dae* (which are almost but not quite here!)

Again, words are wet aren't they? Who would have thought that that
bugger who used to wear the sugar packet on his head would ever
give me money like this? Five pounds maybe ... even fifty pounds.
But fuck! Fifty-eight thousand pounds!!!!!! Now I've got nothing to
lose by talking you out of this!!!!

I won't say anything more. I know that it is soon a done deal.

I wish you love and peace for always.

Thank you for being our friend and for what you have done. We
have and will treasure wonderful memories of you.

Love,

Rob and Margs and Sam and Mike.

That afternoon I phoned Irving for what I thought would be the last time.

"Is that Tucker with a 'T'?" I asked when he answered the phone.

He chuckled. "Yes it is."

"Thank you Irv. From Margie and me, for the money."

"Has it arrived already in your account?"

"No, Irv. I saw the amount on the swift transfer you attached to your
email. I'm sure it's on the way. Thank you."

"Pleasure Robbie. I hope it helps you. Keep it for your retirement. It's not
meant for anything else. Yvonne and I were always worried about what
you were going to do when you stopped working; how you were going
to manage financially. I'm glad that this helps. Yvonne would have been
pleased as well."

"Thank you Irv. It'll be a big help."

"That's good."

"Did you enjoy the rugby on Saturday?"

"Brilliant. We gave those frogs a bit of a lesson. Tough game—but the
better side won."

"Congrats. How did it go with Michael?"

"It went okay. He had to do what I wanted."

"Does he accept now what you are going to do?"

"He has no choice, has he? Not like some of the others, like Murray. He
still won't discuss it. Didn't offer to come over for a chat on Sunday, the
day after we were at his place for the rugby. Never mentioned it. Anyway, I
guess that's his problem, not mine."

There was silence.

Then I said, "So, between ten and midnight your time? That's midnight
to two in the morning our time. Look Irv, I'd better go now." I felt my
throat tighten and my eyes begin to smart. "I'm not saying goodbye, Irv,

you know, we don't say goodbye in my family, I really can't do that ..."

"I know, Robbie, I ..."

I switched off the phone. I couldn't say goodbye. Tears trickled down my cheeks. I brushed them off with my shirtsleeve and stared at the wet marks on my blue shirt. I felt as though someone had placed an iron band around my chest.

Chapter Twenty-five

GOODBYE

For the rest of the day, and throughout that evening I found my eyes drawn to the clock, like a magnet. I felt nauseous at the thought of Irving, on his own in his farmhouse, preparing himself for death.

At about ten o' clock I went to bed but could not sleep. I lay wide awake, staring at the ceiling in the dark. I glanced at the clock. Quarter to twelve. That meant quarter to ten in England. Fifteen minutes to go. I climbed out of bed, put on a dressing gown and walked downstairs, switched on the kitchen light which shone into the lounge and grabbed a beer. In the half-dark I sat in the chair I had used on the night Irving told me he was going to kill himself and dialled his number on my cell phone. The light from the cell phone shone bright in the dusky room. I was relieved when the phone was picked up at the other end.

"Tucker," he answered.

"With a 'T'?"

"Hi Robbie."

"Are you ready Irv?"

"Pretty much. Have a few emails to send and then I'm done."

"What are you doing?"

"Well, I had a very nice dinner. Now I've been watching what our Arab friends are doing on Al Jazeera."

"You are joking aren't you? You can't be serious, watching Al Jazeera?"

"No, I'm not joking," he replied calmly, "you know I'm always interested in what our Arab friends are doing in the Middle East? Then I'm going to have a bath ..."

"Oh! By the way," I butted in, "I had lunch with some friends a couple of days ago and one of the ladies at the lunch is most distressed about your plan. She sent me a letter to send to you."

"Don't waste your time sending it, Robbie. It will just irritate me, if it's what I think. What is the letter about?"

"She gives reasons why you shouldn't go ahead with this madness."

"Exactly. Don't bother sending it. I'm not interested."

I could hear the annoyance in his voice.

"Okay, Irv, okay." I realized that it was futile and did not want to sour what would probably be our last conversation. "Okay, as you were saying, you are going to have a bath. And then?"

"Well, you know, Robbie, then I'll do it."

My stomach knotted. "Are you frightened Irv?"

"Not at all. As I've told you—looking forward to it."

I shook my head. "Just tell me again," I said, "is Yvonne waiting for you on the other side?"

He laughed.

"No, no. Yvonne is gone. I will never see her again. There is nothing where I am going. Absolutely nothing."

"Well, this is the moment that I should offer to pray with you, or something like that, isn't it, Irv?'

He snorted. "Don't waste our time on that Robbie. That's all bullshit."

"How are you going to do it?" I visualized my recurrent dream.

"It won't be messy. That's all I'm prepared to say. I'm not going to tell you."

I sipped my beer.

"You've had a good life, haven't you Irv?"

"Bloody good, Robbie. Lots of laughs, lots of fun. Best time of course was with Yvonne. Had some great times together, never been the same since she went."

There was silence. I sipped my beer.

"Have you got a drink Irv? I'm having a beer."

"No, I haven't Robbie. I had two glasses of wine with my dinner."

"Well, you aren't going to wake up with a hangover tomorrow are you? I don't think that it really matters how much you have to drink. Get a drink, Irv. Let's have a farewell toast together."

He laughed humourlessly. "Okay. I'll get a glass of wine to keep you company."

I waited. After a few minutes he returned. "Okay, got the wine, Robbie."

"I hope it's good South African wine? The least you could do is die with a bottle of South African wine next to you."

"No, actually it's a bottle of good French plonk. After we fucked them up on the rugby field on Saturday I don't mind drinking their wine."

"Jeez, Irv. Even in death you deny us South Africans."

He laughed. I felt a calmness cloak me. My eyes were dry. It was as if it was already over.

"Cheers, Robbie. Thanks for the friendship. You still wearing the copper bracelet—our bond?"

The bracelet glistened in the light flowing from the kitchen.

"Yes, I am, Irv."

"Good."

Silence.

"Remember the song 'Thank you for the music' by Abba?"

"Yes, of course I do. I told you before."

"Well, thank you for the music, Robbie. It's been great."

I swallowed hard.

"Cheers, Irv. Yes, it has. Thank you for singing along. Thank you for your friendship. You've been a difficult old bugger but we love you and are going to miss you like hell. And thanks again for the gift, you have no idea how much we appreciate it and what a difference it's going to make for our *ou dae*."

"I hope it helps you two."

"It will. I can assure you, it will."

I took a deep swig of beer.

"How will I know if you've done it, Irv? If you change your mind between now and then—you can, you know—please phone me, even if it's in the early hours, just to say you are alive. Just so that we know. If I wake up and you haven't phoned, I'll know that you are dead."

"I'll do that. But Michael will let everyone know. He's one of the people getting an email with my instructions."

I heard him take a sip of wine.

There was silence.

"No point in me begging you not to do this terrible thing?"

"Don't even go there. It's over."

"Anything you want done ... after?"

"No. All taken care of."

There was another silence.

"Okay, Irv. This is it then?"

"I suppose," he replied.

"Go in peace and love, Irving. We will never forget you and what you have done for us."

"Goodbye Robbie. It's been good. Thank you for the music."

He put the phone down.

I sat in the chair in the semi-light and began to cry. When I stopped crying I sat and waited in the hope that the phone would ring. It was silent.

⋙

I slept fitfully that night, woke on Tuesday morning with a feeling of dread, looked at Margie and said, "He didn't phone. He must have done it."

"Do you think he has?" she asked, startled and fearful.

I nodded. "I'm certain."

I collected my four guests for a tour which was to include the apartheid museum. I kept looking at my cell phone to see if I had any missed calls. At eleven thirty, still in the apartheid museum, my cell phone rang. My stomach muscles tightened. I excused myself to my four guests and answered the phone. "Hello?"

Brian, Irving's brother shouted: "He's dead. He's dead, Robbie. Irving has killed himself. He's done it! Oh my God Robbie, he's killed himself!"

Brian's scream of anguish seemed to explode in my head. My ears rang. A giant hand squeezed my chest. The world spun as my sight blurred. I felt as though I had been hit by a twelve-foot wave. I fell to the concrete floor. When I opened my eyes my four guests were looking at me with horror.

It was all over.

❦

Irving Tucker died as the result of a lethal dose of pentobarbital early on Tuesday morning, 1 March 2011. He had missed his self-imposed deadline by fifty minutes.

Not that it made any difference.

❦

From: Tucker Irving & Yvonne <IYTUCKER@aol.com>
Subject: DAVID DAVIES
Date: 01 March 2011 12:45:45 AM SAST
To: Michael Hodgson-Hess <michael.hess@machness.co.uk, yvonne@machness.co.uk

Hello Mr and Mrs Hess,
Would you please contact David Davies to come round to Bryn Uchaf tomorrow and collect me. The door will be open.
Please ask Carol to feed Juno in the evening. I have left her food on top of the deep freeze. She can then go back to morning feed as usual.
Thanks and goodbye
Love
Irving

EPILOGUE

As the result of one of the last emails sent by Irving, the police received a call from Michael Hess on the morning of 1 March, at 07h48, informing them he believed that Irving may have harmed himself, and requesting that the police visit Irving's farm, Bryn Uchaf, to investigate

On arriving at the farm the police found the door closed but unlocked. The sound of a radio playing drifted downstairs. They found Irving lying on the bed upstairs, fully clothed and wearing his shoes. He looked as though he had fallen asleep: he lay on his back, his right arm across his chest, his left arm outstretched towards a bedside radio, the source of the music heard by the police when entering the house.

The police found two drinking glasses in the bathroom: one held the remains of a yellowish liquid, the other contained a clear substance. The report of the subsequent post mortem, conducted at Telford and Shrewsbury Hospital, reported that Irving had died from drinking Pentobarbital, which can be used for euthanising cattle and, according to the internet, humans. In fact it has been used in some states in the USA to execute prisoners.

A few months after Irving died I received a phone call from his brother-in-law, Michael Hess. He told me he was in Joburg and would like to see me at my home for a cup of tea. Intrigued, never having met him before, I agreed.

An hour later the front doorbell rang and Michael Hess stood on the steps. I was immediately struck by his resemblance to his late sister, Yvonne. He was tall, black-haired, with angular features and spoke with a distinctive London accent. He was accompanied by his wife, also named Yvonne.

Over tea we discussed Irving and his death. It soon become apparent that, despite the fact that Irving had appointed Michael as a joint executor of his will (with Christine Kendall, a local lawyer), Irving's dislike of Michael was matched equally by Michael's dislike of Irving. In addition, Michael expressed extreme displeasure that Irving, according to his will, was leaving money to his friends and various charities of his choice. Michael felt Irving had no right to bequeath 'his' money to any beneficiary at all—Irving's wealth was really Michael's sister's money, which she had inherited from their father, and Michael was more entitled to the money than Irving.

Then came the bombshell.

"Did you know that you are mentioned as a beneficiary in the will?" he asked, watching me closely.

I was surprised and shook my head.

"No, I didn't. He gave me money before he died. I thought that was all he meant me to have."

"Yes, yes. That's right. I was there and I know about that money. So how do you feel about the fact that you are also listed as a beneficiary?"

"You mean ... I am mentioned in Irving's will ... as well?" My grin was in stark contrast to Michael's unhappy expression. "Shit. I feel like I've just won the pools!"

Michael looked crestfallen.

"But you have already received money ..."

"If my name was left in the will after Irving had transferred money to me, despite having had every opportunity to change his will when you were down there, the weekend before he died, and he *didn't* change his will—then obviously he intended me also to have the money that is mentioned in his will."

There was silence.

"How much did he leave me?"

"I don't know," Michael answered sullenly. "You will be getting a letter from Christine Kendall, my co-executor, explaining his bequest to you. At least you will know what the letter is about when you receive it. She will be communicating with the twenty or more friends and charities to whom Irving has left some money, in varying amounts."

"Did he leave anything to the school at Haga Haga?"

"No. And that really upsets me as well. Yvonne would have wanted that school to receive money. In fact they agreed to help that school and Irving did not leave it one penny. He left money to a school up near Louis Trichardt. That was my sister's money and her wishes should have been carried out—it was Yvonne's money, not Irving's."

A few weeks later I received a letter from Christine Kendall stating that she and Michael felt that Irving had not meant me to have the amount of money he had transferred to me before his death *and* the amount mentioned in his will. She asked me to prove that I was entitled to the amount in the will. A heated exchange of emails took place and after some resistance, Christine Kendall accepted that what was stated in the will was what Irving had intended. I became a minor beneficiary. The major beneficiaries were Michael himself, Irving's brother Brian and his family, and a friend of Yvonne's and her family. At the time of this book going to print, three years after Irving's death, his estate still had not been finalized.

In February 2014 I decided to visit Oswestry and Bryn Uchaf. I attempted by email to set up a meeting with Christine Kendall, as a courtesy, during my visit to Oswestry. She declined, stating that "it would be inappropriate". I emailed Steve Eisenstein to ask if he could establish the names of the new owners of Bryn Uchaf, so that I could request their permission to visit the farm and take some photographs. Unfortunately Steve, who was unaware of the acrimony between Michael Hess, Christine Kendall and myself, approached Michael for the names and contact details of the new owners.

Michael consulted with Christine and following their discussions Steve received an email from Christine. Her message again declined to provide the names of the owners, and stated that it was unnecessary for me to visit the farm as she could provide me with the photographs taken when Irving was preparing to put the farm on the market.

Steve, however, managed to get the names of the new owners, Claire and Andrew Belk, from Emyr and Carol Jones, who had been Irving's next door neighbours. In fact, Emyr had been asked by the police to perform the sad task of identifying Irving's body. Claire and Andrew Belk readily agreed to my visit.

On Tuesday 18 February 2014 I arrived at Heathrow airport on a cold wet grey morning. I collected a hire car and set off on the four hour drive to Oswestry. Although I had once before visited Bryn Uchaf, I had never been into Oswestry itself. It felt strange for me to drive into the little village that I had heard so much about. Irving's words, "Oswestry, the capital of the universe", rang in my ears.

It was delightful seeing Helen and Steve Eisenstein again. They went out of their way to show me the village and to identify places which I photographed for this book. Only then did I realize that Irving's practical jokes had extended to his promotion of Oswestry.

"Can we see Darwin's house?" I asked Helen as we drove through the narrow streets.

Helen smiled and said, in her broad Irish accent, "Darwin's house? He was born in Shrewsbury, about twenty miles southeast from here."

I frowned. "But Irv said he was born here."

She smiled. "That's our Irv, isn't it?"

"Okay then, what about the BAE factory that makes the wings for the 747s?"

She chuckled. "That's at Hawarden, thirty miles north of us."

"Bloody long High Street," I remarked. "Irv said the factory was in the High Street."

"Well, you have to use a bit of imagination."

"Ja, well, the High Street would have to be about seventy miles long for Irv to have been correct. I suppose the biggest fruit and veg market doesn't exist either?"

Helen smiled and stopped opposite the Honeysuckle Fruit and Vegetable shop.

"I think this is what he meant," she said with a wry smile. I chuckled and took my photographs of "the largest organic fruit and vegetable market in the whole of England".

I smiled to myself as we walked the streets of Oswestry. Irving seemed to be with us, chuckling at his over-embellished description of the little village.

We saw the Lindstrand hot air balloon factory, David Davies the undertaker, the old school that dated back to the fourteenth century, the twenty-five-pounder cannon from World War II and the plaque to war poet, Wilfrid Owen, as well as the memorial to Captain Owen Arthur Ormsby Gore who had died in 1852 in the Frontier War in South Africa.

After fitting me out in a pair of Steve's 'wellies' Helen took me for a walk on the remains of the fort that dated back to the Iron Age. From the top we could see over the rolling green hills, dotted with sheep, into Wales. Unhappily, my camera ceased functioning at this stage. Perhaps Irving was still playing tricks on me. The countryside was soft and gentle and, despite the winter weather, the fields were a rich green. It was truly beautiful.

The next morning Steve collected me—my camera had been repaired—and after paying a visit to his Tiger Moth, which he had brought over from South Africa thirty-eight years previously, we set off for Bryn Uchaf, where Claire and Andrew Belk were expecting us. I wasn't sure what I would feel when I arrived at the farm.

As we approached the farm, situated on the border between Shropshire and Wales, the sun broke through the clouds and splashed the rolling fields with an even deeper and brighter green, like a painter putting finishing touches to his work.

The road twisted and turned as we climbed the hill to Bryn Uchaf. The farmhouse came into view. The house that Irving had built. I swallowed hard, thinking about everything that had happened in the last four years.

We entered the yard and were welcomed with smiles and warmth by the new owners, Claire and Andrew Belk, and their neighbours, Emyr and Carol Jones. The Belks threw their home open to us and showed us around. Irving's snooker room had not been changed at all; the posters on the wall, the mementos of concerts attended, were still there.

I looked out over the fields and could see why Irving had chosen this site on which to build a home for Yvonne and himself. The scenery was magnificent: tranquil, isolated and typically English. The undulating hills, green and dotted with white sheep, criss-crossed with dark green hedges, were breathtaking. I busied myself taking pictures until (Irving at his tricks again?) my camera ceased functioning—yet again. Andrew kindly lent me his own camera and I was able to continue taking photographs.

I walked down to Yvonne's grave, accompanied by Emyr. Carol had already left us to go to work as a teacher. The view from the grave was soft and gentle. Irving had planted a small forest of trees around the site and the grave was marked with a large stone taken from the surrounding hills.

"What happened to Irv's ashes?" I asked Emyr.

He shrugged. "No, I don't know. Maybe his brother-in-law scattered them?"

"Pity," I said. "I thought that he wanted to be buried with Yvonne ... I must have been wrong."

Emyr laughed and in his heavily accented Welsh voice said: "Ah well, Irving wasn't one for that kind of thing, he always said to us it didn't really matter what they did with him after he was dead. In fact, he said that they could just dump him on a hill and leave him there to the birds and animals."

It sounded just like Irving—nevertheless I shuddered.

After thanking Claire, Andrew and Emyr and saying our farewells, Steve and I threaded the car through the narrow lanes back to Oswestry. It started to rain. I blinked my eyes to rid them of welling tears. A wave of sadness swept over me, followed by a feeling of immense relief.

It was, finally, all over.

ACKNOWLEDGEMENTS

As always, it is Margie, my wife who deserves my greatest thanks for her unwavering support of my writing. Also for her reading of the manuscript and suggestions made to assist me in conveying the complexities of Irving's character.

To Peter Harris, whose idea it was to write this book and who gave up his valuable time to read the manuscript and make suggestions to improve the story, I owe a huge debt of gratitude.

My friends who read and commented on the manuscript in the early stages of writing and helped me mold the story more accurately are the late Graham de Villiers, Jimmy and Glenda Rangouses, Michael Hook and Bearnárd O'Riain.

Steve and Helen Eisenstein opened doors for me in Oswestry and hosted me when I visited Bryn Uchaf, showing me not only assistance but also friendship.

The new owners of Bryn Uchaf, Andrew and Claire Belk, could not have been friendlier or more helpful. I hope we can reciprocate their warm welcome in South Africa one day.

Irving's neighbors, Emyr and Carol Jones who gave up their time to meet and talk with me, I thank you.

Irving's brother Brian contributed significantly in sharing some of the stories and information about Irving. Thank you. I am indebted to you.

To Chris and Kerrin Cocks, my publishers, many thanks for thinking out of the box and publishing this book. I hope it becomes a bestseller for all of us.

To Joan Cameron who painstakingly edited this book, thank you so much for your significant contribution. If it sells it will be because of you.

Thanks in advance to the many book stores around the country and hopefully in the UK, who stock this book. As they say, "Pile 'em high!" Many thanks for your support and may your tills ring ceaselessly as the public buys this book.

Robin Binckes was born in East Griqualand, South Africa in April 1941. After matriculating in Umtata, Transkei, he did his national service at the South African Navy Gymnasium, Saldanha Bay. In 1970 he opened his own PR company to promote major sporting events, ranging from international cricket to Formula One Grand Prix during the period of sports isolation. In 1990 he started The Gansbaai Fishing Company and spent ten years in the food industry. During the violence that swept South Africa in 1993 he volunteered as a peace monitor in the townships. Sparked by the passion of the late historical orator David Rattray, he qualified in 2002 as an historical tour guide, conducting tours in the Johannesburg–Pretoria region through his company 'Spear of the Nation'. His best-selling books, *Canvas under the Sky* (fiction) and *The Great Trek* (non-fiction) were published in 2011 and 2013 respectively, and continue to fuel lively debate.